MEN OF GOOD HOPE

A Story of American Progressives

. . . .

DANIEL AARON

. . . .

OXFORD UNIVERSITY PRESS

NEW YORK

For Charles Aaron

. . . .

ACKNOWLEDGMENTS

. . . .

The research for this book, begun in the fall of 1947, was made possible by a fellowship from the John Simon Guggenheim Memorial Foundation. I should like to express my gratitude to the Foundation for this grant. Many friends have given me assistance and criticism. I cannot mention them all, but I am particularly indebted to the following: Newton Arvin, for reading and criticizing my manuscript and helping me in innumerable ways; Foster Rhea and Marian Dulles, for reading the manuscript and making valuable recommendations on arrangement and structure; and William Leuchtenburg, for his many criticisms and suggestions.

I am also indebted to George H. Geiger for reading the chapter on Henry George, to Bernard Barber and Charles Page for reading the chapter on Veblen, and to Henry May for reading the last chapter, 'In Retrospect.'

The following people gave me ideas, made corrections, and facilitated the job of research: Henry David, Robert G. Davis, Chester M. Destler, Bernard DeVoto, David Donald, Harold Faulkner, Richard Hofstadter, Howard Mumford Jones, Alfred Kazin, Richard Lewis, F. O. Matthiessen, Stewart Mitchell, John C. Ranney, Max Salvadori, Peter Viereck, and Conrad Wright.

I am grateful to Margaret Johnson, the Librarian of Smith College, for her many services. I should also like to thank Agnes Inglis, Curator of the Joseph A. Labadie Collection of Labor Materials at the University of Michigan Library; Anne S. Pratt, Reference Librarian of the Yale University Library; Robert W. Hill, Keeper of Manuscripts of the New York Public Library; William A. Jackson, Carolyn E. Jakeman, and the late Mrs. Frederick Winslow, all of the Houghton Library of Harvard

University; St. George L. Sioussot, Chief of the Division of Manuscripts of the Library of Congress; Nora E. Cordingley, in charge of the Theodore Roosevelt Collection at Harvard University; and the Librarians of the State Historical Society of Wisconsin.

I am greatly indebted to Agnes De Mille for permitting me to consult her mother's manuscript life of Henry George and for showing me pictures and other mementos of her grandfather; to Marian Bellamy Earnshaw, for reading my chapter on Edward Bellamy and furnishing me with interesting details of her father's life; to Abigail Adams Homans, for giving me access to the letters of Brooks Adams to his brother Henry and for her illuminating comments about the characters and personalities of her uncles; and to Senator Henry Cabot Lodge Jr., for permission to quote portions of the correspondence between his grandfather and Brooks Adams.

Short sections of this book have appeared in modified form in *The New England Quarterly, The Antioch Review,* and *American Quarterly.*

D. A.

Northampton, Mass.
October 1950

This reprint of *Men of Good Hope* is substantially the same as the original published ten years ago. Although I have modified my opinions about some of the reformers treated here, I have resisted making any major changes in the text because I wished to preserve the integrity of the book. I still adhere to its political philosophy.

A number of biographies and monographs have been published or re-issued during the last decade which are relevant to the men and events I discussed in my book. The most important of these are listed in a short bibliographical essay at the end of "Notes on Sources."

D.A.

Northampton, Mass.
September 1960

CONTENTS

. . . .

INTRODUCTION

. . . .

This is a book about American progressives. It is
also an attempt to rehabilitate the progressive tradition, currently
under attack by both liberals and anti-liberals, and to show that
progressivism was not always the shabby thing it is now made
out to be.

'Progressivism' is conceived today either as the sentimental
maunderings of the 'soft-minded' and the 'muddle-headed' or as
communism in disguise. That is not my understanding of the
word. By 'progressivism' I mean a social philosophy that derived
in part from Jeffersonian ideas about popular government, the
pursuit of happiness, and the fulfillment of human potentialities,
and in part from an unorthodox Protestant Christianity more
urgent and more fiercely evangelical than the bland reasonableness
of the Enlightenment. As I see it, progressivism was born at that
moment in our history when a moral and righteous minority began
to observe the social ravages produced by the industrial age and
to protest against what they felt was the betrayal of the republican
ideal.

What distinguished the progressives from the extremists was
their unwillingness to detach themselves from those elements in
society they wished to reform. Their program was conservative
in the sense that it sought to retain the social patterns of an
agrarian democracy with its emphasis upon equality and human
worth. The prospect of a stratified society alarmed them. Throughout their lives they envisaged a kind of democracy in which a
man would not be snared by institutions and where, to quote one
of them, 'the least individual shall have his rights acknowledged,
and the means and opportunities for the fullest expansion of his
faculties guaranteed.' They differed widely in their policies and

xi

attitudes (their political and economic views ranged from the moderate to the radical), but all agreed that whatever form society took, the proper concern of government, as Emerson said, was the care and culture of men.

The amiability and the extravagance of the nineteenth-century reformers, who made large claims for man and who believed Nowhere could be Somewhere sometime, are incongenial to contemporary liberal philosophers. This is regrettable, I think, because the old progressives still have something to tell us. The following propositions (which might be deduced from their writings and their lives) have a bearing on the present course of liberalism:

1. It is the business of progressives and liberals to theorize as well as to act; it is neither necessary nor even desirable for everyone to engage in practical politics. Liberalism needs visionaries and utopians as much as it needs techniques.

2. Utopians believe in a 'potential reality' that is neither a dream nor a description of existing facts but a realistic possibility. 'It must not violate what we know of nature, including human nature, though it may extrapolate our present technology and must transcend our present social organization.' *

3. If the sole aim of liberalism is immediate, tangible results, a political victory or the passage of a particular piece of legislation, then the visionary and the utopian are supernumerary; but if, as John Jay Chapman said, one's concern is for moral standards, then 'idealism pays. A reverse following a fight for principle . . . is pure gain. It records the exact state of the cause. It educates the masses on a gigantic scale. The results of that education are immediately felt.'

4. In some cases, Thoreau writes in *Civil Disobedience,* 'the rule of expediency does not apply . . . a people, as well as an individual, must do justice, cost what it may.' This, Thoreau admits, is 'inconvenient,' but it must be done. 'It is not so important,' Thoreau says, 'that many should be as good as you, as that there should be some absolute goodness somewhere; for that

---

* David Riesman, 'Some Observations on Community Plans and Utopia,' *Yale Law Review,* December 1947. I am greatly indebted to Mr. Riesman for this fine essay.

will leaven the whole lump.' Better 'one virtuous man' than 'ninety-nine patrons of virtue.'

5. Liberalism or progressivism 'fails' when it permits a respect for power to become an admiration for power *qua* power, when it transforms expediency into a virtue and calls a bad thing by a good name. The Mexican War was not a conspiracy of slave-holders, as Emerson thought, but it was a bad war nevertheless. Emerson was not living in a 'progressive dream-world' when he reviled it any more than he was when he called the Fugitive Slave Law (a highly expedient measure) a 'filthy enactment.' In 1846 he entered in his journal: 'The United States will conquer Mexico, but it will be as the man swallows the arsenic which brings him down in turn. Mexico will poison us.'

The nineteenth-century progressives believed in these propositions. They did not always practice what they honored in theory, but, unlike the New Liberal, they possessed that 'humane enthusiasm,' as David Riesman says, from which 'those whose greatest fear is to be gullible, serious, or "soft" are immune.' This emphasis upon 'ethics,' 'virtue,' and 'justice' as the ends of the democratic society is what distinguishes the old progressives from the New Liberals. The latter have modernized their liberalism, stripped off its old-fashioned accouterments, and turned it into something brisk and shiny. It is more efficient now and more impersonal. Something has been gained, but something important has been lost.

The reformers I take up in the first two parts of this book, although wise and practical men, were searching for what they believed to be a discoverable utopia, and they did not let their interest in particular, concrete issues obscure their vision; they knew where they wanted to go. What made them work, as well as speculate, was their conviction that most of their fellow Americans led desperate lives or empty lives. They took for granted that political science was only a branch of something larger, the science of society, and that economics, in the ultimate sense, was transcendental. 'The cost of a thing,' said Thoreau, 'is the amount of what I will call life which is required to be exchanged for it, immediately or in the long run.' The old progressives made an effective appeal to those of their contemporaries who sensed the inadequacies of American life and who were heartened by the prospects of a serene and humane society where 'costs' would be calculated under a different accounting system and 'success' be weighed on a different set of scales.

By the turn of the twentieth century, however, this friendly vision of the old progressives had begun to fade, if not entirely to disappear. The bogus progressivism of Theodore Roosevelt's Square Deal and the sublimated rhetoric of Woodrow Wilson's New Freedom could not revive it. It did not excite the practical-minded New Dealers, nor did it inspire the directors of the Fair Deal. It has not fared well in the Eisenhower age.

This book is written in the belief that the idealistic and ethical concerns of the old progressives are essential to any liberal movement. 'In a day of small, sour and fierce schemes,' says Emerson, we are cheered by aims of 'bold and generous proportion.' I think it is possible that the visions of the nineteenth century can encourage the twentieth and that we may discover in Emerson's 'men who entertain a good hope' a faith and a strategy for today.

. . . .

'They speak to the conscience, and have that superiority over the crowd of their contemporaries, which belongs to men who entertain a good hope.'

EMERSON

PART ONE

. . . .

Precursors

CHAPTER 1

. . . .

Emerson
and the Progressive Tradition

1] In the early days of the Republic, men wrote of the 'national, moral, and political advantages of the United States' with the confidence of believers; they did not need to place their faith in distant utopias, in 'spiritual frontiers.' Before them lay the gigantic outlines of a continent ripe for exploitation and capable of supplying the wants of its restless and ambitious population. Momentary crises might ruin particular sections and classes; injured parties might thunder at the politicians for hindering the march of progress; but behind the extravagances of the boosters and the complaints of the unsuccessful lay what most Americans conceived to be the solid gains of an expanding nation.

Contrasted with the gloomy summations of 1950, some of the national advantages listed by an anonymous writer in 1823 are revealing:

. . . Our territory affords every variety of soil and climate, so as to render us independent of foreign nations as any country whatever.

Our stores of all the important articles of coal, iron, lead, copper and timber are inexhaustible. . .

Our population is active, industrious, energetic, enterprising and ingenious.

Our government is the most free and liberal that ever existed. . .

Our debt is insignificant, not equal to the annual interest paid by some other nations.

Taxes are so light as not to be felt. . .

We have no nobility or gentry, with the enormous annual incomes, derived from the labors of the mass of the community.

3

Our farmers and planters are, in general, lords of the soil they cultivate. . .
Our citizens are unrestrained in the choice of occupation.
We have abundant room for all the valuable superfluous population
of Europe.

During this golden age, American orators quite understandably
saw their country as an area set aside by God for heavenly experiments. They rejoiced in its progress and contemplated a deteriorating Europe with mingled pity and contempt. The American's faith in progress, his utilitarianism, his scorn for precedent
were justified by economics, even if he liked to attribute his country's triumphant march to the magic of democratic institutions. If
all the sections were not equally satisfied and if certain classes en-
riched themselves at the expense of others, most Americans shared
the elation of the times, the sense of movement and progress.

Visitors from abroad who came to look at the Americans during
the early decades of the nineteenth century were struck by the general well-being of the country and impressed by the vast fermenta-
tion taking place in the United States. But the more philosophical
and discerning of the foreign observers, while appreciating the immense significance of the democratic experiment and rarely stoop-
ing to petty recriminations, probed for weaknesses and discovered
them. There was not only the fact of slavery to reckon with. Even
more portentous in some ways was the future of a society frankly
and avidly materialistic, a society adhering to a series of public
truths determined by a sometimes ruthless and mindless majority,
a society agitated by a perpetual restlessness and an insatiable ap-
petite, a virtuous society yet one that revealed on occasion what
Emerson called an 'invincible depravity.'

Alexis de Tocqueville, the most intelligent critic America has
ever had, was on the whole a sympathetic and flattering interpreter,
but his *Democracy in America* more than hinted of corruption in
the American Eden. The advantages of democracy were perfectly
evident to him, and yet he detected certain symptoms in the American behavior that mocked the national aspiration to greatness.
Tocqueville did not draw up any systematic indictment, but the

following series of observations, selected at random from his book, indicate the nature of his criticism:

> What chiefly diverts the men of democracies from lofty ambition is not the scantiness of their fortunes, but the vehemence of the exertions they daily make to improve them. They strain their faculties to the utmost to achieve paltry results, and this cannot fail speedily to limit their range of view, and to circumscribe their powers. They might be much poorer, and still be greater.

(This was also to be the complaint of Emerson, Thoreau, and Whitman: 'the mediocrity of desires,' the inordinate attention to getting and having, so that the true meaning of life is lost. As Thoreau said, Americans have appetites but no passions.)

> A native of the United States clings to this world's goods as if he were certain never to die; and he is so hasty at grasping at all within his reach, that one would suppose he was constantly afraid of not living long enough to enjoy them.

(Tocqueville comments frequently upon the American's restlessness, his chronic dissatisfaction with what he has. He attributes this prevailing feeling to the openness of American society, where no limits are imposed and no holds barred, where the prospects are boundless but where the equalitarian conditions make any discrepancies in individual fortunes all the more glaring.)

> To say the truth, though there are rich men, the class of rich men does not exist; for those rich individuals have no feelings or purposes in common, no mutual traditions or mutual hopes; there are individuals, therefore, but no definite class.

(The American rich are simply a group who willy-nilly and independently have broken through democratic anonymity in the approved way—by making money. Tocqueville did not see this group as constituting any danger to democracy, but the rising industrial aristocracy, which 'first impoverishes and debases the men who serve it, and then abandons them to be supported by the charity of the public,' he regarded as a more serious threat to the country.)

> Selfishness is a passionate and exaggerated love of self, which leads a man to connect everything with himself, and to prefer himself to

everything in the world. Individualism is a mature and calm feeling, which disposes each member of the community to sever himself from the mass of his fellows, and to draw apart with his family and friends; so that, after he has thus formed a little circle of his own, he willingly leaves society at large to itself. Selfishness originates in blind instinct: individualism proceeds from erroneous judgment more than from depraved feelings; it originates as much in deficiencies of mind as in perversity of heart.

(This quotation, taken from Book II, Chapter II of the second volume, makes certainly one of the most important distinctions in *Democracy in America* and expresses the democratic dilemma more succinctly, if less eloquently, than anyone before or after Tocqueville has done. Individualism, Tocqueville goes on to say, although not consciously and impulsively antisocial, begins by sapping public virtue and ends in unmitigated selfishness. What is more important, it is 'of democratic origin' and springs up at a time when class obligations have been removed. Theoretically, from a democratic point of view, 'the duties of the individual to the race' should rightfully supercede the limited allegiances of class, but Tocqueville asserts that in America, 'the bond of human affection is extended, but it is relaxed.' Something has been gained, and something has been lost. At best, 'Aristocracy had made a chain of all the members of the community, from the peasant to the king: democracy breaks that chain, and severs every link of it.')

The great American writers of the nineteenth century recognized these divisive tendencies in their society and were deeply concerned about them. For Hawthorne the unforgivable sin was spiritual isolation, the breaking of the 'magnetic chain of being,' and Melville and Whitman celebrated democratic sociality. And yet these writers and others who preached a similar belief were Americans and children of their times, consciously reflecting the preconceptions of their generation. Hawthorne, despite his ancestral longings, would have found no melancholy implications in Tocqueville's remark that in America, 'the woof of time is every instant broken, and the track of generations effaced.' On the contrary, Hawthorne took a sardonic pleasure in recording the vicissitudes of families and the crumbling away of aristocratic distinctions. Would he have agreed with Tocqueville that democracy breaks the 'magnetic chain'? One wonders how deliberately he made his beloved and innocent country, unshrouded as yet by European gloom, the background for his parables of wickedness. Hawthorne's and Melville's powerful egotists, Ethan Brand and Captain Ahab, damned and destroyed for their pride, are still heroes who carry their creators' benedictions with them into the flaming lime kiln and the ocean grave. Are they not the perfect exemplars of Tocqueville's American individualists?

They owe nothing to any man, they expect nothing from any man; they acquire the habit of always considering themselves as standing alone, and they are apt to imagine that their whole destiny is in their own hands.

Thus, as Tocqueville says, democracy makes 'every man forget his ancestors' (a desirable end from Hawthorne's and Melville's point of view, although both are fascinated by the past) and democracy 'separates his contemporaries from him; it throws him back forever upon himself alone, and threatens in the end to confine him entirely within the solitude of his own heart.' Here, if you will, is the Unpardonable Sin, or, to put it still another way, the great Transcendental fallacy, which emerges most clearly in the writings of Emerson.

Emerson's simultaneous acceptance and rejection of American civilization illustrates the condition of the divided intelligence even more strikingly than the ambivalent positions of Hawthorne and Melville. He was both the critic and the celebrator of his and subsequent generations, the Yea-sayer and the Nay-sayer. By Tocqueville's standards he was the most articulate exponent of democratic individualism, whose philosophy of self-reliance, or self-sufficiency, harmonized with the disintegrative tendencies of American life, and yet at the same time he quite characteristically attacked the social consequences of his own philosophy.

This contradiction also appears, although to a lesser extent, in the ideas of the reformers who regarded themselves as his disciples or who unconsciously reflected his influence; and since Emerson was the real prophet of the progressive tradition—the Scholar without plan or system, who impressed men of all radical creeds—his polarized attitude toward the individual has a direct bearing on the history of progressivism in America. For the progressives who followed him felt his impatience with men in the mass—this 'maudlin agglutination,' as Emerson put it. Like him, they held forth the possibility of human development while noting the appalling evidences of human mediocrity. Like him again, they fervently condemned the shortsightedness and selfishness of the middle class at the same time that they cherished its virtues and faith. Emerson was their perfect representative, and his ambivalent attitude toward man in the aggregate was shared by the progressives who followed him.

II] Consider first his lesser role as the seer of *laisser-faire* capitalism and the rampant individual.

To anyone who has habitually imagined Emerson as the sedentary philosopher invariably upholding with transcendental logic the Ideal-Real against the evanescent Material, his delight in the harmonies of the market-place might appear somewhat paradoxical. A closer survey of his writings, however, show that his communications with the Over-Soul did not always preclude a secular interest in vulgar appearances. His transcendentalism, in fact, provided an ideal explanation for the conduct and activities of the business classes and offered the necessary criteria by which he was able to justify or to criticize them. This leisure-loving beneficiary of a commercial economy, whose antecedents were ministerial rather than mercantile, outlined a rationale for the entrepreneur of an industrial age.

Emerson's fastidious tastes found little that was congenial in the vulgarity and crassness of workaday business. It is all the more remarkable that he was able to sublimate his instinctive distaste for the hucksters in counting-houses and see them finally as exemplifying divine principles. His journals and essays are filled with disparaging references to the business classes; their sordidness, their undeviating pursuit of wealth, their narrow self-interests, and their timidity are bluntly and scornfully arraigned. But he seems to have cherished a particular dislike only for the meaner of the species. Businessmen of larger appetites and bolder ambitions, notwithstanding their faults, often called forth his admiration, and he consistently identified business intrepidity with the exploits of warriors and heroes.

The portrait of Napoleon in *Representative Men* is perhaps the best illustration of Emerson's ambivalent attitude toward aggressiveness and self-seeking; it is not by accident that he saw 'this deputy of the nineteenth century' as the 'agent or attorney of the middle class of modern society; of the throng who fill the markets, shops, counting-houses, manufactories, ships, of the modern world, aiming to be rich.' The essay falls roughly into two parts. In the first section Emerson exalts Napoleon into a superman; in the concluding three or four paragraphs, he dwells fiercely upon his uglier defects—his coarseness and lack of ideality. 'In short,' Emerson concludes, 'when you have penetrated through all the circles of power and splendor, you were not dealing with a gentleman, at last; but with an imposter and a rogue.' But the deflation of the great man undertaken at the close of the essay cannot entirely obliterate the earlier impression of Emerson's enthusiastic admiration, which he shared with thousands of his American contemporaries. In praising Napoleon's practicality, prudence, and directness, his powers of synthesis and cool audacity, Emerson is underscoring precisely those attributes that made up the American success code; his emphasis helps to explain the peculiar fascination Napoleon held for the warriors of American business. Emerson's strictures against the blowhard, the strutting egotist, the low vulgarian are devastating, but the following encomium also represents his settled convictions:

We cannot, in the universal imbecility, indecision and indolence of men, sufficiently congratulate ourselves on this strong and ready actor, who took occasion by the beard, and showed us how much may be accomplished by the mere force of such virtues as all men possess in less degrees; namely, by punctuality, by personal attention, by courage, and thoroughness.

Emerson's respect for power and its achievements is even more glowingly expressed in two other essays, 'Power' and 'Wealth.' Here he reiterates his preference for the 'bruisers' and 'pirates,' the 'men of the right Caesarian pattern' who transcend the pettiness of 'talkers' and 'clerks' and dominate the world by sheer force of character. 'Life is a search after power,' he announces, and the successful men who understand the laws of Nature and respond to the Godhead within themselves, who convert 'the sap and juices of the planet to the incarnation and nutriment of their design,' are unconsciously fulfilling the plan of a benevolent Providence.

In these essays and elsewhere, Emerson was not only synchronizing the predatory practices of the entrepreneur with the harmony of the universe and permitting merchants (as Bronson Alcott shrewdly said) to 'find a refuge from their own duplicity under his broad shield'; he was also outlining a code of behavior that the superior man must follow, and sketching the ideal political economy under which the superman might best exercise his uncommon talents. Specialize, he advised, 'elect your work' and 'drop all the rest.' Do not dissipate your efforts. Concentrate! 'Concentration is the secret of strength in politics, in war, in trade, in short all management of human affairs.' Make up your mind and stick to your decisions. Practice again and again; it is constant drilling that distinguishes the professional from the amateur and enables the 'indifferent hacks and mediocrities' to win out over men of superior abilities. He quoted the business slogans of Poor Richard with warm approval and identified 'counting-room maxims' with the 'laws of the universe.'

Emerson's optimistic faith, his belief that all apparent evil ultimately cancels out into good, allowed him to view the depredations of business more tranquilly than, let us say, a Theodore Parker, less given to transcendentalizing business enterprise. A little wickedness, Emerson believed, served as a kind of energizing principle. 'Men of this surcharge of arterial blood cannot live on nuts, herb-tea, and elegies,' he characteristically remarked. The hot speculators exploiting the country, the 'monomaniacs' of trade who clash in the market-place, build up the country as they enrich themselves. Unworldly moralists who rant against the violence of competition are in reality working against the laws of the world. Were they successful in their efforts to subdue the spirit of competitive enterprise, they would be forced to rekindle the fires of avarice if civilization were to continue. Thus it inevitably followed that any attempt to check the capitalistic incentives was a futile and unjustifiable interference with the iron laws of circumstance:

Wealth brings with it its own checks and balances. The basis of political economy is non-interference. The only safe role is found in the self-adjusting meter of demand and supply. Do not legislate. Meddle, and you snap the sinews with your sumptuary laws. Give no bounties, make equal laws, secure life and property, and you need not give alms. Open the doors of opportunity to talent and virtue and they will do themselves justice, and property will not be in bad hands. In a free and just commonwealth, property rushes from the idle and imbecile to the industrious, brave and persevering.

Quotations like this represent only a single strain in Emerson's thought. Equally eloquent passages might be included in which he affirms his strong democratic attachments and humanitarian sympathies, but the Nietzschean side of Emerson is unmistakable. As a transcendentalist he had to recognize the divine potentialities of all men and to reconcile all social manifestations with the general will of God. Hence his interest in and sympathy with all causes and movements, however absurd, and his tolerance of creeds and men not instinctively congenial to him. His conservative and autocratic biases, however, reasserted themselves from time to time, just as the materiality he philosophically denied anchored his rhapsodic speculations to brute fact. Emerson enjoyed almost sensuously the plump and solid tangibles, and he admired the 'inventive or creative class' that made them possible.

Running through his writings is a constant disparagement of men in the mass, the 'imbeciles,' as he calls them on several occasions, the 'uninventive or accepting class' held down by 'gravity, custom, and fear' and tyrannized by convention. What quickened his faith in the latent capacities of man was the 'grand' talent rising like a huge wave over the placid ocean of humanity. Although Emerson lived in rural Concord during periods of economic and political upheaval, he sanctioned unconsciously the forces of exploitation that were at work in the United States and the powerful men, impelled by what he called a 'keener avarice,' who were directing this exploitation. Rarely does he credit the collective en-

ergies of the common man as the great transforming power. Man
in the mass is inert until galvanized by the great captains of enterprise. Wealth is created by ability, and it is the rich man 'who can
avail himself of all man's faculties . . . The world is his tool-
chest, and he is successful, or his education is carried on just so
far, as is the marriage of his faculties with nature, or the degree in
which he takes up things into himself.'

It would not be too extreme to say that Emerson envisaged the
scholar as employing these 'business principles' in exploiting the
frontiers of the mind, drawing 'a benefit from the labors of the
greatest number of men, of men in distant countries and in past
times.' The function of Emerson's scholar was to mold the plastic
world and shake the 'cowed' and the 'trustless' out of their lethargy.
The scholar was to create an intellectual revolution by gradually
'domesticating' the idea of culture (the metaphor is Emerson's)
and to illustrate the proved maxim that 'he who has put forth his
total strength in fit actions has the richest return of wisdom.' After
a period of worry and doubts, the Emerson who agonized over the
choice of his vocation was able to reconcile the divergent appeals
of practical action and reflection in the vocation of the scholar,
which became for him a symbol of dynamic passivity.

Whether or not there is any truth in the contention expressed
above, it can be plausibly argued that Emerson's 'transcendentalizing' of business conduct testified to his awareness of the growing
significance of commerce and industry in American life. When an
age is dominated by the economic mind, Henry Adams once observed, 'the imaginative mind tends to adopt its form and its faults.'
By temperament, inclination, and circumstance, Emerson belonged
to a class out of sympathy with the rising industrial *bourgeoisie,*
but he was extremely sensitive to the currents of his age and deeply
infected by its omnipresent materialism. Ostensibly preoccupied
with nonutilitarian ends, he nevertheless showed an almost inordinate interest in the practical performances of men and their mundane accomplishments.

Emerson helps us to see the motive forces that drove American
individualists to absorb themselves in money-making; he makes
clear their ambition and self-reliance, their inspired faith in limit-

less opportunities. His emphasis on the value of natural exploitation, of opening the world like an oyster, was only a more articulate and rhetorical expression of what millions already dimly felt, and his celebration of the practical doers was a kind of transcendental concession to those who scorned the useless visionary. He had been impressed by the magnificence of American commercial and industrial enterprise, by the dramatic implications of a continent unsubdued. To a romantic and poetic nature, such a phenomenon helped to compensate for the drabness and sameness of American life, to reduce the tedium of democratic anonymity. It allowed him to celebrate audacious individual accomplishment, and it gave a martial air to a nation of civilian traders. 'Whatever appeals to the imagination, by transcending the ordinary limits of human nobility,' Emerson said in speaking of Napoleon, 'wonderfully encourages and liberates us.' Emerson encouraged his countrymen to cultivate their inward greatness, and one of the ways he did so was to glorify the characters and deeds of the world's heroes who followed transcendental impulses.

III] Neither Emerson nor his disciples, oddly enough, saw any connection between the cult of self-trust and the mercenary paradise about to be revealed after 1865, although a closer perusal of Tocqueville might have hinted as much. Emerson was simply acknowledging, perhaps unduly, a side of the national character that was aggressive and rapacious, that hated physical impediments, whether things or people. The significance of the frontier has been exaggerated, but the fact that for two centuries it represented a challenge and an obstacle as well as an opportunity to generations of 'go-getters' is of crucial importance in understanding the American experience. If the frontier did not make the American character, it whetted the appetites and aggravated the assertive compulsions of the men who camped along its fringes.

Another kind of individualism, however, that took root and flourished in America did not express itself in a compulsion to dominate, to impose by force. Rather it emphasized the need for individual fulfillment and enlargement, for self-containment and passive growth. Individualism, taken in this sense, did not manifest itself in gouging the outer world, in fighting and scrambling in order to keep one's identity. It encouraged inner cultivation, and in so far as it was concerned with external realities—the problems of government and economics and culture—it conceived of them in terms of individual welfare. This kind of individualism or Personalism regarded the 'self' as a rare and tender thing. Thoreau caught its spirit when he wrote: 'The finest qualities of our nature, like the bloom on fruits, can be preserved only by the most delicate handling.' And Emerson reflected this passive and humane conception of individualism even more unmistakably than he did its aggressive antitype. If as a Yankee he sympathized with the latter and vicariously enjoyed the coups of the unshrinking entrepreneurs, as a Poet and Seer he repudiated them and their philosophy.

Emerson, a radical wedded to principle, never intended his exhortations to justify the practices of 'robber barons.' In fact Emerson came to have a supreme contempt for the commercial mentality. He made fun of State Street timidity. He charged the bankers with fearing transcendentalism, because it would unsettle property and impair the obligation of contract. The businessman, he said, preferred slavery to illegality. Emerson addressed himself, finally, to democrats and humanitarians, not to property-worshippers, and for every conservative who hailed him there were a dozen reformers who constructed their systems upon his radical assumptions.

Emerson's political philosophy—it might be called transcendental democracy—had marked Jeffersonian and Jacksonian overtones. Strongly individualistic, it also spoke for equality of opportunity in economic and political affairs, and it lent support to the belief in *laisser-faire* and the necessity of the minimized state. But it was more spiritual and intellectual than the organized movements for political democracy and less concerned with political and economic considerations, less a matter of economic rationalization. Its chief proponents tended to be professional and literary people; ministers, writers, teachers, and reformers made up its ranks rather than businessmen, office-holders, or lawyers. This is not to say that the Transcendentalists played down political and economic questions —far from it—but they were not defenders of an 'interest' or a

'faction.' If they had no desire to capture and operate a government, they stubbornly protested when government overstepped its
limited confines and by its acts trespassed on their spiritual domain.
The men and women who made up this transcendental corps
were mostly of New England origin, although a handful were born
outside New England. As children of the professional or commercial classes or of the sturdy farming yeomanry, they received
educational advantages above the average of their day, and for the
most part they came from families distinguished neither by great
wealth nor by poverty. Almost all of them seemed to have been
reared in homes where the business of life was taken seriously and
idealistically. It was this group that, disgusted by the prevailing
materialism of the day, turned to culture and to reform.

Although the reformers shared their contemporaries' faith in
progress, they could not accept the corollary that America was the
best of all possible worlds or that the American experiment could
be called a complete success. Shocked by the materialism and the
inhumanity they saw everywhere about them, they found themselves in the position of condemning the social practices and behavior of a class with whom they were closely connected by birth
and education and of speaking for an underprivileged group with
whom they had little in common. Like the intelligentsia in societies
before and after, they deliberately alienated themselves from the
moneyed interests who had nurtured and sustained them. Because
they still took seriously the Puritan tradition of stewardship, of
class obligations, at a time when community responsibilities were
being increasingly ignored, they could not be oblivious to the
ruinous consequences of 'enlightened self-interest.' Many of them,
moreover, believed quite literally in natural rights and other
eighteenth-century humanitarian doctrines that proclaimed the necessity of the mutual concern of every man for another. Since the
Transcendentalists respected the sacredness of the human individuality, the crassness and the insensitivity of the employing
classes, indeed most of the values of the rising business elite, were
personally distasteful to them.

Although Emerson was the most famous exponent of the tran-
scendentalized democratic philosophy, his was neither the most

original nor the most incisive mind among the New England reformers. William Ellery Channing had prepared the way for him;
Thoreau and Whitman developed certain strains of his thought
more acutely and profoundly; and Theodore Parker, as we shall
see, surpassed him as a political and economic analyst. But Emerson, the master transcendentalist, somehow subsumed them all
and most successfuly comprehended his age. In him, as Howells
wrote, 'conscience and intellect were angelically one.'

Emerson's political ideas emerged quite logically from transcendental principles. He believed in a divine power sometimes referred
to as the Over-Soul, and he taught that all men shared in that
divinity or at least were capable of establishing a rapport with it.
Men's joint participation in this Spirit, their common share of the
divine inheritance, made them brothers and gave the lie to artificial distinctions. In the great democracy of spirit that Emerson
conjured up as a kind of Platonic archetype of the imperfect American model, all men were potentially great. Men were not great
in fact (Emerson had no such leveling ideas, as we have seen),
but every man could be great if he harkened to the admonition
of the Over-Soul in himself.

Like John Adams and Thomas Jefferson, Emerson believed in a
natural aristocracy, although his *aristoi* bore little resemblance to
Jefferson's. Society divided itself into the men of understanding
and the men of Reason. The former, the most numerous and the
most ordinary, lived in 'a world of pig-lead' and acted as if 'rooted
and grounded in adamant.' Sunk in this profound materialism, they
lacked the imaginative penetration of the true aristocrats, the men
of Reason, who plumbed the spiritual reality behind the world of
fact. The men of Reason—poets, seers, philosophers, scholars—
the passive doers, served humanity as the geographers of the 'super-
sensible regions' and inspired 'an audacious mental outlook.' They
formed no inflexible caste, but they wonderfully 'liberated' the
cramped average afraid to trust itself.

Emerson did not intend his political theories to provide a sanction for social lawlessness, even though his celebration of the individual intuition, abstracted from the body of his thinking, seemed
to justify an aggressive individualism. If it encouraged the predatory

entrepreneur, it also invalidated contracts. It dissolved the power of tyrannical authority; it undermined tradition. If carried to its logical conclusion, the Emersonian theory that every person should act as a majority of one would result in anarchism, but he never pushed this idea to its end. Although his writings are filled with disparaging remarks about the state as the 'principal obstruction and nuisance with which we have to contend,' he opposed it only when it sought to supervene the higher laws, when it prevented men from living naturally and wisely and justly.

His views on the function of government were by no means entirely negative. Government, he said, 'was set up for the protection and comfort of all good citizens.' If the withered state represented his ultimate ideal, he could subscribe to Thoreau's remark: 'To speak practically . . . I ask for, not at once no government, but *at once* a better government.' He explained the community experiment at Brook Farm as proceeding

in great part from a feeling that the true offices of the state, the state has let fall to the ground; that in the scramble of parties for the public purse, the main duties of government were omitted,—the duty to instruct the ignorant, to supply the poor with work, and . . . the mediation between want and supply.

Emerson reached this mature and liberal view of government and its purpose after a considerable amount of candid self-examination and after a long look at his own country. But Emerson came to believe that the Democrats had the best principles if not the best men, and the more he dirtied himself with politics (for he regarded the demands of the social world with resentment and anger) the more disgusted he became with the 'thin and watery blood of Whiggism.'

Instead of having its own aims passionately in view, it cants about the policy of a Washington and a Jefferson. It speaks to expectation and not the torrent of its wishes and needs, waits for its antagonist to speak that it may have something to oppose, and, failing that, having nothing to say, is happy to hurrah.

Emerson's contempt for timid conservatism is best conveyed in his sarcastic description of its doctrine: 'Better endure tyranny according to law a thousand years than irregular unconstitutional happiness for a day.'

iv] That he could feel this way about a conservatism continuously on the defensive and still retain his affection and respect for the 'active, intelligent, well-meaning and wealthy part of the people' who made up its party is characteristic not only of Emerson but also of the middle-class reformers who succeeded him. Like Emerson, they belonged to that corps of sensitive intellectuals who placed spiritual values above material ones and human considerations above the rights of property. Like him, they made the flowering of the individual personality their ultimate goal and estimated all political and social ideologies, whether conservative or radical, by this single test. They had no quarrel with the machine nor did they advocate a return to a smokeless, factoryless America. They repudiated Thoreau's remedy by isolation, for they agreed completely with Mazzini's repeated injunction that the only way an individual man could fuse with his fellows was through social institutions. Although desiring a more equitable distribution of the wealth produced by the new technology, they did not stop with material consideration. To preserve the integrity of 'souls' suffocating in the impersonal fog of the market system, to eliminate the evils so inextricably bound up with industrialism, these seemed to them the most pressing responsibilities of the reformer.

Their sensitiveness to the blights caused by the industrial revolution and to capitalistic methods is the trait that distinguishes them most sharply from their thicker-skinned contemporaries. The shabby and sordid slums, creeping like an infection across the face of their cities, repelled them. So did the intemperance and pauperism and vice that inevitably accompanied the overcrowding of towns and deadened human sympathies. This revulsion, aesthetic as much as ethical, turned them toward reform at a time when community obligations were increasingly ignored and successful go-getters justified themselves by drawing false analogies from Darwin. In a sense these men were artists appalled by a disorderly world and driven by some kind of creative compulsion to reshape it and give it meaning. As Lester Ward observed with his usual acuteness,

> if the social artist is moved more by pain to be relieved than by pleasure to be enjoyed in his ideal society, this is only a difference of degree, since there can be no doubt that one of the strongest motives to creative art is the pain caused by the defects, maladjustments, discords, jars, and eyesores that the real world constantly inflicts upon the hyper-sensitive organization of the artist.

It was this aesthetic aspect of the reformist impulse that William Morris felt in himself, but which he failed to detect in American reformers like Edward Bellamy. 'The only ideal of life which such a man can see,' Morris concluded in a review of *Looking Backward,* 'is that of the industrious *professional* middle-class men of today purified from their crimes of complicity with the monopolist class, and become independent instead of being, as they are now, parasitical.' There is a good deal of justice in such a statement, as anyone familiar with the character and personality of George or Bellamy or Howells or Lloyd can attest; capitalism and its fruits made them morally uneasy. And yet who would attribute their zeal and unselfishness, their association with unpopular causes merely to a queasy conscience?

Most of the progressives, of course, were not extremists and malcontents camped outside the bastions of respectable society. Their programs must in no way be construed as incendiary attacks against private property or the family or the state. Society, they felt, needed to be reformed, to be brought into closer correspondence with American democratic precepts; it did not need to be uprooted. To conserve the best and eradicate the wrong, to redirect the social energies without disturbing fundamental social laws, to maintain an open society and to oppose the tendencies in national life that made for rigid class stratifications, these were the real aims of most of the reformers. If their proposals sounded revolutionary (as, in certain respects, they certainly were), their objectives were conservative in the sense that they were intended to provide stability in an insecure social order.

The progressives conceived of themselves as mediators reconciling the interests of the exploited and the exploiters and seeing

to it that the America so enthusiastically pictured by the intoxicated booster should more closely approximate his roseate description. With a few exceptions they shared the general optimism of
the day, not because they felt the laws were perfect, as Andrew
Carnegie did, but because they had faith in the resources of human
nature and a profound belief in the limitless power of the unfettered individual. This optimism, if excessive, was not unreflective. It
rested on a conviction that something could be done with the stuff
of the world and with man who molded it. Their vision of the
good society made them angry and impatient with the men and
forces who they felt prevented its emergence. But they never ceased
their agitation nor doubted the final victory. Their affirmations
grew out of knowledge and experience, out of defeat and humilia-
tion.

Although the progressives carried on their programs with an
untroubled assurance that their values were sound and their goals
attainable, they rarely sentimentalized human nature or failed to
consider the inertia of prejudice, ignorance, and viciousness that
had to be overcome. For the most part they looked to their own
class to provide the shock troops for the battle of reform, since they
distrusted both the plutocratic few who had been corrupted by success and the masses of the propertyless who had never been given
the opportunity to cultivate their latent virtues. The latter were to
be the trusted citizens of the future, but until they demonstrated
their God-given capacities, the reformers refused to celebrate them
uncritically. Yet the reformers never deserted the leaderless majority to whose cause they had consecrated themselves, and they
concurred with the spirit of Emerson's fervid condemnation of the
apostate-scholar who abandoned his trust:

Meantime shame to the fop of learning and philosophy who suffers
a vulgarity of speech and habit to blind him to the grosser vulgarity of
pitiless selfishness, and to hide him from the current of Tendency; who
abandons his right position of being priest and poet of these impious
and unpoetic doers of God's work. You must, for wisdom, for sanity,
have some access to the mind and heart of common humanity. The
exclusive excludes himself. No great man has existed who did not
rely on the sense and heart of mankind as represented by the good
sense of the people, as correcting the modes and over-refinements and
class prejudices of the lettered men of the world.

. . . .

CHAPTER 2

Theodore Parker:
'The Battle of the Nineteenth Century'

1] Emerson is a protean figure; his works are a composite of many views and attitudes, often conflicting and yet finally reconciled. He is the rebel and the conservative, the man of action and the man of thought, 'the doubter and the doubt.'

His spiritual sons and daughters, however, seized upon certain characteristically Emersonian positions or roles and then proceeded to carry them further and to live them more consistently than the Master. Thoreau, for all of his brave independence, was an extreme illustration of certain Emersonian precepts subsumed in the idea of the Scholar. Walt Whitman was Emerson's poet conjured up in 1842 when Emerson called for the genius 'with tyrannous eye' who would capture the poetry of American geography and culture in his meters. Theodore Parker chose to be the rebel and the political man, the transcendental systematizer. Emerson unwittingly described him in 1841 in his portrait of the reformer, ready

to cast aside all evil customs, timidities, and limitations . . . a free and helpful man, a reformer, a benefactor, not content to slip along through the world like a footman or a spy, escaping by his nimbleness and apologies as many knocks as he can, but a brave and upright man, who must find or cut a straight road to everything excellent in the earth, and not only go honorably himself, but make it easier for all to follow him, to go in honor and with benefit.

And Parker was only speaking the truth when he wrote to Emerson in 1851: 'Much of the little I do now is the result of seed of your own sowing.'

Parker is the link between Emerson and the postwar reformers. He is among the first of the middle-class radicals to recognize and to protest against the signs of the coming business age. He is not the Harmonizer or the Poet or Sardonic Critic but the armed prophet who announces to his country that it must give up 'the pursuit of wealth and the pursuit of power' lest it degenerate into a 'Christian feudalism of gold.'

II] When Louisa May Alcott arrived in Boston in 1855, awkward, unfashionable, and friendless, she found her first refuge in the parlor of 'the terrible Theodore Parker,' who remained for her ever after 'a great fire where all can come and be warmed and comforted.' Parker gave this 'large, bashful girl,' as she described herself at this time, the confidence she badly needed, and his sermon on 'Laborious Young Women' helped her to understand and to accept her role of spinster. She later acknowledged the kindness of her 'beloved minister and friend' when she introduced him as the magnetic preacher, Mr. Power, in her autobiographical novel, *Work*.

The heroine of her story, Christie Devon, has been warned against this 'rampant radical and infidel of the deepest dye,' but she soon agrees with the opinion that Louisa Alcott wrote in her own journal: 'He is my *sort;* for though he may lack reverence for other people's God, he works bravely for his own, and turns his back on no one who needs help, as some of the pious do.' Christie finds him as eager to comfort and advise the perplexed as he is to castigate the Pharisee. 'He tells the truth so plainly,' she says to her friend Mrs. Wilkins, 'and lets in the light so clearly, that hypocrites and sinners must fear and hate him. I think he *was* a little hard and unsparing, sometimes, though I don't know enough to judge the men and measures he condemned.'

Mrs. Wilkins assures Christie that Mr. Power can be 'as gentle as a lamb,' but her own evaluation is more interesting. Mrs. Wilkins is a washerwoman. To her, 'folks is very like clothes, and a sight has to be done to keep 'em clean and whole.' Mr. Power does the 'scrubbin' and the bilin'; that's always the hardest and the hottest part. He starts the dirt and gits the stains out, and leaves 'em ready for other folks to finish off. It ain't such pleasant work,' she admits, 'as hangin' out, or such pretty work as doin' up, but some one's got to do it, and them that's strongest does it best, though they don't git half so much credit as them as polishes and crimps. That's showy work, but it wouldn't be no use ef the things warn't well washed fust.'

What Mrs. Wilkins is stating so inelegantly here is really the dilemma that Louisa Alcott's and Parker's contemporaries constantly faced: the seeming impossibility of harmonizing the reformist temper with urbanity and grace and good taste. Man was born to be a reformer, Emerson announced, but the impulse and the theory were more beautiful than the practice. Most of the passionate advocates 'urging with the most ardor what are called the greatest benefits of mankind,' he concluded, 'are narrow, self-pleasing, conceited men, and affect us as the insane do. They bite us, and we run mad also.'

Emerson and Hawthorne, and Thoreau too, arrived at their separate conclusions about reform and reformers after having studied as motley a crowd of healers, dieticians, religious prophets, and social architects as any American was ever privileged to observe. The horde of men and women who attended a convention of Friends of Universal Reform at Boston's Chardon Street Chapel in 1840, for instance, represented the reformist movement in its most freakish and disorderly aspect; and we are not surprised that sober spirits disassociated themselves from the picturesque maniacs who came, as Emerson said, 'to chide, or pray, or preach, or protest.'

The Come-outers and Groaners, however, did not comprise the entire body of reformers. Many men and women living in New England—quiet, sensible, conscientious people for the most part—showed a chronic tendency to examine their society and to dissent from its conventions. They asked simple but fundamental questions about the sources of wealth, the disparity in economic rewards, the nature of business and competition, the changing status of men, the meaning of government. They began to realize with Emerson that most men were prisoners of society. They, too, learned to say with him: 'I pay a destructive tax in my conformity.'

Theodore Parker belonged to this class of reformer rather than to the bizarre and flamboyant variety. He did not 'prescribe for the globe' nor did he expect Paradise in ten years. God was a good worker, Parker would say, but He liked to be helped. Parker helped God, working methodically and realistically and following a program of action at once too radical for the conservatives and too conservative for some radicals. Unlike his friend Alcott, he did not cultivate aspiring vegetables at Fruitlands. He joined no utopian community. He made no mystical pronouncements. Still, he was a reformer, perhaps the greatest among the Transcendentalists, and possessed most of the virtues and some of the defects of the reformist temper.

The reformer is very likely to be uncompromising, opinionated, and blunt. He is apt to have strong feelings about what is right and what is wrong. When to these qualities are added a talent for invective and phrase-making, a devotion to humanity, and a consecrated love of righteousness, one can readily see why such a man arouses strong antipathies and enthusiasms.

Even Parker's friends deplored his sarcasm and the bitterness and harshness of his denunciations when he struck at 'the Ahabs and Herods of State Street.' His enemies, vocal and numerous during his lifetime and even after his death, singled out this unchristianlike failing to justify their poisoned assaults. To the *Boston Traveller* he personified the raucous heretic 'announcing his judgments, sometimes with brutal coarseness, though oftener in a tone that shows he is, after all, rather holding political caucuses on Sunday morning, than anything else, and that his hearers so understand him by answering his appeals to their passions with clapping of hands and other signs of caucus-like applause.'

Parker's friends countered these accusations by saying that his fierceness, his 'Moral Irascibility,' came naturally to one who was 'wroth with wrong.'

His commanding merit as a reformer is this [Emerson declared], that he insisted beyond all men in pulpits,—I cannot think of one rival,—that the essence of Christianity is its practical morals; it is there for use, or it is nothing, and if you combine it with sharp trading, or with ordinary city ambitions to gloze over municipal corruptions, or

private intemperance, or successful fraud, or immoral politics, or unjust wars, or the cheating of Indians, or the robbery of frontier nations,
or leaving your principles at home to follow on the high seas or in
Europe a supple complaisance to tyrants,—it is a hypocrisy, and the
truth is not in you.

Revering men as he did and never happier than when making a
eulogy, Parker could smash a reputation to bits when he felt it
necessary, regretfully as in the case of Webster, but none the less
thoroughly. He did not enjoy his reputation of washing down his
dinner with sulphuric acid, but there were times, Parker told himself, when silence could be a violation of God's law. 'If you do not
say what you think,' he wrote in his commonplace book, 'soon you
will dare to say what you do not think.'

His devastating candor when discussing the faults of sacrosanct
personalities and his relentless exposures of hypocrisy and wrong-
doing partly explain why this Paul of the Transcendentalists became the most popular preacher of his day. A soft-spoken, genteel
sort of man, as one of his friends correctly pointed out, 'a man of
decencies and proprieties,' would not have been able to fill the
Music Hall week after week. Parker, without trying to be sensational, refused to differentiate social evils in the abstract from the
men who committed them, and the thousands of visitors who came
from all over America and from Europe to hear him declaim
against the iniquities of the times were not given tepid homilies on
morality but specific names and facts and issues.

They saw a short stocky man who read from a manuscript, ac-
centuating significant points with ungraceful gestures. His face was
homely and rugged, his forehead high. A slightly protruding lower
lip added a touch of pugnacity to his face, which a strong chin,
later concealed by a beard, seemed to reinforce. In some of his
pictures he looked like an Indian fighter, in others like a man of
affairs. He suggested Franklin and Daniel Boone rather than Alcott or Emerson; the plowman, as Lowell said, more than the priest.

Parker talked simply, drawing his allusions from the world of
Boston and its environs, enlivening his long discourses with humor,
satire, and invective. He once told Thomas Wentworth Higginson
'that the New England people dearly loved two things,—a philo-

sophical arrangement and a plenty of statistics,' and Parker gave
them what they wanted. He would stuff his sermons with widely
assorted facts and bolster his moral appeals with a sometimes incredible infusion of corroborative testimony taken from historical,
scientific, and sociological sources. He would inject this mass of
detail even though it made his sermon or discourse topheavy, but
the close attention with which his congregation (numbering between two or three thousand in Boston) heard his two-hour talks
showed that his listeners did not resent the demands he placed
upon their patience or their faculties. No matter who had spoken
on an issue, Higginson tells us, the majority of the 'progressive'
thinkers in New England wanted to hear what Theodore Parker
had to say about it before making up their minds. And not simply
New England. Parker made the whole country his parish. During
one winter in the 'fifties, shortly before his breakdown, he lectured in every northern state from Maine to Wisconsin, and eighty
thousand people are said to have heard him.

An enormous following who did not have the opportunity to
hear 'the notorious Christian infidel' read him with avidity. His
printed sermons, Frothingham says, 'were sold by the thousands
and read by the ten thousand. Strangers from afar— carried his
thought all over the land. His name was spoken in the places of
power by men who had the political and social destinies of the
country in their charge—by statesmen, senators, governors of
States.' And Frothingham did not exaggerate, as a glimpse into
Parker's correspondence will prove. His letter books contain hundreds of communications from men and women all over the United
States, from Europe, from as far off as India. The tributes and testi-
monials that deluged him came mostly from the humbler sorts of
people, men and women who wished to thank him for his advice,
money, or encouragement, but leading statesmen from his own section and from the outside acknowledged his leadership—public
figures like Horace Greeley and Charles Sumner, Seward from New
York, Salmon P. Chase from Ohio, George Bancroft the historian,
and Lincoln's law partner, Herndon, who passed on Parker's pamphlets and sermons to his friend.

Successful in his dealings with men of affairs, his genius also triumphed over the respectability of Boston and Cambridge and the conservative elements, lay and clerical, who had tried to muzzle him. As his friend Wendell Phillips pronounced somewhat grandiloquently,

> They said, 'He shall not have the sounding board of Brattle Street, nor the walls of Chauncey place for an audience': and when they denied him these, they gave the Rocky Mountains for a sounding board, and the hearts of every hopeful and oppressed man for an audience.

Parker, who had planned at the outset of his career 'to do more through the *Press,* than the *Pulpit,'* hardly exaggerated when he told his congregation in 1859: 'In the last dozen years, I think scarcely any American, not holding a public office, has touched the minds of so many men, by freely speaking on matters of the greatest importance, for this day and for the ages to come.'

The astonishing popularity of his written works, the published sermons and discourses, cannot be readily explained by his style. He was not really a gifted writer, as any reader of his sermons will discover. Hastily composed, often repetitive, and lacking charm and finish, they suggest the mind of a person more interested in what he says than how he says it. The orotund passages that studded his sermons must have pleased audiences who relished elaborate rhetoric, but they seem a little self-consciously poetical to modern ears. Parker liked to think of himself as a frustrated bard and philosopher drawn by necessity into reform movements for which he had no special talent, but actually his imagination was thoroughly practical, and his fondness for the conventionally poetic does not strike us as genuine.

When Parker wrote naturally and in the spirit of Poor Richard, his prose took on a freshness and distinction at times almost Emersonian. Unusual metaphors and phrases revealed an observant mind well stocked with images of farm and city. His prose became earthy as he described a heap of potatoes or roots ('what homely and yet what comely things they are! nay, the commonest of them all has a certain rather hard, but masculine beauty and attractiveness') or Daniel Webster, whom he damned with epithet and epigram. Webster's course, wrote Parker, 'was as crooked as

the Missouri,' his later speeches smelled of bribes, he had 'been
on all sides of moral questions, save the winning side,' he had degenerated into a decrepit lion whose mane 'draggled' in the dust,
'his mouth filled with Southern dirt.' This same lion 'poisoned the
moral wells of society with his lower jaw, and men's consciences
died of the murrain of beasts, which came because they drank
thereat.' The cause of slavery, which Webster defended, threatened to silence Parker himself, but he warned his listeners that 'the
thread which is to sew my lips together will make your mouths but
a silent and ugly seam in your faces.' This is not language for posterity, but there is something in this hard talk that suggests, as Higginson pointed out, Parker's own description of Luther's eloquence:

> The homely force of Luther, who, in the language of the farm, the
> shop, the boat, the street, or the nursery, told the high truths that
> reason or religion taught, and took possession of his audience by a
> storm of speech, then poured upon them all the riches of his brave
> plebeian soul, baptizing every head anew,—a man who with the people
> seemed more mob than they, and with kings the most imperial man.

Parker was too busy to polish or refine his prose, but at its best it
brings back to us something of what he called 'the strong, rank life
of the nineteenth century' and justified Phillip's remark: 'How direct and frank his style! just level to the nation's ear.'

One is occasionally annoyed by his air of martyrdom, by his
patronizing references to inferior races and nations. But his sermons and discources are not seriously marred by these intrusions.
For the most part they are lusty, sensible, and honest. The ideas
they contain are seldom very deep or original, and yet they are
often acute and stated freshly and vivaciously. Finally, Parker is a
consistent if not a systematic thinker, and his political and social
theories can be presented without the kind of apologies and qualifications that follow as a matter of course when writing about
Emerson.

III] Theodore Parker came from what is familiarly
known in success-story language as 'sound stock'—native and
Anglo-Saxon. Parker men had helped to found Massachusetts Bay
and his grandfather commanded a handful of farmers at the Battle

of Lexington. Proud of his Anglo-Saxon heritage ('this Anglo-Saxon people . . . has many faults, but I think it is the best specimen of mankind which has ever obtained great power in the world)' he frequently mentioned his warlike grandpa and liked to quote his famous order: 'Don't fire unless fired upon; but if they mean to have a war, *let it begin here!*' Something of the doughtiness of Captain John Parker could be seen in his grandson Theodore, who some seventy-five years after Lexington helped fugitive slaves to break federal laws and advised one of them to kill if there were no other way to preserve his liberty.

The birth of Parker on 24 August 1810 swelled the size of his father's family to eleven. Families came much larger in those days than now; even so, his father, a versatile and industrious Lexington farmer, was no money-maker and far too poor to smooth things over for his children. Nevertheless he seems to have been a rather unusual man, if not by the standards of Van Wyck Brooks's New England renaissance, at least by ours; and Parker's precocity and intellectual gourmandizing can be attributed in part, perhaps, to the influence of his solid and many-sided parent—farmer, mechanic, and amateur metaphysician—who reverenced the scholarship and erudition later amassed by his indefatigable son.

We might hurry through these biographical details, slight as they are, together with the accounts of Parker's preparatory training, his attendance at Harvard, his schoolmaster days before he entered the Divinity School at Cambridge, his subsequent calls to West Roxbury and finally to Boston, his struggles in the Unitarian ministry, for they are not, taken by themselves, always germane to Parker's political views. And yet some of these facts, or at least their implications, help to explain how the phenomenon, Theodore Parker, emerged and why he thought and acted as he did.

Superficially Parker's career follows the familiar pattern of the American success story: the poor boy rising by pluck and determination to become the greatest preacher of his times. He is a radical and a reformer because he has come up 'the hard way'; he has sweated and suffered and now carries within him the burden of responsibility for a community that had sustained him through his dreary apprenticeship.

All this is true so far as it goes, and yet just enough considerations are left out to distort the picture. Had Parker been an Irish immigrant just off the boat and reared in the Boston slums, or had he been even the son of a Lowell factory hand, already discriminated against and underprivileged, his life would be at once more remarkable and more readily explained. But Parker was none of these things. He belonged to a homogeneous community still relatively unmarred by class lines, a community welded together by common beliefs, still independent, confident, self-contained. His family was poor, to be sure, but at the same time respected and able to give him a name and a position in New England society that outsiders could attain only with difficulty. The great influence he later exercised over his countrymen, especially in New England, lay in his power to draw upon the moral presuppositions of a people he understood and who in turn understood him. Parker articulated his society's neglected ideals—republicanism, the equality of every man before God, the right to work and be happy—and if he drew the anger of his conservative contemporaries, they stoned him with the particular kind of vehemence a people reserves for its own prophets. His radicalism was autochthonous. He did not suffer as does the subversive alien, the importer of the new and the strange, even though he might have been lynched if he had ventured into some southern districts during the 'fifties.

This is not to say, of course, that Parker remained unscathed by the conservative opposition or that his road was an easy one. No reformer's is. New truths, he realized, 'seem destructive as the farmer's plough,' even though they herald a harvest. Parker had too many things to say that were not congenial to his generation, and from the earliest days of his West Roxbury ministry when he admonished his congregation, consisting mostly of farmers, on the sins of dairymen to the last years when he infuriated the money-captains of State Street, he engaged in a rough-and-tumble controversy that would have broken a softer man.

Long before he joined with Phillips and Garrison against the 'foul monster' of slavery, he had shocked orthodox Unitarians with his rationalistic treatment of what he deemed permanent and transient in the Christian religion and had amplified and developed Emerson's bland infidelities. He had never been a pliant student—formalism of any kind, religious or political, irritated him—and he welcomed Emerson's dissolving logic as a reagent that would crystalize the real out of the apparent. By 1836 Parker had completed his studies at the divinity school, and two years later he was criticizing the conventional treatment of the miracles of the Pentateuch.

Nature had delighted him, although he questioned Emerson's doing away with matter entirely and for several years regretted the Transcendentalists' penchant for confounding God and man, but the 'Divinity School Address' impressed him even more deeply. 'It was the noblest of his performances,' he wrote shortly after, 'a little exaggerated with some philosophical untruths . . . but the noblest, the most inspiring strain I ever listened to. . . It caused a great outcry, one shouting "The Philistines be upon us," another, "we shall all be *dead men*," while the majority called out "Atheism." ' Parker enjoyed especially Emerson's thrusts against the organized churches, already under fire from Orestes Brownson, and felt obliged to carry on the campaign. But where Emerson seemed content to write subversively from his Concord study, Parker, perhaps impelled by the tempestuous Brownson, insisted on proclaiming transcendentalist heresies from the pulpit, and it was on this issue that he split from his more orthodox Unitarian brethren.

The experience of being snubbed by ministers and scholars, dropped by his friends, and excluded from certain respectable circles—especially during the years between 1837 and 1846 when he preached at West Roxbury—was an important one for Parker, although hardly beneficial in every respect. The copious abuse he received warped him a little, made him unduly sensitive to criticism, and perhaps even accounted for some of his vitriolic judgments; it brought too frequently a note of self-pity into his discourses and letters, which his critics and even his close friends felt obliged to comment on. Samuel Gridley Howe, one of his warmest friends and a candid, perspicacious man, constantly chided him for being thin-skinned and oversensitive. It was time, Howe said, that he stop attributing 'unworthy motives' to people who disagreed with him, that he remove 'some spots of *hard grit*' from his 'warm and loving heart,' and that he become more charitable in thought and word.

But if persecution brought out this grit in his personality and made him want to kill rather than to put to death, as Howe said, 'the moral vermin it is your mission to remove,' it sharpened his convictions about the right conduct of a Christian minister. In accepting the pastorate of Boston's Twenty-eighth Congregational Society in 1846, he preached his own ordination sermon on 'The True Idea of a Christian Church' and removed whatever doubts anyone might have had about his firmness and determination as a reformer:

In the midst of all these wrongs and sins, the crimes of men, society, and the state, amid popular ignorance, pauperism, crime, and war, and slavery too—is the church to say nothing, do nothing; nothing for the good of such as feel the wrong, nothing to save them who do the wrong? Men tell us so, in word and deed; that way alone is 'safe'! If I thought so, I would never enter the church but once again, and then to bow my shoulders to their manliest work, to heave down its strong pillars, arch and dome, and roof and wall, steeple and tower, though like Samson I buried myself under the ruins of that temple which profaned the worship of God most high.

He exhorted his congregation to engage in practical religion, perform good works, become martyrs if necessary. The Christianity of Christ, he assured them, would 'build up a great state with unity in the nation, and freedom in the people; a state where there was honourable work for every hand, bread for all mouths, clothing for all backs, culture for every mind, and love and faith in every heart.' A decade before he probably would not have said these things, for he had not expected to be a reformer; he knew now that a Christian minister, if he abided by his professions, could be nothing else. He saw now the connection between religion and politics and economics, and he became increasingly obsessed with the political implications of his new role.

He had much to learn about politics and his fellow Americans. The security of place and family and profession that made it easier for Parker to say unpopular things accounted also for his parochialism, for what might almost be called a regional complacency. He had an exaggerated notion about the nature of his own section and a deep scorn for parties, native or alien, that offended his political code. Like Emerson, he disparaged the Irish and the American Democratic politicians who exploited them. He felt more at ease with what he chose to regard as the busy, decent natives of his beloved New England and always returned home from his peregrinations more certain than ever that only Massachusetts could provide the indispensable moral tone for the rest of the Union.

One might think that Parker's radical bias would have made him a staunch advocate of Jackson and his 'wool hat' boys, but he never felt at home with the Democrats despite his confession, made in 1837 and probably under the spell of Orestes Brownson, that 'I grow more loco-foco-ish every day.' He agreed pretty largely with Emerson's conclusions—the Whigs had the best men, the Democrats the best principles—and actually voted the Whig ticket in 1844 and 1846. But he did so reluctantly, because he had no love for the negations of Whiggery, or, as Parker usually called it, Hunkerism. Had the Democrats followed the gospel of Jefferson, had they weeded out the mercenary, tobacco-chewing, and envious elements from their ranks and substituted for their present watchword, 'I am as good as you, damn ye,' the more fitting, 'You are as good as I, may God bless you,' there would have been no question about his allegiance.

Neither party, in Parker's opinion, met the real responsibility of government: to make Americans *'a wiser people* and a *more moral* people.' The country was economically sound enough, he believed, to withstand a bad administration or two, but when the Capital stank 'with such creatures as Polk, Pierce, Buchanan and the like of them!' and party leaders habitually perverted the ends of government to their own advantage, America was ready for the despot. The Daniel Websters and even the Abraham Lincolns who held back or compromised enraged him. Confronted with the great wrong of slavery, no honest man need hesitate to declare himself, and if the extirpation of that wrong meant the end of the Union,

why then Americans must give up their chimerical faith that a
civilization half slave and half free could last. Dissatisfied with
the leadership in both of the major parties, he decided that he
could make himself most effective by keeping clear of party allegiances and devoting himself to "education—*intellectual, moral,
and religious* education—everywhere and for all men.'

With such a goal, he could contemplate the breaking up of the
United States with few qualms, not only because he hoped to see
the cancerous South cut out of the body politic but also because
he regarded a nation of a hundred million Anglo-Saxons as an
anomaly. 'We do not like centralization of power,' he wrote, 'but
have such a strong individuality that we prefer local self-govern-
ment; we are social, not gregarious like the Celtic family. I, therefore, do not look on the union of the States as a thing that is like
to last a great length of time, under any circumstances. I doubt if
any part of the nation will desire it a hundred years hence.'

Thus Parker with characteristic assurance described the future
course of a country he frequently misunderstood. He could be
strikingly wrong on occasion—impatient, pig-headed, and undis-
criminating—but enough has been said of his unmistakable limitations. Our task now is to reconcile the provincial, myopic, and
sometimes querulous martyr with the transcendental and democratic Parker who overshadowed the first and belied his own prejudices, who championed unpopular causes with impressive energy,
and who put aside his theological speculations when the times
called for a stump orator.

          IV] Believing as he did that all men partook of God
and shared His glory and dignity, the transcendentalist by the logic
of his position had to support political theories that placed human
rights above material rights and to judge all institutions by their
value to man. Parker's comment on Emerson might stand for the
transcendentalist creed in general:

> On earth only one thing he finds which is thoroughly venerable,
> and that is the nature of man; not the accidents, which make a man
> rich or famous, but the substance, which makes him a man. The
> man is before the institutions of man; his nature superior to his his-

tory. All finite things are only appendages of man, useful, convenient, or beautiful. Man is master, and nature his slave, serving for many a varied use. The results of human experience—the State, the Church, society, the family, business, literature, science, art—all of these are subordinate to man: if they serve the individual, he is to foster them, if not, to abandon them and seek better things.

Parker's emphasis upon the body as well as upon the mental well-being of man deserves some attention here, not only because it foreshadowed the notions of postwar reformers like Edward Bellamy but also because most of his fellow transcendentalists looked upon the body in the same ambivalent way in which Hawthorne pictured the attractiveness and the menace of Rappaccini's sensuous garden. We cannot say that he subordinated the ideal to the physical, and yet his practical interest in marriage, sex, and physiology clearly differentiates him from Emerson (who found the body an uninspiring if not a distasteful subject) and Thoreau, repelled by sensuality. The appetites of man, Parker felt, could no more be ignored than his spiritual cravings, and if we find no catalogues of 'the Body Electric' in his writings, he exhibits on occasion a Whitmanesque frankness in discussing human passions:

> God put no bad thing there; it is full of good things; every muscle is a good muscle; every nerve which animates the two is good nerve. . . Trust your own flesh and your own soul, not the words of Paul,—a great brave man, but sometimes mistaken like you and me.

His celebration of the body had a close bearing upon his social theories and kept him from making the mistake of devoting himself too exclusively to the spiritual problems of society.

As a transcendentalist Parker naturally turned to the individuals, 'the monads, the primitive atoms, of which society is composed,' but he saw the individual as a component of the community, the culmination of the individual collectivized. The community was secondary, to be sure. 'Destroy the individuality of those atoms, human or material, all is gone. To mar the atoms is to mar the mass. To preserve itself, therefore, society is to preserve the individuality of the individual.' And yet to Parker, far more than to Emerson or Thoreau, the community, or the individual enlarged, tended to comprehend its constituent parts. 'Nobody,' he said, 'is as great as everybody.' He could exalt the community and remain consistent with his premises, because only in the well-ordered community did individual man most satisfactorily realize himself. Thoreau notwithstanding, man could not escape his contemporaries and their influence. 'He may, indeed,' Parker noted, 'withdraw himself from their meetings, and refuse to co-operate with them, but to attempt to retire from all sympathy with them is silly, and to pretend to have done it is preposterous.' Society at once quickened and channelized human energies. It worked imperfectly, to be sure, but he anticipated the immense forces available to mankind once it had harnessed 'the great rivers of humanity . . . forever overflowing their banks, raging and tearing and committing destruction.'

v] Having more respect for the complexities and mundane concerns of day-to-day living than most of the Transcendentalists and distrusting anarchistic notions, Parker took a greater interest in the practical details of government than his solipsistic friends did. But if government amounted to something more than Emerson's 'useful cow,' it existed only for the convenience of man and succeeded or failed according as it served or neglected his interests. He had no mystical notions about its origins. Because human society was divinely ordained (men naturally united and formed societies), it did not follow that government shared that divine origin. Men organized governments because they needed rules to live by and officers to administer them. Governments depended finally upon the desires of men; they could claim no other excuse for being. 'A state *has no right to enact wrong*,' Parker insisted, and he reminded those who made a fetish of the state that it could perfectly well operate in the interests of the Devil.

If governments stood only as temporary and worldly systems dependent on the people who erected them and to the eternal laws that transcended them, how could they justify themselves? Parker answered that question to his own satisfaction—and it was here that he parted company with most of his contemporaries—by ascribing to government certain vital 'positive' functions: to facilitate the organization of 'the powers of Nature for the service of man,' to fuse 'the social powers of humanity, so as to have national unity of action,' and 'to develop the individual man into a great variety of forms.'

Parker's contemporaries, generally speaking, did not share his views on the positive role of government. They argued over the power of government to underwrite internal improvements, charter banks, and regulate commerce, but even if their attitude toward a particular national or state policy depended upon the degree to which they suffered or benefited, the idea of a socially responsible government such as is envisioned, let us say, in Paine's *Agrarian Justice,* or even in the mind of John Quincy Adams, seldom entered their thoughts. Parker, who had read Paine with profit, did not bother very much about constitutional niceties. He got down to the point at once. Government overstepped its functions only when it prevented a people from carrying out good and expedient programs and when it tried to make statutes superior to higher laws. Parker never conceived of government as the impartial or impersonal umpire; he neither feared nor worshipped it. Government, in Parker's view, became simply a social instrument; its effectiveness depended upon the intelligence and virtue of its users.

Now it is true that any form of government presented a potential threat to popular liberties, but the true and legitimate ends of government, Parker felt, were most likely to be gained under a democracy, a term he defined before Lincoln as 'direct government over all the people, for all the people, by all the people.' Democracy, committed to secure these inalienable rights never relinquishd by the citizen, was by Parker's definition the only form of government prepared to guarantee these rights with a minimum of personal restraint.

Democracy derived its ultimate sanction from the will of God, but Parker noted its slow acceptance by mankind and traced its gradual rise in America from the time when it existed as a vague sentiment until its final practical application. He did not join his contemporary, Daniel Webster, in imputing democratic ideas to the Puritans. The Puritans, he recognized, 'had no fondness for a Democracy,' and he shrewdly observed that the 'road to the ballot box lay under the pulpit, only church members could vote, and if a man's politics were not marked with the proper stripe it was not easy for him to become a church-member.' Puritanism sanctioned slavery and upheld the 'claims of gentility' against 'the spirit of freedom,' but nature and history gradually undermined the influence of the oligarchy. New ideas smothered in Europe, where 'the old stubble still choked the rising corn,' but in America great political ideas took root and flourished. The wilderness-bred freeman judged a person by his accomplishments and ignored his origins; the Old Testament freshened the democratic idea by teaching its advocates 'forms of denunciatory speech'; and Europe furnished congeries of political ideas eventually welded together in the Declaration of Independence, 'the most remarkable and important State paper in the world.'

Out of the American experiment came a new and powerful conception, which Parker called 'industrial democracy.' This phrase, 'industrial democracy,' which came into greater currency during the closing decades of the nineteenth century, appears frequently in Parker's writings. Since it is probably his most interesting contribution to American political thought (and the most germane for modern readers) as well as a very early expression of what was to be the linchpin of American progressivism, it deserves closer attention.

According to Parker, a democratic society, if it were ever to approximate its aspirations, could not be content with a mere superstructure of political and social equality.

Democracy is not possible except in a nation where there is so much property, and that so widely distributed that the whole people can have considerable education—intellectual, moral, affectional, and religious. So much property, widely distributed, judiciously applied, is the indispensable material basis of a democracy; as military power is indispensable to the existence of an unnatural oligarchy—priestly, monarchic, nobilitary, or despotocratic; and as those tyrannical rulers must have military power to keep the people down, so in a democracy the people must have property—the result of their industry—to keep themselves up, and advance their education; else, very soon there will be a government over all, but by a few, and for the sake of the few; and democracy will end in despotism.

A considerable part of Parker's reformist writings centered in the analysis and exposure of those subversive influences—religious, political, and economic—threatening the democratic state, but Parker placed the chief responsibility for social obstruction on the mercenary values of his generation. In the new industrial age, money became the criterion for success, 'the symbol of power, for the individual and for the nation,' and when this itch to acquire money reached a point where 'the generic rights of human nature' became secondary to property, industrial democracy passed away.

The Revolution, Parker said, forced Americans to ponder metaphysical questions, but the absence of despotic pressure and the huge growth in national wealth since 1776 had accentuated the country's preoccupation with material things. He did not inveigh against wealth as such but only against its improper distribution. Certainly the lack of it undermined his health during his student days, and he reflected bitterly on the truth that wealth often painlessly confers what genius struggles to attain. Wealth had become the sole measure of value, the justification for social prestige.

The unremitting quest for the 'almighty dollar' destroyed industrial democracy and set up in its place a kind of industrial feudalism that produced the terrible sores of the factory age. Parker did not deplore the economic revolution; its coming, he recognized, heralded a new age of plenty. But he was not so sanguine or myopic that he failed to see the social and cultural effects of industrialism, which even more than the incidental injustices jeopardized 'spiritual individuality, all freedom of mind and conscience.' New England was 'a monumental proof thereof.' The finest talent of the nation, which in an industrial democracy might be turned to public business, now engaged almost entirely in commerce and manufacturing, strengthening the capitalist feudality, aggravating class antagonism.

Such a system, he soon became convinced, was irrational and unchristian, and he feared that if the deification of property continued at the present rate, it would only be a matter of time before the Yankee nation would resemble the English—'a mass of cloth and food' with 'many naked backs and hungry mouths.' It was Orestes Brownson, most probably, who started him thinking about the inequalities of wealth, and while he confessed that Brownson's 'property notions agree not with my view,'

certainly the present property scheme entails awful evils upon society, rich not less than poor. The question, first, of inherited property, and, next, of all private property, is to be handled in the nineteenth century, and made to give its reason why the whole thing should not be abated as a nuisance.

The new commercial and industrial order was building a parvenu elite, a mass of 'practical atheists' and slaveholders, the conscious and unconscious enemies of industrial democracy and their host of lackeys. Parker knew these children of darkness and their works. He did not let his respect for human nature deter him from his prophetlike denunciations, and his analysis of the then prevailing business ethics—the greed, indolence, selfishness of the ruling groups—indicated his awareness of the extent to which human nature, good in itself, could become infected by corrupt institutions.

vi] The acquisitive elements in American society, the 'regressive forces,' as Parker called them, became the object of his fiercest diatribes, because collectively they represented the poisoned fount from which all social contagion flowed. The stewards of wealth debauched education, literature, religion, and politics; they sanctioned slavery. Although they included among their numbers the cruel, the mercenary, and the ignorant, Parker, in his milder moods, did not blame them as individuals but only as a blind and thoughtless class. 'Here wealth is new,' he wrote in 1849, 'and mainly in the hands of men who have scrambled for it adroitly and with vigour. They have energy, vigour, forecast, and a certain generosity, but as a class, are narrow, vulgar, and conceited.' Their devotion to their own self-interest, moreover, precipitated offenses against the property and the lives of their own countrymen and the people of other nations. 'There is no country in Christendom,' he said, 'where life is so insecure, so cruelly dashed away in the manslaughter of reckless enterprise.'

Business touched the lives of men more intimately than any

other social institution and was for this reason, Parker realized, a most influential educator. In other countries rival hierarchies with different sets of values diminished the potency of business, but here in the United States business owned and controlled all channels of opinion-making: 'so it subtly penetrates everywhere, bidding you place the accidents before the substance of mankind, and value money more than men.'

Parker belongs among the first of the early observers of competitive capitalism who noticed how the assumptions of business became national assumptions, and how the businessman supplanted the minister and the statesman as the articulator of American ideals. In the spirit of the later progressives, he pointed out the dangers of unreflective economic individualism, dangers that were to become more crucial as the century drew to a close. Business, however idealistic its motives and well-meant its intentions, too often injured the community in the process of getting what it wanted. And as for the ravages of unrestricted enterprise, were they the inevitable price a nation had to pay for the luxury of political democracy? Parker did not think so. The rule by 'despotocrats'—later generations were to name them 'malefactors of great wealth' and 'economic royalists'—he saw as a disease and the abuse of the principle of leadership.

Here again it should be pointed out that Parker did not condemn the activities of commerce and industry as such. But Parker questioned the ultimate value of their calling, because it placed a premium upon self-aggrandizement and smothered all inclinations for community service and self-sacrifice. Jesus had said that 'he who would be the greatest of all, must be most effectively the servant of all.' Business ethics hardly complied with this credo.

As a general rule, Parker said, the men of great property in American cities, seemed 'strangely debauched in their morals' and never could be found on 'the moral side of any great question.' The great technological improvements, 'the property of mankind,' they used for their own advantage and imposed upon the community a new tyranny of machinery, a new feudalism of money, which stole a man's work if not his person. Opposed to them stood the large masses of the working people 'with no capital but muscles or skill,' but in this clash of interests the weaker party always lost out. Following the sacred injunction—buy cheap and sell dear— the merchant-traders and merchant-manufacturers disregarded the social effects of their acts and either countenanced or ignored the pauperism, crime, and oppression that accompanied the radical industrial changes they helped to introduce. 'The weaker class,' wrote Parker, 'can seldom tell their tale, so their story gets often suppressed in the world's literature, and told only in outbreaks and revolutions.' For this reason he assigned himself the role of spokesman for the repressed producers and summed up the case against the business classes.

Parker's charges have become familiar even though he made them some hundred years ago when capitalism in this country was young and uninhibited. First of all, he stated baldly that the trading classes dominated politics and owned the government. The laboring men had no such machinery. On rare occasions the people interfered and tried to 'change the traders' rule,' but ordinarily the merchant elite had its way:

Acting consciously or without consciousness, it buys up legislators when they are in the market; breeds them when the market is bare. It can manufacture governors, senators, judges, to suit its purposes, as easily as it can make cotton cloth. It pays them money and honours; pays them for doing its work, not another's. It is fairly and faithfully represented by them. Our popular legislators are made in its image; represent its wisdom, foresight, patriotism and conscience. Your Congress is its mirror.

Business not only made the statutes and kept the government in its pocket; it also muzzled the professions and saw to it that the molders of opinion—the clergy, the journalists, and the educators —advocated safe and cautious doctrines.

Hireling ministers, or, to use Parker's phrase, 'ecclesiastical blowbags,' preached in business churches and in endowed theological schools; 'hence,' he said, 'metropolitan churches, are, in general, as much commercial as the shops.' The church in America, he concluded scornfully, 'is based on the letter of the Bible and the notion of its plenary inspiration. It is the hospital of fools, the resort of rooks and owls. The one thing it does well is the baptizing of babies.'

The press, too, had thrown away its right to speak freely and independently. Servile, vulgar, materialistic, it reflected the morals of the class it represented: 'Our newspapers seem chiefly in the hands of little men, whose cunning is in a large ratio to their wisdom or their justice.'

And finally the schools knuckled under to the mercantile interests by excluding the controversial issues from the classroom and serving as training grounds for the rich instead of educating the majority for industrial democracy. For Parker, the nursery of academic reaction was 'the Alma Mater,' Harvard College, full of students undergoing a process of senilification and dedicated to the following academical creed:

1. *Riches* is the summum bonum; 2. *Respectability* i.e. the praise of men, is the bonum secundum; 3. *Education* is to give a man power to use men for his own purposes, i.e., to get the summum and secundum bonum. 4. Education consists in having a good deal of what every body not educated has a little of. 5. *Religion* means attending the most respectable church in the neighborhood, but without belief in the real God, or actual men. 6. *Democracy* is to be tolerated— because 'established by the Constitution of the United States.' 7. *Philanthropy* is to be ridiculed at all times,—it is a Fanaticism. 8. Daniel Webster is the greatest man that ever was, or is, or will be, and the Fugitive Slave Law saves the union.

Thus Parker concluded his arraignment of the merchants, the class that formerly had fought in the vanguard against conservatism and had helped to usher in a new era of trade and industry. The businessmen had forsworn their revolutionary birthright and now opposed the abolition of debtor laws, temperance reform, antislavery legislation. They had become at last the force of regression, the guilty sponsors of poverty and popular ignorance.

vii] Parker's indignation against the practices of the rapacious rich was balanced by an equally intense concern for the laboring poor, the men and women unrepresented in the press, excluded from the upper-class churches and colleges, and submerged by the trading classes. During the 'forties and 'fifties when Parker preached to eager congregations in the Melodeon and the Music Hall, factory towns were already beginning to nestle comfortably into the New England landscape, and the slums in his beloved Boston grew more rank and crowded. Parker, with his usual realism, saw the hopelessness of the workingman's position and recognized that the surface prosperity of the times concealed the plight of the producers. He had come to the conclusion quite early that the laborer did not receive a fair share of the wealth he produced. But even more important to him, as it also seemed to the post-Civil-War progressives, were the alarming signs that the laboring man had lost his sense of personal identity, that the operative had become merely a tool serving an industrial purpose.

Looking into the past and comparing with customary thoroughness the workingmen's status in Massachusetts a half or three quarters of a century earlier with their present state, Parker found no cause for optimism. In the statistical evidence he saw not only a decline in 'size, health, and longevity' but, even more important, a diminution of freedom of thought and manly independence. The change in working conditions, he believed, had much to do with this transformation. 'A large part of the men are now at work under cover, in factories or shops, and are also dependent on some man or corporation who employs them.' Material progress had followed as a matter-of course, but man, warped by the new machine discipline, paid a price for this progress. 'The industrial battle, like other battles, is won with a loss.'

If the conditions of the skilled operative, day laborer, or factory hand seemed bad, the circumstances under which the submerged or 'perishing classes,' as Parker called them, struggled to exist were infinitely worse. That such conditions could obtain in such a young country seemed to Parker inexcusable. Poverty might result from natural, political, or social causes; unfertile land, a bad climate, an enervated race of inhabitants might produce it, or bad laws or injurious prejudices—such as the prejudice against manual labor—but poverty in the United States could not be explained by any of these causes. God had stocked America with wealth and intended it 'to serve the great moral purpose of human life; to make the mass of men better off, wiser, juster; more affectionate, and more holy in all their life, without and within.' And yet with this rich trust, the nation was breeding a class of unemployables kept in a state of helpless degradation. Ignorant not out of choice but from necessity, this class lived like grubs in the crowded slums (they averaged thirty-seven to a house, he methodically observed) and paid rents that gave tenement owners from 12 to 30 per cent and over on their investments. These were the people demoralized by the glaring extremes of wealth and poverty, unjustly taxed, and ostracized from their so-called betters. Society met the threat of lower-class violence by administering an antiquated and barbaric system of penology instead of placing these prisoner-victims in moral hospitals and eradicating the conditions that bred them. It was perfectly characteristic of the Boston *bourgeoisie,* Parker noted bitterly, that they did not ask what could be done *for* these people but what could be done *with* them.

Parker had no illusions about poverty disappearing overnight, but he did know that it would remain until its causes had been removed. If he could not accept the conclusions of the Fourierites, he sympathized with their hopes and agreed with them that something must be done if America were to escape the convulsions almost certain to engulf Europe. There, he suspected,

a change must come. . . If powerful men will not write justice with black ink, on white paper, ignorant and violent men will write it on the soil, in letters of blood, and illuminate their rude legislation with burning castles, palaces, and towns.

America had not yet reached that point of crisis, but conditions were bad enough even here to make imperative something stronger than palliatives.

He proposed, as an illustration of what might be done, that the municipal authorities provide cheap and adequate housing for the poor if the capitalists neglected their responsibilities. The city would find it cheaper, he believed, to own and rent houses at a small profit than to spend huge sums on almshouses and on jails like the new 'Tombs' in New York City. The social order could not be Christianized by indiscriminate charity; broad economic

reforms were needed and a spiritual regeneration as well, for society's sin lay not so much in the unjust transmission of property,
as George Ripley believed, but in 'the *love of low things,* and in the
idea that work degrades.'

In the as yet unattained industrial democracy, Parker hoped
to escape the moral cannibalism that disfigured his own society.
In Massachusetts, he saw men dishonored and human abilities
wasted and repressed by the terrible tedium of work. Work in
itself was good (no one ought to eat who did not work) and
was not necessarily distasteful; yet labor through excess became a
curse and a punishment:

> Too much of it wears out the body before its time; cripples the
> mind, debases the soul, blunts the senses, and chills the affections.
> It makes a man a spinning-jenny, or a ploughing-machine, and not
> 'a being of a large discourse, that looks before and after.' He ceases
> to be a man, and becomes a thing.

In the good society that Parker anticipated, a man would do what
he was best fitted to do, and the number of crippled and aborted
natures, the direct consequences of excessive work and narrowing specialization, would decline.

Anticipating the later Utopians, he suggested that if all men
worked two hours a day, the nation as a whole would be better
housed and fed than it was, and the disgraceful situation would
no longer prevail of having one class crushed by the oppressive
indolence of another. He looked to the increased use of machinery to lighten the burdens of the workers. Thus far, machines had
not really benefited the men who operated them. The 'Hands'
continued to work fourteen hours a day when five would have
sufficed, because new technology, privately owned, only increased
the savageness and extensiveness of human exploitation. Parker
took the same illustrations that Henry George was to use for a
later generation. Like George, he drew the ugly paradox of poverty amidst plenty, the 'melancholy back-ground to the success
and splendid achievements of modern society.'

Yet Parker, by temperament and philosophy an optimist, did
not despair. 'It is curious,' he wrote shortly before his death,

'that Progress is never in a straight line for any length of time: There are bendings and windings and crossings backward—but still the general course is *on* and *up.*' He foresaw the time when Christianity would be applied to social life, when the drone would be treated as a robber and a pest, and no man would have a natural right to any more than he could earn or use. In the meantime, however, Parker consecrated his talents to combatting those ideas and practices that postponed the arrival of industrial democracy.

VIII] Parker's reputation today rests largely upon his fame as an antislavery agitator, so much so, it seems, that the fundamentally radical nature of his thought has been obscured by humanitarian sentiment. It is sometimes overlooked that his loathing for slavery inevitably sprang from certain views about man and society, ideas that his followers applied after the freeing of the slaves had been effected.

From approximately 1846 until his death in 1860, the slavery question absorbed more and more of his energies. Here was practical atheism in its worst form—the ownership of men by men, the conspiracy of property against the higher law. Slavery betrayed democracy and demoralized society.

The marriage of convenience between the northern commercial interests and the slave owners and their joint domination of the government did much to shape Parker's notions about the American political system: the nature of the Union, the courts, and the rights of the states. These are aspects of Parker's political thinking that seem the most topical and accidental. This provincialism in no sense invalidates his charges against slavery as a system any more than does his personal, almost physical distaste of Negroes as individuals. It was typical of Parker that he could risk his life and liberty to rescue a fugitive slave and at the same time refer to the Negro as an 'equatorial grasshopper.'

Many rabid abolitionists lost their radical fervor after 1865. So far as men like Whittier were concerned, the great blot upon democracy had been removed once and for all, and they renewed their interests in less controversial matters. Had Parker lived, however, it is more than likely that he would have carried on his crusade for human justice in the spirit of his close friend and co-worker Wendell Phillips.

But Parker could not keep up the destructive pace he had set for himself, nor would he take seriously the warnings of his friends to conserve his strength. Weakened by the strain of early privations and self-denials and constantly overtaxing himself, he broke down in 1858 and was forced to drop out of the fight. The trip to Europe that followed perhaps prolonged his life a short while, but his consumption was far too advanced to be checked. Parker spent his last months in Italy, reading Mommsen and brooding over the decline of the Roman Empire. The city of Rome spread out beneath his windows, but Parker's thoughts turned naturally to America, where another tragedy threatened. 'How young we are!' he wrote to a friend. 'Yet we have a more difficult problem to settle than the oldest European State is now vexed with —a Democracy with 4,000,000 Slaves—mocking at the first principles of all human society.' The episode at Harper's Ferry did not surprise him. 'It is only the beginning,' he said, 'the end is not yet. But such is my confidence in Democratic Institution⸗ that I don't fear the result.'

Parker died in 1860 on the eve of the war he had helped to bring about. 'There is a great deal of work to do,' he had written home before he died. 'I enlisted "for the whole war" which is not half over,' and yet he could regard his accomplishments with a certain amount of satisfaction. His last letter to his old friend George Ripley, composed on the eve of his death, closed with this apologia:

Oh George, the life I am slowly dragging to an end—tortured but painless—is very, very imperfect, and fails of much I meant of it, and might have reached, nay should, had there been ten or twenty years more left for me. But on the whole it has not been a mean life, measured by the common run of men, never a selfish one. Above all things I have sought to teach the true Idea of Man, of God, of Religion—with its Truths, its Duties and its Joys. I never fought for myself, nor against a private foe, but have gone into the battle of the nineteenth century and followed the flag of Humanity. Now I am ready to die—tho' conscious that I leave half my work undone—and much grain lies in my fields waiting only for him that gathereth sheaves.

Others were to gather in the unharvested sheaves.

Parker's social and political philosophy continued to be preached by a group of reformers imbued with his evangelical fervor and motivated by the same passionate concern for industrial democracy. They shared his view that the 'social evils which result from the struggles of competitive labour seem to outweigh all its benefits,' that the 'providential impulses of human nature were being forced to act in subversive ways and directions, when they might all be harmonized by their own inherent laws, and the blessings of mutualism succeed to the bane of antagonism.' Above all, they insisted with him on the too often neglected 'duty of the State to watch over the culture of its children.'

Parker's influence among the postwar reformers is difficult to trace directly, for to his contemporaries he was not a man with a special plan or message so much as a popular oracle for the dissemination of radical truths. From the tributes of his friends one is chiefly impressed by the general recognition of his powerful personality and of the galvanic energy his very presence seems to have communicated. Bronson Alcott, a very shrewd and sensitive observer—despite Parker's contemptuous opinion of him—testified to his 'formidable abilities,' and Samuel Gridley Howe expressed a similar thought when he wrote to Parker:

What a Terrible Turk you would have become, if your blessed mother had not set your face toward the Cross and given you an impulse thitherward! What a hard push the dear woman must have given you, to have got you so far along the uphill road! How lucky it is that there are evil institutions and wicked men in the world, for you to assail and belabour with your iconoclastic hammer, or you would have smote the good, and even struck upwards against the sky.

To see him as a great reformer, as the *Vir generosus,* to quote Phillips again, is perfectly proper so long as the bonfire of his personality does not distract us from what he had to say. For the sake of discussion, Parkerism must be abstracted from Parker.

Parkerism was at once a philosophy and a program of action. It assumed first of all that the business of man was not to amass property but to live. Whether a man realized his powers to the fullest, whether he had 'lived,' depended not only upon himself but also upon society. That is why Parker saw politics as the religion of a nation and economics as a branch of applied Christianity.

In the industrial democracy, no group withdrew itself from the economic and political work of society; no functionless class of drones made work seem ignoble. A man received his pay for the service he gave. He could even become rich. But industrial democracy did not permit the capitalist to occupy 'the chief seat in our Christian synagogue,' and it eliminated the grossly rich as well as the grossly poor. An industrial democracy, he hoped, would eradicate those conditions that made even political democracy an impossibility and end the formidable and as yet unknown power of consolidated property. It would extend material prosperity ('No nation was ever too well fed, housed, clad, adorned, and comforted in general') and lay the 'indispensable foundation for a spiritual civilization in some future age, more grand, I think, than mankind has hitherto rejoiced in.'

The later progressives implemented and restated these sentiments, improving upon them and adding new features, too, for the battle of the nineteenth century continued after Parker fell by the way. Parker's disciple and lieutenant, young Thomas Wentworth Higginson, worried at the close of the Civil War about the paucity of good causes left for the fighting reformer. 'We seem nearly at the end of those great public wrongs,' he wrote, 'which require a special moral earthquake to end them. There will be social and religious changes, perhaps great ones; but there are no omens of any fierce upheaval.' But Higginson soon realized, along with Wendell Phillips, that a new struggle was taking shape, potentially more explosive than the sectional war that preceded it. Both men bridged the gap dividing the century, carrying on Parker's battle, and fighting the corporate wealth ('bare, naked, shameless, undisguised,' in Phillips's words) that now seemed ready to impose an industrial slavery on the country. Most of the old abolitionists had either died or retired, but a new generation of reformers replaced them, men ready to speak out for 'the great mass, chained to a trade, doomed to be ground up in the mill of supply and demand, that work so many hours a day, and must run in the great ruts of business.' So Phillips described the undefended population in 1876.

Phillips, Parker's brother-in-arms, died in 1884. By that time, the 'patient armies of the poor' had discovered new leaders, such as Henry George, who reiterated Parker's conclusions with different emphases and yet who revealed the same concern for the predicament and potentialities of man in the modern world.

PART TWO

. . . .

'Prophetic Agitators'

. . . .

CHAPTER 3

Henry George:
The Great Paradox

1] The feeling of doubt and apprehension about the so-called benefits of the machine economy antedates, as we have seen, the post-Civil-War years in America. Many of General Jackson's supporters, in the words of Arthur Schlesinger, Jr., 'felt themselves the victims of baffling and malevolent economic forces which they could not profit by or control.' In the 1830's men were disturbed by the growing class divisions, by the pride and the snobbery that accompanied the increase of wealth, by the effects of aggressive individualism and the consequent weakening of the community spirit.

The majority of the discontented during this period did not advocate any revolutionary scheme of property redistribution, although there were some groups who did. What seemed to attract them the most were the movements that promised to insure equal social status and equality of opportunity. Public education, it was anticipated, would reduce the traditional handicaps of the poor in the race for success. Shorter working hours would allow the operative or the day laborer more time for self-improvement, so that he too could compete for the high offices. Early trade-union movements (especially the interesting but abortive flurry of activity in the 'thirties) sought not only to unite workers against the encroachments of organized capital but also to preserve their individuality. So, too, the community experiments of Owen and Fourier can be seen as fruitless attempts to redeem the frustrated and aimless citizen trapped, as the exuberant Utopians believed, in a savage and a chaotic society.

Evidences of insecurity or 'alienation,' already discernible before 1865, became more apparent during the last half of the nineteenth century. And as the impersonal economic order grew less
and less concerned with the vast changes it was effecting on the
American scene, and as the business community grew increasingly
irresponsible, it became necessary, as Walter Rauschenbusch said,
for the state 'to step in with its superior Christian ethics' before
unadulterated capitalism destroyed the social order. The reform
movements that agitated the country at this time, which increased
in turbulence and finally culminated in the wild eruption in 1896,
are less explainable by Marxian dialectic than by a kind of unconscious mass awareness of the community that it was being endangered by inhuman social forces.

One man who voiced this fear and proposed to circumvent the
threat to community welfare was Henry George. He is an ar-
resting and important figure in the progressive tradition, not because his program had much practical significance but because he
exerted a vast influence as a social philosopher and caught the
surge of unarticulated public despair and hope in a single book. In
an age of trusts and millionaires, of labor violence and depression,
George compounded the agrarian radicalism of Jefferson with the
humanitarian transcendentalism of the 'forties. He revived an old
American dream of equality and plenty and made clear to hundreds
of thousands the menace and the promise of nineteenth-century industrial society.

ɪɪ] Professor William Graham Sumner, who during
the last three decades of the nineteenth century rescued several
generations of Yale students from what he called 'the domination
of cranks,' once wrote an essay about a person he called 'the forgotten man.' Sumner's 'certain man who is never thought of' was
no kin to Franklin Roosevelt's lost citizen but an unsung embodiment of middle-class business virtues, a less flamboyant and more
respectable Poor Richard, the solid citizen who works hard, minds
his business, and pays for the stupidities and indiscretions of
the masses. Sumner worried about the forgotten man and spoke
for him whenever he could, because the forgotten man, patient and

long-suffering, had no other champions. Drunkards, criminals, and misfits successfully appealed to soft-headed reformers; the man who lived quietly, educated his children, and paid his debts never sank low enough to arouse their sympathies. Instead he was perpetually robbed by the philanthropists and nostrum-peddlers. His savings provided the capital for their absurd attempts to remodel the world.

Sumner also took an angry pleasure in portraying the vicious, shiftless, inefficient brother of the forgotten man. This improvident fellow possessed all the traits of the man in the street. He was a fool, a bungler, a band-wagon jumper. He believed that life was a banquet and that he had a natural right to a large portion of nature's feast. He envied the rich and wanted the advantages of wealth without working for them. He spoke about a golden age. He flattered human nature. In his personal life he was likely to be imprudent or intemperate. He usually married when he was too young and always had too many children. He could not support them. He never had any money in the bank. He chattered a good deal about 'injustice' and paid no taxes. He supported the crazy schemes of the Greenbackers or the Populists or the Socialists, gave lectures on the crimes of capital and on human equality, and dumped his badly disciplined progeny into a world already burdened with an excess of the same breed.

These sentiments came naturally from one who made a fetish of hard fact and whose entire life had been devoted to puncturing abstractions. Like other armchair realists dealing with particulars removed from their contents and carefully dusted, he sounded more practical than he really was, and the gospel of Herbert Spencer that he preached (with a few revisions) permitted him to consign the drunkard to the gutter and defend the millionaire with a tranquil conscience, assured that what God or nature had ordained, no human scheme could modify.

It is proper to mention Sumner in these introductory remarks not merely because he was a contemporary of Henry George and later his vigorous antagonist, not because of the curious parallels and contrasts of their respective careers, but because George might have served as Sumner's horrid example of the improvident man.

It was only coincidence that the essay series in which the phrase 'the forgotten man' first appeared (characteristically entitled 'What the Social Classes Owe Each Other') should be answered by George himself in *Frank Leslie's Illustrated Newspaper,* but a poetic significance lay hidden in George's rejoinder, which the Yale professor undoubtedly missed.

In the first place, Henry George never made any money in spite of the tremendous sales of his books; in fact he usually owed money and accepted loans and gifts of cash from his friends. From his birth in 1839 until his death fifty-eight years later, he lived a helter-skelter sort of life—working as a clerk, a sailor, a printer, a peddler—searching for gold, sleeping in barns, agitating, writing what Sumner would have considered nonsensical editorials, lecturing, pamphleteering, and in general doing everything that the forgotten man rigorously eschewed. As Sumner might have suspected, George proposed marriage with fifty cents in his pocket. He was twenty-two years old at the time, with no job and very meager prospects. He wore borrowed clothes to the wedding ceremony and barely managed to keep alive during the next five years. Like other improvident men, however, he promptly began to raise a family and on one occasion, after the birth of his second son in 1865, he had to beg five dollars from a stranger to keep his wife and children from starving. It is true that bad times had something to do with his early misfortunes, but Sumner, had he been reviewing George's career, would have dismissed this excuse with contempt. 'Here you have,' he might have said, 'the classic type of the improvident man, half-educated [George's education stopped when he was thirteen], restless and impractical, and totally devoid of those steady habits without which no man can succeed in the battle of life.'

Before George exploded into fame with *Progress and Poverty* it is quite likely that he would have humbly accepted these Sumnerian rebukes. He had too much of the middle-class ethic in himself not to be ashamed of his poverty and his aimlessness, and he constantly exhorted himself to save, to avoid running into debt. His eighteen years spent in ante-bellum Philadelphia, before the fateful journey to San Francisco, had stamped into him some of

the morality of the Quaker City's merchantdom, which even fourteen months aboard an old East Indiaman could not eradicate.
George's parents, like Sumner's, were devout Episcopalians, and
George was raised on the Bible and the Book of Common Prayer
and the Episcopal Sunday School books published, incidentally,
by his father. Although he drank whiskey with his friends, played
cards, and swore when away from his father's strait-laced household, the odor of respectable Protestantism clung to him nevertheless, and the guilty feelings he experienced during the early California days were quite possibly induced by his earlier pious associations.

Had his father been a more gifted man, or even a richer one,
had George's home atmosphere been less drab and more intellec-
tually stimulating, or had some discerning person recognized his
remarkable potentialities, George might have become an Episcopal
minister like Sumner and gone on to Göttingen and Oxford. Set
adrift at fourteen, George educated himself, but with all of his
wide reading he remained an uncultivated man with a feebly developed artistic sense and the instincts of a Philistine.

And yet Henry George did not end up in the gutter or in jail,
where, according to William Graham Sumner, improvident men
usually landed; on the contrary, he became a world-famous man.
His masterpiece, *Progress and Poverty,* was a work of genius,
but it was also the culmination of intense and varied experience
—experience quite alien to the bookish Sumner and far more real
than the obdurate facts he professed to deal with.

III] When George set sail for San Francisco aboard
a United States Lighthouse steamer in 1857, he had already
traveled and seen more sights than most eighteen-year-olds. Two
years before he had signed up as foremast boy on a ship captained
by a friend of his father's. On the voyage of the *Hindoo* he did not
see the opulent and exotic scenes he had anticipated, but he observed the unemployment in Melbourne and watched dead bodies,
covered with crows, float down the Hooghly River. To judge from
his recollections, life in the forecastle was no more glamorous than
the seamy Orient. 'There were so many cockroaches and bed bugs

on the vessel,' he wrote afterwards, 'and they got so black and thick that you could not get a drink of water or eat a piece of pie or eat soup without getting a mouthful of them. It was on this trip that I began to like cockroaches for they would eat the bed bugs up.'

George had one more short experience as a sailor after he returned from India, but parental pressure and the advice of the *Hindoo's* captain induced him to forget the sea. During the next few years he learned the trade of typesetter, drank 'red-eye' and smoked cigars with his friends, argued with his father and mother about slavery, and began to weigh the possibilities of going to Oregon. His friends there assured him that jobs were plentiful, and since thousands of 'hard fisted mechanics'—among whom he numbered himself—were being discharged daily from Philadelphia shops, the prospects of high wages in the West sounded especially alluring. The offer of a steward's berth on the Lightship *Shubrick,* bound for California, settled the matter, and on December 22 he left Philadelphia and all it contained with few misgivings. 'I know, my dear parents,' he wrote the next month from the West Indies, 'that you felt deeply the parting with me—far more so than I did. But let the fact that I am satisfied and that my chances are more than fair comfort you. As for me, I, for the first time in my life, left home with scarcely a regret and without a tear.'

If he had known what was to await him in San Francisco and what kind of life he was going to lead during the next decade, he might have written less jauntily to his grieving family. But George had already formed quite a good opinion of himself, if we can judge from a phrenological self-analysis he made while still in Philadelphia. This examination revealed a tendency toward rashness and over-zealousness which needed to be checked, but it also showed that the subject possessed an ardent, generous, and discriminating temperament, an audacious imagination, and a fearless, resolute spirit. One notation appearing in the phrenological report deserves special scrutiny, for it was uncomfortably substantiated in San Francisco: 'Desires money more as a means than as an end, more for its uses than to lay up; and pays too little attention to small sums.'

The question of money, or rather the absence of it, figured prominently in George's mind during the following years. He searched for it in the Frazer River gold fields; he shifted from job to job, to the concern of his family and friends, and he tramped around the state. All of these discouraging experiences helped to mature him and stock his mind with information, but they did not make him rich. What galled him particularly, he confided to his sister, was 'the fierce struggle of our civilized life,' and it was at this time that he began to dream about

the promised Millennium, when each one will be free to follow the best and noblest impulses, unfettered by the restrictions and necessities which our present state of society imposes upon him—when the poorest and meanest will have a chance to use all his God-given faculties, and not be forced to drudge away the best part of his time in order to supply wants but little above those of the animal. . .

George had not yet pondered the question of why work was scarce and hard to keep; he only knew, he wrote home in 1861, that 'the want of a few dollars . . . keeps us separate . . . forces us to struggle on so painfully . . . crushes down all the noblest yearnings of the heart and mind.' Some sixteen years later he began to formulate a reason and a solution for the dilemma, to raise the specter of poverty and lay it to rest; but a long time of trial remained before he was ready to announce the glad tidings to the world.

IV] After the first shock of discovering the rarity of windfalls and the improbability of picking up gold nuggets on the streets, George settled down to the job of staying alive. The city in which he had chosen to make his home was rapidly losing the look of an isolated coastal port and showing unmistakable signs of its future importance. When George got there in 1858, San Francisco depended on the ocean-going steamer for its communication with the outside. Two years later George wrote to his sister Jennie about the arrival of the Pony Express and his expectations of a transcontinental telegraph system by 1862. He thus found himself in the unusual position of watching the evolution of a society from 'incoherent homogeneity to coherent heterogeneity' (as his one-time idol, Herbert Spencer, phrased it) and drawing invaluable conclusions from this phenomenon. George Bernard Shaw, himself 'swept into the great Socialist revival' after hearing George speak many years later, subsequently wrote of George's California sojourn:

> Some of us regretted that he was an American, and therefore necessarily about fifty years out of date in his economics and sociology from the point of view of an older country; but only an American could have seen in a single lifetime the growth of the whole tragedy of civilization from the primitive forest clearing. An Englishman grows up to think that the ugliness of Manchester and the slums of Liverpool have existed since the beginning of the world: George knew that such things grow up like mushrooms, and can be cleared away easily enough when people come to understand what they are looking at and mean business. His genius enabled him to understand what he looked at better than most men; but he was undoubtedly helped by what had happened within his own experience in San Francisco as he could never have been helped had he been born in Lancashire.

As Shaw correctly observed, George might not have reached his solution if he had not been a close reasoner with an ability to see beneath the glittering surface of progress and to detect its latent consequences. An unreflective booster might have drawn the unwarranted conclusion that he automatically profited from the growth of his city or section and would have accepted the coming of the railroads and the resulting expansion of trade and population with complacence if not delight. But George early deduced that only the property holders or people with established businesses and special skills could expect to benefit. 'Those who have only their own labour,' he wrote in 1868, 'will become poorer, and find it harder to get ahead.'

The responsibilities of a marriage entered into with customary thoughtlessness may have provoked these sober reflections, and certainly the gloom of the early war years had something to do with them. But perhaps the real explanation was simply that Henry George was growing up. Resisting the impulse to join the Federals, he had taken a job as typesetter in Sacramento after his wedding.

He lost this job after quarreling with the foreman, and then he failed completely as a clothes-wringer salesman. The operation of a small job-printing business which followed earned him a precarious livelihood in the middle 'sixties, but it was not until 1868 that he secured a decently paid position on the San Francisco *Times*. George emerged from these dreary and seemingly interminable misadventures a more mature person and a more confident one. He had found out that he could write well, a piece of information any reader of his vigorously written log books and letters should have been able to give him, and he sensed that his opinions, hitherto scattered and unrelated, were beginning to shape into a coherent philosophy.

He had not yet developed his powers as a speaker, but in his newspaper work he now came face to face with organized wealth in the guise of autocratic railroad executives and the Associated Press monopoly. A trip to the East in the winter of '69 not only furnished convincing proof that no small individual concern could survive a contest with a monopolistic and influential organization like the Associated Press, but also illustrated for George the dramatic paradox of wealth and scarcity which he was to exploit so brilliantly in another ten years. In New York at this time, overcome perhaps by the sight of so much want and misery, he experienced what he later described as 'a thought, a vision, a call—give it what name you please' to devote himself to the eradication of poverty. But still the solution lay hidden. That monopoly, especially monopoly in land, had something to do with the great paradox, he was now ready to believe; by 1877, he became certain at last that land monopoly lay at the root of all social and economic ailments.

v] George's disciples, the more devout ones at any rate, have attached the same reverence to his vision and its subsequent embodiment in *Progress and Poverty* that the Israelites gave to the revelation of Moses on Mt. Sinai. His own account of the genesis of his ideas did not discourage this attitude, for although he was in many respects a modest man and disinclined to plume himself at the expense of his movement, he occasionally gave the impression of being the Lord's holy vessel. It would be possible, for instance—although unfair—to write his life as hagiography, to describe his youthful follies, his soul-searchings, his pilgrimage through the valley of the shadow, and then to conclude with the flood of irresistible grace and the transfiguration.

His first vision, it will be remembered, came to him in New York when he made his vow of social dedication. The second, and perhaps more important, vision occurred several years later when it suddenly burst upon him that 'with the growth of population, land grows in value, and the men who work it must pay more for the privilege.' He afterwards described this seemingly humdrum observation as 'one of those experiences that make those who have them feel thereafter that they can vaguely appreciate what mystics and poets have called the "ecstatic vision." ' That many of his followers sensed the transcendental origins of his book is borne out by the number of letters he received from 'believers' all over the world, in which they thanked the 'Master' or the 'Prophet,' as many of them addressed him, for vouchsafing his more than human message.

Putting aside these supra-rational explanations for the moment and turning to more verifiable facts about the events immediately preceding the writing of *Progress and Poverty,* we know that George sat down to work on September 18, 1877, after several years of active crusading against political corruption and social cruelty. Women's rights, prison reform, the treatment of sailors, honest elections—any issue bearing on the rights of the underdog or having any humanitarian implications—inspired his pen. During this period he built up and lost a promising newspaper, inspected gas meters, campaigned for Tilden (developing at this time his forensic talents), offended the political scientists at the University of California by impugning the value of 'all this array of professors, all this paraphernalia of learning,' thrilled San Francisco with a magnificent Fourth of July address, and speculated unluckily in mining stocks. The gambler kept pace with the seer.

In the early fall of 1877, Californians suffered from one of those periodic economic disturbances which economic philosophers disposed of very easily but which meant real privation for the wage earners. Denis Kearney founded his Workingmen's party and a 'citizens' committee retaliated characteristically by organizing a vigilance group of five thousand volunteers armed with the traditional pick handles and guns. At this point George began what was to be a magazine article on the question of poverty and progress. His personal affairs were rather unsettled, but neither the arrival of a fourth child nor the lectures he gave in the interests of the family larder interfered seriously with the writing of *Progress and Poverty* as it gradually lengthened into a book. Dressed in a shabby robe of saffron yellow, so a visitor described him, and surrounded by his books and papers, he seemed quite oblivious to what someone euphemistically called the 'rolicking disorder' of his dingy house. Anyone who has tried to work under similar conditions may well marvel at his self-possession and inward serenity, which enabled him to write one of the most lucid and logical of books in a house filled with small children. But George pushed along, and at the end of fourteen months of intermittent work, the book was done. He finished the last page in the middle of the night. Then, as he himself records it, he flung himself on his knees 'and wept like a child.'

The finished product did not satisfy him completely. The chapters dealing with the development of civilization were not so detailed as he had originally intended them to be, and he had a few misgivings about the intelligence of his west-coast audience; but George never doubted that the ultimate reception of his book would be favorable. Difficulties arose about getting it published, as George might have expected, and recognition did not come immediately, but its sensational popularity a few years later must have gratified his vanity even if it did not greatly surprise him. He had sent a copy of his book to his father, informing him with sublime assurance that although *Progress and Poverty* might not be accepted for some time, 'it will ultimately be considered a great book;—will be published in both hemispheres, and be translated into different languages.' What seems like conceit merely indicated a quiet faith in the truths he believed his book embodied; he had simply transcribed God's word and Nature's laws. Once published, *Progress and Poverty* ceased to be a personal thing for George. There it stood like any other natural object. One did not question a mountain or an ocean. 'My work is done,' he wrote to a friend; 'the rest is not my business. . . I do not think anything that could be said of it could either flatter or abash me.'

He was perfectly justified, to be sure, in attributing the success of *Progress and Poverty* to its intrinsic merits, but other circumstances had something to do with its tremendous vogue. It appeared toward the close of a long depression and served as a kind of literary equivalent to the bumper wheat crop of that year, which revived America's flagging economy. The poverty and unemployment he so bitterly arraigned, however, and the angry outbursts of a discontented laboring class were still fresh memories to a public now thoroughly alarmed about the growing class antagonism earlier discerned by Theodore Parker. Writers and publicists, perhaps with the Paris Commune in mind, hinted at vast working-class conspiracies and eyed such a sprawling inchoate organization as the Knights of Labor with wonder and fear. Actually, this body, formed secretly in 1869 to promote a friendlier public attitude toward the labor movement, had by 1879 lost any revolutionary zeal it might have possessed and was simply a loosely joined and ineffective aggregation of wage earners agitating for a conventional program of reform. But the Knights augured the rebirth of a more aggressive labor spirit in the 'eighties, and George, though he usually sided with labor, did not hesitate to point out to his middle-class audience what lay in store for them if the movement for reform fell into the wrong hands.

Progress and Poverty was, among other things, a lecture to the middle class on the tactics for survival. George, of course, presented his case as a moderate and democratic American who detested violent and illegal remedies, but he refused to minimize the dangers that might conceivably result from stupid inaction. Civilizations advanced or retrogressed; they did not stand still. And the dry-rot invariably set in as power and wealth tended to become unequal. George, following in Parker's steps, pointed out that technological progress in a plutocratic society increased inequality and accelerated national decay, thus giving the lie to the Andrew Carnegies, and he reminded stubborn conservatives that their refusal to scrutinize the rotten foundations upon which American prosperity rested endangered the lives of their children and their children's children. He threatened them finally with his prophecies of the new barbarians now breeding in noisome slums who would solve in their own way the problems ignored or mismanaged by their betters.

Had *Progress and Poverty* confined itself to these negative appeals alone, it would not have evoked such a universal response. George always emphasized the positive and constructive features of his plan. The real success of his book lay in its warmth and optimism, in the convincing way he demonstrated how the application of his one simple measure—the appropriation of rent by taxation —would 'substitute equality for inequality, plenty for want, justice for injustice, social strength for social weakness' and 'open the way to grander and nobler advances of civilization.' His book, in one sense, might be described as a dramatic poem justifying the ways of God to man.

VI] Anyone who has read *Progress and Poverty* can understand George's excitement in undertaking so tremendous a book and his exaltation on completing it, for it was indeed an astonishingly bold attempt. George proposed nothing less than to explain why poverty exists and how it could be abolished without disorganizing the economy or provoking social upheaval.

He aimed his book, moreover, at an audience hitherto bored by the doctrines of political economy or confused by the jargon of the professionals, who did not write their books for the average reader. He did not expect to reach directly the poverty-stricken and the hopelessly ignorant. They had been deprived of their natural rights so completely that they had lost their power to regain them without the help of luckier men. Their amelioration had to come from above. George preferred to address himself to a large number of business and professional men and to artisans, merchants, and skilled workers, who possessed the natural wit to comprehend the grand truths of the political economy he set out to expound. Stripped of its abstract terminology and the vicious distortions of its academic purveyors, the science of political economy was easily grasped. In *Progress and Poverty* George brilliantly succeeded in demonstrating this contention.

The ideas expressed in his masterpiece turned out to be less original than George had at first believed (many others had anticipated his solution) and his economic assumptions were not unassailable, but *Progress and Poverty* remains nevertheless one of the greatest popular primers ever written. George later discounted the question of originality as being of no importance. What really mattered, he said, was the fact that his book placed old truths in new relations, that 'it shattered the elaborate structure that under the name of political economy had been built up to hide them, and restoring what had indeed been a dismal science to its own proper symmetry, made it the science of hope and faith.' He made it at once a lesson in economics and a message of hope. As a treatise, it unfolded with clarity, logic, and simplicity; as an exhortation and a call to action, it throbbed with an emotion that unquestionably sprang from the author's sincerity but was heightened none the less by his skill as a popular rhetorican. *Progress and Poverty,* with its alliterative title, its dramatic structure, its theatrical set-pieces, fused fact and feeling and suggested through emotion what it did not convey by sense.

George opens his book with a presentation of his famous paradox—'the great enigma of our times,' the 'central fact from which spring industrial, social, and political difficulties that perplex the world, and with which statesmanship and philanthropy and education grapple in vain.' He sketches swiftly the glaring discrepancies between want and plenty and indicates that he will try to answer the riddle posed by the sphinx of fate. *Progress and Poverty* thus begins darkly and with a note of urgency, for the barbarians are already beginning to stir.

Before the prophet can cut down the tree of error, much underbrush must be removed. George is obliged to expose the false teachers who through their economic hocus-pocus have made poverty seem inevitable and permanent. The wage-fund theory of the classical economists—that wages are drawn from a limited stock of capital—and the gloomy pronouncements of Malthus, which attribute scarcity to a niggardly nature, are reviewed and demolished.

In this examination, carrying George almost one third of the way through his book, he discusses the issues in a quiet conversational tone and proves his points by the kind of homely analogy most reassuring to the average reader. He domesticates economics, removing it from the academic groves and bringing it to the firesides and offices and country stores. At intervals he stops and recapitulates, making certain that his basic axioms are completely understood, for *Progress and Poverty,* as George was fond of saying later, is a 'linked argument,' and he wants to make sure that no doubts remain before he mounts the next step.

Having struck off the gyves of Manchester, George proceeds to correlate and co-ordinate the laws of distribution. He has shown what poverty is *not* caused by, but he must still weed out other false distinctions and re-define such misinterpreted words as *wealth, capital, value, land,* and *rent* before the problem of poverty can be solved and its remedy suggested. The crux of this section lies in his definitions. The *value* of anything does not depend upon its mere exchangeability but on the degree to which it can command the product of labor. *Wealth* consists of *real* natural products 'modified by human exertion . . . labor impressed upon matter' and nothing else. *Capital* is stored-up wealth, an accumulation of the product of labor. But *land* is not the product of labor; unlike wealth, it cannot be reproduced, and its supply is limited. Moreover, it is the primary substance without which there could be no wealth or capital. The value of land ownership, then, lies simply in the privilege it confers of withholding the use of something that is not man-made but God-made. When the rentier commands a share of wealth—the results of production—by virtue of mere ownership, he is taking without returning a commensurate contribution.

George's arguments have been oversimplified here and the connections loosely drawn, but it can be seen now where he is heading. The true wealth producers, the wage earners, or the man 'who by any exertion of mind or body adds to the aggregate of enjoyable wealth, increases the sum of human knowledge or gives to human life higher elevation or greater fullness,' are collectively drained by the evil monster George is now ready to disclose—the Vampire of Rent. Labor and capital lie at the mercy of rent. They receive their

share of production only after the Vampire has seized a large portion for himself.

George is now already beginning to formulate his answer to the
sphinx. Why, he asks next, does rent advance? And then he offers
these reasons. Rents go up after the increase in population reduces
the margin of cultivated land. The landholder benefits not only
from the heightened demand for an inelastic and irreplaceable
commodity but also by the imponderable values that society by its
mere presence confers. 'The most valuable lands on the globe,' he
writes, 'the lands which yield the highest rent, are not lands of surpassing natural fertility, but lands to which a surpassing utility has
been given by the increase of population.' Every advance in culture or technology enhances the value of land by aggravating the
insatiable demand for it. The pre-emption of large acreage by
speculators is another important cause he does not fail to mention,
but the real force of his explanations lies in its implied answer to
those optimists who place their hopes in science and technology.
Increased wealth, like population, forces down the margin of cultivation. 'This being the case,' he concludes, 'every labor-saving
invention, whether it be a steam plow, a telegraph, an improved
process of smelting ores, a perfecting printing press, or a sewing
machine, has a tendency to increase rent.'

The problem is solved. Now George can show why periodic depressions paralyze the country and why poverty persists as wealth
multiplies. The real enemy, he has demonstrated, is rent. Robber
rent levies a constant toll on productive labor:

Every blow of the hammer, every stroke of the pick, every thrust
of the shuttle, every throb of the steam engine, pay it tribute. It levies
upon the earnings of the men who, deep under ground, risk their lives,
and of those who over white surges hang to reeling masts; it claims
the just reward of the capitalist and the fruits of the inventor's patient
effort; it takes little children from play and from school, and compels
them to work before their bones are hard or their muscles are firm;
it robs the shivering of warmth; the hungry, of food; the sick, of
medicine; the anxious, of peace. It debases, and embrutes, and em-
bitters. It crowds families of eight and ten into a single squalid room;
it herds like swine agricultural gangs of boys and girls; it fills the gin
palace and the groggery with those who have no comfort in their

homes; it makes lads who might be useful men candidates for prisons and penitentiaries; it fills brothels with girls who might have known the pure joy of motherhood; it sends greed and all evil passions prowling through society as a hard winter drives the wolves to the abodes of men; it darkens faith in the human soul, and across the reflection of a just and merciful Creator draws the veil of a hard, and blind, and cruel fate!

George's style, growing lush and almost revivalistic when he writes of injustice or the iniquities of rent, lapses back again to cool expository prose as he constructs an argument and clinches a point.

George now reveals his remedy for the unequal ownership of land: the confiscation of rent by the nation. Society at last can profit from the value that it alone confers and the Vampire, deprived of its sustenance, will shrivel away. The owners of land, to be sure, retain title to the property or the 'shell,' as George puts it, but the community takes the kernel. This appropriation of rent is the famous Single Tax which will finally do away with the necessity of any other tax, restore the harmony of interests intended by nature, and prepare for the glorious destiny that lies in store for the emancipated society.

The effects of the remedy on production will, of course, be enormous after the parasite growth is removed, but George writes even more enthusiastically about the prevention of waste at last possible in a povertyless society. It will no longer be necessary to spend vast sums on charity. Vice and crime and corruption will disappear. And most important of all, individuals who have hitherto been a drain on the community can become active working members. George regarded men too highly to think that the acquisitive mercenary 'men with muckrakes' were following their natural instincts. Approbation, the esteem of their fellows, is what they seek primarily, he insists—'the sense of power and influence, the sense of being looked up to and respected,' and not money for its own sake. Abolish the fear of want and the passion now wasted in the quest for riches may be harnessed for the welfare of the community.

By this time George has transcended the dubious mechanics of his land tax and is now reaching the ethical and spiritual part of his treatise, which links him with the other middle-class progressives of his generation. Poverty is condemned, finally, not because of the physical suffering attendant upon it, but because it brutalizes the spirit and destroys the sympathy latent in everyone:

> The wrong that produces inequality; the wrong that in the midst of abundance tortures men with want or harries them with the fear of want; that stunts them physically, degrades them intellectually, and distorts them morally, is what alone prevents harmonious social development.

Down-to-earth people may scoff at 'the dream of impracticable dreamers,' but George assures his readers that it is really a utilitarian consideration for men not to kill themselves with drudgery and to release the mental power, the 'infinite diversities of aptitude and inclination' lying unused and unrecognized. He presents an alluring picture of a society in which human resources are conserved, in which want and ignorance and degradation have vanished, and he asks the property holder if the future of his children would not be safer in such a state.

Having held forth the golden prospect of a new day, George dramatically suspends the final apotheosis while he offers an either/or choice to the world—to retrogress and decay or to go forward. Progress is by no means inevitable, he argues, despite the 'hopeful fatalism' of the Spencerians, nor is there any justification for imputing human advances to wars or slavery or famine as exterminators of the unfit. Civilizations rise and fall; 'the earth is the tomb of the dead empires, no less than of dead men.' Hereditary modifications, George suspects, and changes in the nature of men explain neither progress nor retrogression. And the line of reasoning that attributes a life cycle to nations or races paralleling the growth and decay of individual lives is no less superficial than all such analogies. A community, unlike the human body, is being constantly refreshed by new members and cannot be corrupted 'unless the vital powers of its components are lessened.' Yet the central truth remains: that civilizations engender their own poisons.

George has swept away the claims of racial chauvinists and boldly asserts that human development depends largely on the

matrix of culture in which the individual finds himself, what Veblen
was later to call 'the state of the industrial arts.' This web of institutions, this storehouse of human achievement, while it often
acts as a barrier to progress, accounts for the transmission of
knowledge and 'makes progress possible.' But still George with-
holds his revelation. He has not yet explained the dynamics of
civilization's mobility forward and backward.

The answer when it does come is not anticlimactic. Nations grow
or deteriorate depending on the extent to which they make use
of or vitiate the collective mental powers. When societies are running downgrade, mental energies are being consumed for what
George calls 'non-progressive' purposes. That is to say, men's lives
are consumed in aggressive enterprises of their own or in resisting
the aggressions of others. George illustrates this thought with one
of his characteristic nautical analogies:

To compare society to a boat. Her progress through the water will
not depend upon the exertion of her crew, but upon the exertion devoted to propelling her. This will be lessened by any expenditure of
force required for bailing, or any expenditure of force in fighting
among themselves, or in pulling in different directions.

Mental power, in short, is most effective when men associate in
equality.

George does not minimize the importance of natural circumstances in determining the kind and quality of a civilization. Following a lead of Buckle's, he emphasizes the importance of physi-
ography and admits that uncontrollable physical phenomena—
deserts or jungles or mountains—not only isolate men and prevent
association but directly inspire national conceits and prejudices that
ultimately promote wars, 'the negation of association.' But he attributes the chief reason for a civilization's decline to the ever-
present tendency toward inequality. The institutions that take root
at the dawn of a civilization may later strangle it by retaining obsolete ideas and by funneling off the benefits derived from the 'collective power' of the society to a special class in the community.
The community in turn is deprived of the advantages achieved by
men commingling in free association; progress stops and retrogression begins:

On the one side, the masses of the community are compelled to expend their mental powers in merely maintaining existence. On the other side, mental power is expended in keeping up and intensifying the system of inequality, in ostentation, luxury, and warfare.

When a society has reached such a pass, any innovation, of course, is considered dangerous; the rulers permit no experiment that may ultimately unseat them, and the masses are too preoccupied with the problem of staying alive to take up 'progressive' considerations.

The lesson for America is quite obvious. It is the inequality of wealth that finally brings about the petrifaction of civilization, divides society into a plutocracy and a mob, and sweeps away the middle class for which George speaks and from which he believes most good derives. He has revealed the cause for social decay and has offered a plan to circumvent it. Now he presents a stark picture of what America may expect if present tendencies are allowed to continue unchecked. The threat follows the promise. Our boasted political democracy has not prevented economic inequality nor can mere political forms sustain a democracy. Tyranny sprouting out of decayed republican institutions can be the most vicious of all, 'for there despotism advances in the name and with the might of the people.' The very democratic stratagems that in the equalitarian society insure popular will become devices ideally suited to plutocratic manipulation. Universal suffrage becomes a positive evil when granted to a broken-down, will-less corrupt proletariat.

George does not conclude his book on this painful note; a heavenly vision must follow the apocalypse of destruction. He is no fatalist, no Brooks Adams charting the course of civilization's decline. 'The Central Truth' is most reassuring despite the possible menace it involves, for if men will only act, a utopia whose golden spires have been seen only by a few poets and seers will become at last an earthly habitation. Political economy, far from being the dismal science, becomes under George's supervision 'radiant with hope,' and the reader is pleased and comforted to discover at the end that everything George has been discussing is subsumed under the golden rule, dear to Christian and democrat alike. We see finally 'that the truth which the intellect grasps after toilsome effort is but that which the moral sense reaches by a quick intui-

tion,' that nature is bounteous, not stingy, and that earthly salvation lies in the minds and hearts of men. George's eschatology is
optimistic in the best transcendental vein. His investigation has
convinced him that though the race and the individual die and the
world shall someday 'resolve itself into a gaseous form, again to
begin immeasurable mutations,' a passage exists 'from life behind
to life beyond.' Man at last is redeemed, and the ways of God are
justified.

       VII] The almost instantaneous popularity of *Progress
and Poverty* had nothing to do with its originality—or rather un-
originality, for in many ways it was a most derivative book. Like
the Declaration of Independence from which it stemmed, it was
largely an amalgam of ideas already long familiar (the echoes of
Condorcet, Comte, Fourier, Bastiat, Mill, Jefferson, Emerson, and
many others are deafening), but it was at the same time so intensely personal and sincere and presented with such an enraptured
finality that it seemed more novel than it actually was. George had
really enlarged upon his own experiences and written a kind of
sublimated autobiography calculated to attract even those readers
—and there must have been many—who had neither the interest
nor the ability to follow his chain of thought.

John Jay Chapman, describing 'the New Jerusalem of Single
Tax' that George unfolded in the last chapter of *Progress and
Poverty,* could think of nothing else but Don Quixote:

> He is rapt. He is beyond reach of the human voice. He has a harp
> and is singing—and *this* is the power of the book. It is preposterous.
> It is impossible. It is romance—a rhapsody—a vision—at the end of
> a long seeming scientific discussion of rent, interest, and wages—(in
> which discussion of his *destructive* criticism of other people must be ad-
> mitted to be very strong—conclusive—but which leaves his own work
> subject to his own criticism). This burst of song, being the only lyric
> poetry of this commercial period, is popular.

But with all of his facetiousness, Chapman gave more credit to
George's destructive criticism than did most of the academicians,
who never treated George as a serious economist.

George expected the hostility of the propertied interests and tried to meet it. If he seemed carried away by the significance of his revelation, he never dropped out of his role of the cautious advocate. 'A great wrong always dies hard,' he wrote, and George tried carefully not only in *Progress and Poverty* but also in his subsequent works to play down those ideas that were likely to antagonize his audience if presented in too bald a fashion. For instance, if George had proposed outright confiscation of land, it would have involved, as he said, 'a needless shock to present customs and habits of thought—which is to be avoided.' He did not like to hedge when great principles were at stake, for that was not real wisdom, but he apparently had no illusions about the social inertia holding back reform or the stubborness of the masses. With all of his idealism and his Jeffersonian expressions of human equality, he showed an almost hard-boiled awareness of human stupidity, which suggests, at times, Emerson's contemptuous opinion of the 'imbecile' mob.

No matter how outrageous the wrong, George believed, society accepted it and grafted it into the social system:

. . . the majority of men do not think; the majority of men have to expend so much energy in the struggle to make a living that they do not have time to think. The majority of men accept, as a matter of course, whatever is. This is what makes the task of the social reformer so difficult, his path so hard. This is what brings upon those who first raise their voices in behalf of a great truth the sneers of the powerful and the curses of the rabble, ostracism and martyrdom, the robe of derision and the crown of thorns.

He likened mankind to a great stupid bull with a ring in its nose, all tangled up in its own rope and struggling vainly to reach the green pastures a few yards away. Like the bull, man can only bellow ineffectively, and he will never be able to use his great power 'until the masses, or at least that sprinkling of more thoughtful men who are the file-leaders of popular opinion, shall give such heed to larger questions as will enable them to agree on the path reform should take.' That George regarded himself as one of these prophets or file-leaders is quite clear. Quietly and skillfully he disentangled the bull, taking particular precautions not to alarm it and leading it by the nose into Elysium.

The zeal, always tempered with discretion, that made *Progress and Poverty* radical but somehow safe, characterized the speeches he now began to make in great profusion after 1880. He had developed during the previous ten years from a halting and awkward speaker into a natural orator of extraordinary charm and persuasiveness. His public writing had always been oratorical in tone, mingling the plain words and simple phrasing with rhetorical flourishes, and his speaking took on the same quality. George, first drawn to the lecture platform in order to supplement his meager income, grew to believe that his spoken words would gain more converts than his written, and his short sturdy figure and his red beard and dome-shaped head soon became familiar to people all over the United States. But it was in the British Isles that his eloquence drew the admission from the London *Times* that as an orator he was superior to Cobden and Bright.

In the spring of 1881, afloat once more and poorer than he had been at twenty-one, 'The Little Gamecock,' as the reporters called him, became actively concerned with the agitation for land reform in Ireland, and seeing an opportunity for propagandizing his own views on the question, began to speak and write for the Irish Land League. The pamphlet he published on this issue received considerable attention, and in the fall of 1881, he sailed for Ireland as a reporter for the *Irish World*. This trip marked the beginning of George's enormous vogue in Ireland and England. He was quickly identified as one of the leaders of the Irish movement, hobnobbed with celebrities, lectured to large audiences, and returned home a year later a famous man. His friends and well-wishers, including some New York politicians who thought George was an Irishman, tendered him a fancy dinner at Delmonico's.

Progress and Poverty in the meantime had been selling by the thousands, and even though George's growing reputation brought him little cash (he was lax about his copyrights and gave away as many books as he sold) and he continued to live, as he said, 'literally from hand to mouth,' he now found plenty of opportunities to write and speak. The series in *Frank Leslie's Illustrated Newspaper* appeared at this time, and he started his book on the tariff, but an invitation by the Land Reform Union to deliver a

number of addresses in England put an end to his writing for the
time being. In January of '84, George found himself once again
in London, eager to convert the gentiles.

George Bernard Shaw, who heard George in 1882, has recorded
his impressions of the American prophet:

> One evening in the early eighties I found myself—I forget how and
> cannot imagine why—in the Memorial Hall, Farringdon St., London,
> listening to an American finishing a speech on the Land Question. I
> knew he was an American because he pronounced 'necessarily'—a fav-
> orite word of his—with the accent on the third syllable instead of the
> first; because he was deliberately and intentionally oratorical, which
> is not customary among shy people like the English; because he spoke
> of Liberty, Justice, Truth, Natural Law, and other strange eighteenth
> century superstitions; and because he explained with great simplicity
> and sincerity the views of The Creator, who had gone completely out
> of fashion in London in the previous decade and had not been heard
> of there since. I noticed also that he was a born orator, and that he had
> small, plump, pretty hands.

For all of his levity, Shaw attested to the importance of George as a
social revivalist, and although he and his friends outgrew the sim-
plicities of the Single Tax, Shaw, at any rate, never minimized his
debt to Henry George. It was enough for Shaw that George made
them see the importance of economics in the battle for reform prior
to their discovery of Marx and that he stimulated such men as
Sidney Webb and H. G. Wells to complicate the problem for themselves and pass beyond the elementary outlines of *Progress and
Poverty*. It was a good thing, said Shaw, that George was not overly
burdened with information when he arrived, for 'the complexity
of the problem would have overwhelmed him if he had realized it,
or if it had not, it would have rendered him unintelligible.' As it
turned out, his book served as an introductory text to the nature
of society for these budding socialists and Fabians; without it, perhaps, they would not have advanced so quickly to more sophis-
ticated levels of economic thinking.

In England as well as in America George became the popular
instructor in political economy not only because he was a gifted
teacher—patient, lucid, and persuasive—but also because he possessed to a high degree what J. A. Hobson called a 'certain capac-

ity of dramatic exaggeration.' During George's first English visit
in 1882, liberal M.P.'s, non-conformist leaders, and ministers
looked upon his views with horror. Seven years later these same
men were presiding over his lectures and advocating his ideas in
Parliament. No one, Hobson believed, exercised so much influence
on English radicalism in the 'eighties and 'nineties as Henry
George.

George's own effectiveness and influence were not lost upon
him, and despite his modesty and his conscious desire to subordinate his fame and fortune to the land-reform cause, he came
more and more to think of himself as God's right arm. After he
had been scornfully denounced by the Duke of Argyll as the
'Prophet of San Francisco,' his friends happily borrowed the designation and henceforth referred to George in terms that suggested
he was more than mortal. He emerged, in the words of one of his
ardent followers, as 'the hero,' the 'commander in chief in the contest of ideas . . . for me, and doubtless for future generations,
the greatest man of the 19th century.'

By the middle 'eighties, the Single Tax had hardened into a religion, with George in the role of the not always genial Pope when
it came to the question of refuting minor heresies. Organized
churches, he believed, offered men 'stones instead of bread,' and
from Protestant to Catholic preached 'alms giving or socialism.'
He now grew more certain 'that the time is ripe for our doctrine,
and that it is being forced forward by a greater power than our
own.' Convinced of the truth of his own particular vision, George
began to regard other reformers who ranked their pet projects as
of equal or of more importance than his own as upstarts. He closed
the columns of his newspaper, *The Standard* (the parent organ of
the Single Tax, established in 1887) to rival ideas, and fired two
of his editors for insubordination. George was justified in dis-
missing these men on many counts, yet he showed an impatience
and an absence of generosity in this episode not consistent with
his earlier magnanimity.

The men who took the leadership in the movement at this time
were largely business and professional people. Some of them, like
Thomas G. Shearman, a successful corporation lawyer, and Tom

Johnson, a Cleveland industrialist, seemed to be more interested in the economics of the Single Tax and free trade than in the more deeply radical implications of George's theories, and George himself became increasingly chilly toward socialism and its proponents as the radicals grew more vociferous about the inadequacies of the Single Tax.

At the beginning George had been tolerant of socialism and had agreed with its objectives; but, he argued even then, 'it is evident that whatever savors of regulation and restriction is in itself bad, and should not be resorted to if any other mode of accomplishing the same end presents itself.' The confiscation of rent, he was sure, would bring about the benefits of socialism without inviting the dangers likely to occur with its installation.

Realizing the looseness of the term 'Socialist' and acknowledging that he too had been classed as one, he neither admitted nor disclaimed the name, because he saw 'the correlative truth' in the principles of both individualism and socialism. But he made it quite plain that Marxian socialism as expounded by the British socialists and in America by Laurence Gronlund was nothing more than 'a high-purposed but incoherent mixture of truth and fallacy, the defects of which may be summed up in its want of radicalism—that is to say, of going to the root.' In so far as socialism increased international solidarity and taught the advantages of associated action, he concurred. He fully admitted that as society grew more complex, the domain of social action would enlarge. He pointed out that much evil had resulted from the habit of leaving to individuals what ought to be undertaken by the state, and he called the *laisser-faire* gospel of the Spencerians a 'stench in the nostrils.' Nevertheless, he distrusted deeply the 'super-adequate' socialism that allowed the state to 'absorb capital and abolish competition' and that saw labor and capital as irreconcilably opposed. Super-adequate or scientific socialism, moreover, brought up visions of the authoritarian state, where the workers had everything provided for them, 'including the directors themselves.' It lacked a guiding principle, and, most important of all, it failed to define 'the extent to which the individual is entitled to liberty or to which the state may go in restraining it.'

It is not always easy to discover what prompted George's feelings toward the Socialists. Some of his misgivings were in all probability honestly arrived at, and these have been confirmed by history. And yet his annoyance with the Socialists was not always warranted. He complained that they tried to wreck any movement they could not dominate and that they blurred the Single Tax by introducing irrelevant issues, but George and his followers did not try very hard to maintain a basis of agreement with them. His unfortunate stand against the Haymarket Square anarchists, unjustly convicted in 1887, alienated the Socialists even farther, and it is no wonder that they deserted him in the same year when he ran a very poor third in the New York contest for Secretary of State. In view of the fact that he had nearly won the mayoralty of New York City the year before with Socialist help, his defeat was particularly humiliating.

No man who led as active and public a life as George could avoid making occasional blunders, and the adulation he received would have hopelessly ruined a smaller man. George threw himself into politics and engaged in public debates ostensibly to publicize his cause, but he unquestionably enjoyed the limelight and the thrill of conflict. Yet despite his piques, his unconvincing rationalizations, his sectarian bickering, and his downright errors, his public record is impressively good.

Unfortunately, as many of his friends continually told him, the hours devoted to journalism and politics and the forum prevented him from rethinking the weaker portions of his theories and from writing the books he might have written had he allowed himself the necessary leisure. Even so, George did manage to find time to write several other important works besides *Progress and Poverty*, most notably *Social Problems* (1883) and *Protection or Free Trade* (1886), and his collected writings are well worth studying as a rich and perceptive expression of American progressive philosophy. The lesser writing of George derives, of course, pretty much from *Progress and Poverty*, for he never seriously modified any of these theories, but frequently they are specific and concrete where the parent book is general.

VIII] The nub of George's social philosophy is his sympathetic view of man. 'To him,' as a friend wrote after his death, 'every human being, no matter how high or how low, was an immortal soul with whom his own immortal soul could come into sympathetic contact. It was as easy for him to converse with a hod-carrier as with a philosopher.' This conviction of man's innate goodness led him, as it did most of the other middle-class reformers of Jeffersonian or transcendental origins, to accept an oversimplified psychology that exalted instinctive benevolence and played down human perversity, yet at the same time it saved him from the even more naïve and untenable utilitarianism of the so-called realists who invented a dehumanized integer they called 'man' and created a folklore of their own.

Since man was a social animal, the virtues residing within him developed harmoniously only when he associated with others on a basis of equality. George did not discount the importance of individual genius, but he attributed progress to 'the larger and wider cooperation of individual powers; to the growth of that body of knowledge which is a part, or rather, perhaps, an aspect of the social integration I have called the body economic.' The experience of the race could be stored and transmitted only after individual man had merged with the social body, the great repository of human knowledge. Co-operation not only helped men to overcome social problems; it also quickened the religious spirit and the springs of human sympathy and dramatized the truth of mutual dependence. No one class could be emancipated, he kept insisting, at the expense of another; every person's happiness was the concern of all. And he regarded all legislation or pressures exerted for a particular body of people as dangerous to the interests of the whole.

According to George, it required no special knowledge to grasp these truths. One did not have to be a college graduate to reason correctly; indeed, he observed, 'There is no vulgar economic fallacy that may not be found in the writings of professors; no social vagary current among "the ignorant" whose roots may not be discovered among "the educated and cultured." ' And the successive arguments he proposed followed logically from his initial premises about the duties and capacities of man.

The Social Darwinists, the followers of Spencer and his school, George felt, blurred these central truths with their specious talk of 'survival of the fittest' and 'nature's remedies,' and thereby sinned against the divinity in man. In valuing man for his muscles rather than his mind, in treating him like a commodity, 'a thing, in some respects, lower than the animal,' they made themselves culpable on practical as well as moral grounds, because, for George, the physical strength of the human frame counted as nothing when placed against the 'resistless currents' flowing from unleashed intelligence.

The Spencerians talked of progress (and George himself grew lyrical about technological advances) but they canceled out its human costs. George, like Parker and the other humanitarians, did not interpret the word 'progress' in its material sense or call progressive a civilization that excluded so large a portion of society from physical and spiritual benefits. Inventions and discoveries in themselves were not unmixed blessings so far as the workingman was concerned. They hastened the march toward monopoly; they made employer-employee relations increasingly indirect and impersonal; they deprived the worker of his independence; they cramped his mind and body. 'We are reducing the cost of production,' he wrote, 'but in doing so, are stunting children, and unfitting women for the duties of maternity, and degrading men into the position of mere feeders of machines. We are not lessening the fierceness of the struggle for existence.'

George no more hungered for the pre-industrial golden age than Parker did, but he was impressed by the findings of such men as Professor Thorold Rogers of Oxford, whose *Six Centuries of Work and Wages* (a work of immense influence among the progressives) confirmed George's contention that the workingman had lost more than he had gained by the industrial revolution. The great factories, housing thousands of hands, produced with miraculous economy as compared with the old handicraft system, and yet the modern worker performed the most monotonous labor 'amid the din and the clatter, and whir of belts and wheels,' and had about as much chance of becoming a master of the plant as of becoming 'King of England or Pope of Rome.' Circumstances remote from his personal life threw him out of work, and during the boom times he and his fellows could increase their share only by striking or threatening to strike.

The callous disregard for men in a country that mouthed the sentiments of the Declaration of Independence was reprehensible on moral grounds, but George also saw the dangerous political consequences of such an attitude. The industrial revolution, breaking the bonds that had formerly tied the individual to the community, had precipitated a kind of mass alienation, and produced a type of rootless man who could fall an easy prey to the demagogue. The 'dangerous classes politically' are not only the 'very rich' but the 'very poor':

It is not the taxes that he is conscious of paying that gives a man a stake in the country, an interest in its government; it is the consciousness of feeling that he is an integral part of the community; that its prosperity is his prosperity, and its disgrace his shame. . . Men do not vote patriotically, any more than they fight patriotically, because of their payment of taxes. Whatever conduces to the comfortable and independent material condition of the masses will best foster public spirit, will make the ultimate governing power more intelligent and more virtuous.

The corollary was equally obvious. Deprive a man of that sense of identification, facilitate the piling up of huge fortunes, aggravate the tendency toward inequality, and you have a disoriented and menacing proletariat.

George assumed that the tendency toward concentration, which produced the disparities of wealth and divided society, was not necessarily an artificial one. As men associated together in larger groups, production naturally took place on a larger scale. But he refused to admit that the evils following in the wake of the factory system were either natural or inevitable. 'The concentration that is going on in all branches of industry,' he wrote in *Social Problems,* 'is a necessary tendency of our advance in the material arts. It is not in itself an evil. If in anything its results are evil, it is simply because of our bad social adjustments.' The whole question hinged on

whether the relation in which men are thus drawn together and compelled to act together shall be the natural relation of interdependence in equality, or the unnatural relation of dependence upon a master.

George's trustful acceptance of the principle of bigness may seem to contradict his defense of competition, but he had no difficulties in reconciling the ideas of co-operation and competition. The trouble heretofore, he argued, was the myth of the free market. A slave class cannot be said to compete. But once assure natural rights to everyone,

then competition, acting on every hand—between employers as between employed; between buyers as between sellers—can injure no one. On the contrary it becomes the most simple, most extensive, most elastic, and most refined system of cooperation, that, in the present stage of social development, and in the domain where it will freely act, we can rely on for the coordination of industry and the economizing of social forces.

When competition failed to work properly and the economic machinery broke down, when the natural processes of concentration degenerated into hoggish monopoly, George never blamed the defective laws of nature. Political economists euphemistically disposed of depressions and unemployment by inventing concepts like 'overproduction,' but to George such reasoning was nothing less than blasphemous. How could there be overproduction with so many wants unfilled? Fallible men created artificial scarcity by interfering with the natural laws of trade—strangling production through monopoly, tariffs, and other hidden taxes—and by engaging in piratical ventures against the community. The waste in men and machines, the vice and crime accompanying and resulting from the 'masked war' of business, stemmed directly from 'our ignorance and contempt of human rights.' Nature remained bountiful. Plenty of work always remained to be done. Clearly, then, the blame lay with man himself, and he would never pull himself out of his mire until he took to heart the truth taught by both religion and experience—'that the highest good of each is to be sought in the good of others; that the true interests of men are harmonious, not antagonistic; that prosperity is the daughter of good will and peace; and that want and destruction follow enmity and strife.'

The salvation of society depended ultimately on a moral revival, but at the same time a society had to be constructed in which these benevolent virtues might be permitted to flourish. The Single Tax, George was certain, would transform disintegrative forces into life-giving ones, but in the meantime, the state had to quicken the ameliorative process. It was not the business of the state to make man virtuous, but it did have the responsibility of securing 'the full and equal liberty of individuals.'

George modified, with some reluctance, his earlier views on the role of governments. To the last he retained certain Jeffersonian prejudices against the large army and navy, expensive and un-democratic; and the abolition of the diplomatic service, he felt, 'would save expense, corruption, and national dignity.' He urged that we hold tenaciously to local liberties, for no outside authority, either state or national, knew as much about local affairs as the residents themselves. But as he observed the 'growing complexity of civilized life and the growth of great corporations and com-binations, before which the individual is powerless,' he became convinced 'that the government must undertake more than to keep the peace between man and man—must carry on, when it cannot regulate, businesses that involve monopoly, and in larger and larger degree assume co-operative functions.' If any means of curtailing monopolies, other than federal intervention, had presented itself, George would have preferred it, but he could see no other.

Natural monopolies, he believed, ought to be taken over out-right by the state instead of being regulated. Such a proposal might seem inconsistent with George's moderate views and his distrust of socialism, but he took the stand, anticipating some of the later re-formers, 'that any considerable interest having necessary relations with government is more corruptive of government when acting upon government from without than when assumed by govern-ment.' The railroads provided a notorious illustration for this argu-ment. Actually, the kind of governmental control George advo-cated really applied the free-trade principle to keep open the channels of trade. For, he concluded, 'if we carry free trade to its logical conclusions we are inevitably led to what the monopolists, who wish to be "let alone" to plunder the public, denounce as "socialism," and which is, indeed, socialism, in the sense that it recognizes the true domain of social functions.' Enlarging the sphere of government, he was perfectly aware, always carried with it an element of danger and he dreaded the hypertrophy of federal bureaus, but he expected the substitution of a single tax for all the myriad taxes hitherto collected to simplify the job of government and even permit it to extend its activities into the domain of public health, libraries, recreation, and scientific research.

Distrusting as he did large concentrations of power, he was finally persuaded by experience and observation that the welfare state had to come if the democratic individualism he believed in so passionately was to survive in America. The risks were great, but George concluded that the only thing to do was to load the state with popular controls and assume 'that there must be in human nature the possibility of a reasonably pure government, when the ends of that government are felt by all to be the promotion of the general good.'

America had no other course anyway. The frontier was gone, as George announced some years before Professor Frederick Jackson Turner, and with it our period of national probation. Now that we had impoverished our soil, dumped our fertility on European shores or flushed it into the sea, or allowed it to pass into the hands of absentee landlords, we had to resign ourselves to the consequences. The treasures we had exhausted during this national debauch were irretrievable. Meanwhile, we had aroused 'the aspirations and ambitions of the masses' while accelerating the tendencies that thwarted them, and we could no longer fall back on the consolation that our magical republican institutions would somehow carry us through. Forms meant nothing when the substance was gone.

IX] Georgian philosophy spread during the 'eighties and 'nineties, taking root especially in the British radical movement and enlisting the support of many prominent Americans in business, politics, and the arts. George's trips to England and his Australian tour not only enhanced his reputation abroad but made him a more considerable figure for those Americans who needed a foreign seal of approval to convince them of George's greatness. After all, not many Americans were admired by Tolstoy, Ruskin, Shaw, Wallace, and Gladstone. Even Karl Marx felt George important enough to despise. And in this country he could claim the friendship of Mark Twain, Howells, Henry Demarest Lloyd, Hamlin Garland, William Jennings Bryan, Henry Ward Beecher, Samuel Gompers, and hundreds of other prominent men and women who admired his character and sincerity even though they may not all have accepted his entire program. Few reformers in our history have managed to attract so diverse a following and appeal to so wide a variety of groups whose interests ordinarily clashed.

Ex-President Hayes, visiting New York during the first George campaign for mayor in 1886, discovered to his great astonishment that a considerable number of respectable Republicans—well-dressed, well-fed men who carried gold-headed canes—planned to vote for George. The arguments they gave for supporting a radical like George coincided with Hayes's own views at this time: the dollar had acquired too much power and threatened the republic; monopoly (Hayes cited the Standard Oil trust as a notorious example) had grown too insolent. These men, disliking George's remedies, nevertheless found themselves for the time being on the same side as the labor unions and credited George with being 'a thoroughly sincere, honest man with the welfare of his fellow men at heart.' Whatever doubts he may have had about the Single Tax, Hayes believed that George was 'strong where he portrays the rottenness of the present system.' He placed George with the other 'Nihilists'—himself and Mark Twain and Howells and Abraham Lincoln—who 'opposed the wrong and evils of the money-piling tendency of our country, which is changing laws, Government, and morals, and giving all power to the rich and bringing in pauperism and its attendant crimes and wretchedness like a flood.'

But a political and economic program that tried to harmonize all interests and rigorously excluded ideas not in keeping with the views of its sponsors inevitably invited dissent from conservative and radical alike. George, in his turn, felt obliged to discipline the recalcitrant of both wings, and the skirmishes he engaged in during his last years revealed a talent for polemics as well as a zeal for his cause. Herbert Spencer had to be answered, and the Pope, too; and so did the Socialists and the Populists and the false ministers.

George blundered badly in the Haymarket affair when men like Howells and Bellamy and Lloyd behaved magnificently, and he sanctioned the execution and imprisonment of the anarchists without studying the case honestly or courageously. He blundered again in 1888 when he swerved to Cleveland and broke for a time with his friend, Father Edward McGlynn, a brilliant and incorruptible priest who had devoted himself to the Georgian movement and had risked excommunication for his beliefs. And yet George denounced Cleveland in 1894 against the wishes of his friends and bitterly criticized the use of federal troops in the Pullman strike. The Democratic party had reneged on its pledge to reduce the tariff and opposed the income tax that George, the leading Single Taxer, believed temporarily necessary. It had sponsored the anti-anarchist bill, which George (although the anarchists hated him and attacked him at every opportunity) called worse than the Alien and Sedition Acts. Finally, Cleveland had ratified the infamous extradition treaty with Russia and sealed the entrance to America against such great men as Kropotkin and Reclus. George joined other reformers and humanitarians in condemning these acts and demonstrated that his liberalism had not been tarnished by his association with property holders.

In 1896 he campaigned for Bryan, again grieving his conservative backers, and toured the Middle West as a reporter for the New York *Journal*. Once more his articles took on the radical tinge that had colored the essays he had written fifteen years before. George, like Bellamy and Lloyd, was actually neither a gold nor a silver man. He played down the money issue and chose to interpret the election as a struggle for power between a ruthless plutocracy, dominating their sham republic, and the people. Bryan, for all his limitations, represented Jeffersonian principles—equal rights for all, special privileges for none; all other issues of the campaign were small compared to this. 'I shall vote for Bryan,' George confided to a correspondent, 'with greater satisfaction and firmer confidence than I have voted for a Presidential candidate since Abraham Lincoln.'

George had expected Bryan to win—at least his articles give that impression—but he did not let the disappointment of McKinley's landslide discourage him. If the plutocracy still controlled the banks and the government, reform might begin in the municipalities, and George accepted the independent nomination for the New York mayoralty in 1897 with the idea that once again Jeffersonian principles might be injected into a political campaign. Exhausted already by his strenuous efforts of the last year, and looking, according to one report, 'like a racked and wounded saint,' George entered the New York race against the advice of his physicians. Such a step, they assured him, would undoubtedly kill him. He accepted the verdict quite philosophically, telling one of them that he knew he had to die sometime and that he preferred to die while serving the people. Five days before the election, for which he had campaigned in his usual vigorous spirit, George's spent body broke under the strain, and he suffered a fatal apoplectic stroke.

The city turned out to pay tribute to the dead reformer and thousands filed past his bier in the Grand Central Palace. They were honoring the man, if not the theorist, and spontaneously recognizing a leader who throughout his short life had consistently stood for what he called 'the principle of true Democracy, the truth that comes from the spirit of the plain people.' To his disciples, of course, George remained a saint and a social deliverer, but his humanitarianism and integrity carried over into groups of people who had never read the bible of the Single Taxers and who never would.

An indefatigable corps of followers remain today, propagandizing Single Tax ideas and preparing for the millennium, but George's lasting greatness, fortunately enough, does not depend upon the validity of the Single Tax as a social panacea. 'Nobody,' as Bernard Shaw put it so well, 'has ever got away, or ever will get away, from the truths that were the centre of his propaganda: his errors anybody can get away from.'

George's criterion for the good society is still valid—a society where the non-progressive forces do not dam up mental energy and where monotonous labor does not deprive man of his 'godlike power of modifying and controlling conditions.' Perhaps he asked for too much. Most certainly his own solution for the paradox of want amidst plenty enormously oversimplified the causes of man's plight—a condition George so compellingly described. But he was right in trying to strike a balance between the claims of those who emphasized the necessity of personal regeneration and the environmentalists relying entirely on the results of external reform. He never divorced religion and science, for he was certain that the deeper religious instincts of the multitude, scarcely touched in modern society, would be reached only through a genuinely social application of scientific principles. No fairyland would grow up from a slag heap, no race of saints from festering slums. The geniuses who had distinguished themselves in the relatively short annals of human history betrayed, George believed, the vast untapped veins of power society had not begun to scratch. He hoped to exploit that hidden wealth by convincing his contemporaries of the practicality of the golden rule, by showing that through virtue men could be free.

CHAPTER 4

. . . .

Edward Bellamy:
Village Utopian

1] As Henry George became convinced that he alone
possessed the answer to the economic riddle and grew more impatient with any program that minimized the importance of the
Single Tax, a number of his former supporters—especially the
more socialistically inclined—regretfully turned against him. If
they retained their respect for his eloquence and magnetism and
admitted the sincerity of his sympathy for the workers, they nevertheless were forced to conclude by the middle 'eighties that George
was incapable of growth, that he was mentally inflexible.

Until 1886, the socialists and the more class-conscious trade-
unionists found him useful and worked for him, because (despite
his claims to the contrary) his land theories and tax system struck
at the bastions of capitalism. But George's refusal to condemn the
wage system and his unwillingness to accept the socialist program
of nationalization disappointed the Marxians, who saw a basic
cleavage between the interests of the capitalists and the workingmen. 'What Henry George demands,' Engels wrote in 1884, 'leaves
the present mode of social production untouched, and has, in fact,
been anticipated by the extreme section of Ricardian bourgeois
economists who, too, demanded the confiscation of the rent of land
by the state.' Engels erred in saying that George advocated public
ownership of land, but he correctly analyzed the conservative aspects of George's proposals. To the American as well as to the
European socialists, George was the modern Rip Van Winkle, who

'instead of sleeping twenty years had been sleeping ever since the adoption of the Declaration of Independence.'

Among George's severe critics in America was a Danish-born lawyer named Laurence Gronlund, an emotionally unstable but brilliant social thinker whose writings were much in vogue during the 'eighties and 'nineties. Like so many other radicals, Gronlund had been an enthusiastic admirer of George but had resented George's war against the socialists. Although strongly influenced by Marx, he was neither a revolutionist nor a communist. He merely wished to legislate capitalism out of existence and to establish in its place a democratic-socialist economy (described in his widely read *The Co-operative Commonwealth,* 1884).

Gronlund's goals differed little from George's, but owing perhaps to his European background, he could not appreciate the average American's aversion even to the most benevolent conception of the omnicompetent state. George's belief that no irreconcilable differences divided capital from labor, that 'the true conflict' was 'between *labor and monopoly,'* undoubtedly approximated the views of the majority of American dissenters more closely than the philosophy of out-and-out socialism. Socialism, as George conceived it, was a European importation unsuitable for the American scene; prior to Edward Bellamy, no socialist could make the scheme of government ownership of the means of production anything less than a conspiracy against the individual. Gronlund's books, to be sure, demonstrated convincingly that co-operative ownership need not degenerate into tyranny and that his kind of socialism emphasized the ideals of good will and mutual aid rather than hatred and the lust for spoliation, but they reached only a specialized audience. The most fruitful result of *The Co-operative Commonwealth,* as Gronlund himself recognized in 1890, was that it 'led indirectly, and probably unconsciously, to Mr. Bellamy's *Looking Backward,* the novel which without doubt has stealthily inoculated thousands of Americans with socialism, just because it ignored that name and those who had written on the subject.'

Gronlund might have added that Bellamy succeeded in domesticating socialism by removing its 'objectionable' and 'disreputable' features and by making it palatable for masses of Americans intimidated by the name of socialism while yearning for its promised benefits. He might have said, too, as W. D. Howells was later to point out, that Bellamy wrote in a language and employed a terminology that the average American could understand.

II] The American 'average,' Howells had written in his appreciation of Edward Bellamy, 'is practical as well as mystical; it is first the dust of the earth, and then it is the living soul; it likes great questions simply and familiarly presented, before it puts its faith in them and makes its faith a life. It likes to start to heaven from home.' Bellamy, according to Howells, was the unwitting interpreter for this average, so 'intensely democratic' and 'inalienably plebeian,' that he seemed able to reflect its aspirations with a kind of will-less fidelity.

Bellamy's invincible parochialism and his preference for the village mentality increased his merit in Howell's eyes. Even if he sometimes winced at the commonness of his diction and felt a slight distaste for, it seemed to him, his friend's undue interest in the creature-comforts of the middle class, he recognized the nobility of Bellamy's purpose and saw the ideal gleaming through the gadgetry of his utopia. *Looking Backward* stimulated the appetites of its readers for material things, but it held them out as a bait, as a reward that could be secured only after a thorough-going application of the village ideals of equality and neighborliness. Bellamy, with his unerring insight into the heart of the 'divine average,' knew perfectly well what he was doing, Howells concluded, and 'could not have been wrong in approaching it with all that public school exegesis which wearies such dilettanti as myself.' He knew for a certainty 'what it wished to know, what problem will hold it, what situation it can enter into, what mystery will fascinate it, and what noble pain it will bear.' He spoke always for this middle group, for the villager rather than for the country or city dweller, the unpretentious man with a regular occupation rather than the rich or the poor; it was among this class, Bellamy believed, that 'the virtues of a people will be always found to dominate.' To Howells, who agreed that 'in this as in everything else we are a medium race,' Bellamy's appreciation for the average made him 'distinctively American' and one of our most deeply rooted writers since Hawthorne.

Henry George, possessing the same insights and predilections, had tried perhaps more consciously than Bellamy to reach the middle classes, but he missed that sizable proportion who could not bring themselves to read even *his* seductive popularization of political economy. It remained for a novelist to lure the less scholarly. 'Those not able to follow Mr. George's earnest pages,' wrote William T. Harris, the American Hegelian, educator, and antisocialist crusader, 'find themselves quite equal to undertaking the story of the new Rip Van Winkle, who sleeps for a century or more and awakes in a new world at the close of the twentieth century.' Harris declared that Bellamy had simply taken his cue from George and had then proceeded to outdo his master.

But George and Bellamy merely approached their common goal from different directions and with different emphases. George stemmed most immediately from Jefferson in respect to his views on property, natural rights, and the functions of government. The radicalism of Bellamy was also in part Jeffersonian but tinged more markedly than George's with a particular brand of Yankee communism, or, to be more precise, 'Associationism,' which linked him with the pre-Civil-War disciples of Charles Fourier. As Fourier's heir, he succeeded even better than Albert Brisbane or Parke Godwin—Fourier's principal popularizers during the 'forties —in presenting the flamboyant Frenchman's theories to the American middle class. They had reached and influenced only a limited audience; fifty years later Fourier's ideas, trimmed of their eccentricities, made sense to millions. The people had not changed, but their environment had. Refracted through the middle-class consciousness of Edward Bellamy, Fourier's visions seemed down-to-earth and perfectly feasible.

The unmistakable trace of Fourierism in *Looking Backward* does not necessarily mean that Bellamy's brand of socialism or 'Nationalism,' as it came to be called, derived solely from Fourier. His modifications and additions are certainly as significant as his borrowings, but Bellamy's social theories are a continuation of Brisbane's doctrines of Association (by no means dead when Bellamy began to write) and tie him very definitely to a particular school of New England reformers and the traditions of a region.

He was a Yankee, with all of the connotations that go with that word, just as Theodore Parker was, and Emerson, and Mary Baker Eddy, and he possessed what might be called the Brook Farm temperament, 'the age old belief in the millennium,' as Mr. Van Wyck Brook says, 'that has always lurked in the depth of the Yankee mind.' Boston served as the locale for *Looking Backward* and Bostonians organized the first Nationalist club to spread his ideas. Massachusetts' strong-willed feminists backed him to the hilt. The Yankees above all others savored his Chicopee concoction of science and mysticism.

III] In the spring of 1888, the year *Looking Backward* appeared, Bellamy sent a short autobiographical notice to Ticknor, the Boston publisher. Because of his great horror at the prospect of being 'boomed,' only his desire 'to spread this book and the ideas it suggests' persuaded him to send even this meager sketch:

> Born at Chicopee Falls 1850, direct line of descent from Dr. Joseph Bellamy the brimstone divine . . . for a short time of Union College but not a graduate; after college a year in Germany; educated as a lawyer but never a practitioner; by occupation journalist and fiction writer; in 1871-2 outside Editorial contributor to *N.Y. Evening Post;* for half-year after that editorial writer and Lit. critic on staff of *Springfield Daily Union;* 1876-7 Voyage for health to Sandwich Islands; subsequently *one* of the founders of *Springfield Daily News;* published four books, some dozens of stories . . . several barrels of editorials.

This brief paragraph was 'enough for a tombstone,' as Bellamy put it, but hardly more than that. Had Bellamy been writing for posterity, he might have added some interesting commentary to this bare outline. He could have said, for instance, that Chicopee Falls was a thriving and partially industrialized New England village a few miles from Springfield; or he might have gone on to say that while he respected his Calvinist ancestor mentioned in the letter, who took part in the Great Awakening and dreamed a utopia of his own, he was prouder of Joseph Bellamy's contemporary and namesake, a Captain Samuel Bellamy, supposed to have conducted piratical operations off the coast of New England and in the South Atlantic. He makes no mention here of his father, Rufus King Bellamy, a fat, approachable Baptist divine, or his mother—thin, sensitive, and tenacious—from whom, so he told Frances Willard, he derived his 'mental and spiritual constitution.' There are no references to his three older brothers and the affectionate and amiable household, nothing about the family arguments or of his hopes for a military career or of his father's ward, Emma Sanderson, whom he afterwards married.

All of these details and more would have to be included to round out the portrait of Edward Bellamy before he wrote *Looking Backward,* but the clues to his character during this growing-up or apprentice state may be found in his journals and notebooks and his autobiographical writings in which he reveals his moody, rebellious, and unconventional thoughts. That Bellamy at this time was trying 'to find himself,' as the phrase goes, is perfectly evident from such unpublished works as *Eliot Carson.* Eliot, like his inventor, is a dissatisfied dreamer and intellectual who prefers desultory reading to organized study and gives up a law career because he has 'become utterly disgusted with the dirty trade of a local pettifogger.' He follows the advice of Thoreau and chucks his well-paid but soul-warping job in the mill in order to cultivate himself, to become a 'success' in the transcendental sense: that is, to enlarge his mind, develop the chords of sympathy, and to pulsate with 'the rhythm of infinity.'

Bellamy realized that society condemned as ne'er-do-wells young men who seemed to have no definite purpose in life, but he reassured himself in his diary: 'I hold that the object of life is to live, and nothing else save as a means thereto. We are not to work but to live, to live the fullest freest most developed life we can. Life is its own end.' If this were true, men ought not to dissolve themselves in their occupations and live for work. Bellamy never lost this interest for what he called 'the economy of happiness' and made it the chief consideration for his ideal state.

In trying to recall for his admirers and friends what had prompted him to write *Looking Backward*, Bellamy mentioned several incidents in his life that provided the initial impulses. In 1889 he made the rather startling and wholly inaccurate admission that his book had begun as 'a real literary fantasy' and that he had never before given much thought or sympathy to social reform. Somehow, he explained, he 'stumbled over the corner-stone of the new social order.' A conflicting and more truthful account appeared four years later. In this essay entitled 'How I Wrote *Looking Backward*,' Bellamy recollected the 'vivid realization of the inferno of poverty beneath our civilization' which came to him during his European travels in 1868 and 1869 and his early radical effusions before the Chicopee Lyceum. Undoubtedly, as he told Howells, concern for his children's future drove him on. Quite possibly, too, the idea for his industrial army furnished the imaginative catalyst, but these explanations are all arguments after the fact. No one can read through Bellamy's published and unpublished writings without seeing immediately that *Looking Backward* began to take shape in his mind from the time when he first put pen to paper.

If this assumption is valid, then all of the arguments over Bellamy's sources and the mystery of from what utopia he did or did not borrow become interesting but not particularly relevant. Given his dissatisfaction with the present order and his will to free men and women from thralldom, no further esoteric clues or influences need be dug out. John Macnie's interesting novel, *Diothas*, which preceded *Looking Backward* by five years and which projected the hero into the future by the same device of mesmerism later employed by Bellamy, is perhaps an important source, but here as elsewhere Bellamy selected details that confirmed and complemented his own preconceived ideas. His belief, expressed many times, that we ought to look at ourselves from without rather than from within presages the scheme of looking backward from utopia to the present; and long before he had come across the works of Macnie, Gronlund, Blanc, Cabet, Bebel and the numerous other books he is supposed to have pilfered, he had anticipated his own masterpiece. Sometime in the 'sixties, he conjured up a people living in 'a happier futurity' and looking back 'upon the social barbarism of these times with abhorrence,' and although he had not yet conceived of his hero, Julian West, and the voluble Dr. Leete, Julian's host and guide into the twenty-first century, he was already making preparations for an expedition into what he described then as the 'undiscovered country' of socialism. He had no blueprint for the new economy, he told his Lyceum audience: 'no human foot has ever trod on its shores. But I know that it exists and we must find it. I see the countless difficulties which envelope the task, but I feel this to be the great problem of humanity propounded by the sphinx-like fates which we must solve or perish.'

In *Looking Backward* and more particularly in its sequel *Equality,* published in 1897, Bellamy nailed down the vision of his youth and illustrated what he had professed to Howells in 1884. The romancer, he declared then, must derive his sustenance from the earth: 'Though he build into the air, he must see to it that he does not seem to build upon the air, for the more airy the pinnacles the more necessary the solidity of the foundations.'

ɪᴠ] Bellamy began to clear the ground for his grand edifice about 1886, when he was finally ready to put to use the experiences of the past fifteen years. Not that he had done very much or traveled very far. From 1872 on, he had lived in Chicopee almost continuously except for a six-months' trip to Hawaii with his brother Frederick, but he had married Emma Augusta Sanderson in 1872, and marriage, an important event in the lives of most men, was a particularly significant one for Bellamy. Women had always symbolized for him everything that the rebel rebels against, the embodiment of those stable, conservative habits of life he feared. Whether we interpret this step as a capitulation to the world or as a sign of maturity, his marriage and the children that followed transformed him from a detached onlooker of the social scene into an active partisan for social equality.

The strikes and conflicts that flared up in the months preceding the writing of *Looking Backward* must also have absorbed his attention at this time and suggested to him an appropriate subject for his talents. Certainly his book is filled with an urgency and a sense of crisis which bespeak the times and which reflect not only the anger of the 'toilers of the world engaged in something like a world-wide insurrection,' but also the exasperation and apprehension of his own middle class, in revolt, as he put it, 'against social conditions that reduce life to a brutal struggle for existence, mock every dictate of ethics and religion, and render well-nigh futile the efforts of philanthropy.'

This feeling of crisis, which George also exploited so cleverly, strongly pervades *Looking Backward*. Bellamy himself, in explaining the book's immense popularity, made a great deal of the vague but unmistakable public fear of catastrophe which it articulated; it was 'a bare anticipation or expression,' he wrote, 'of what everybody was thinking and about to say,' interpreting the drift of social conditions and making the movement towards Nationalism 'henceforth a conscious, and not, as previously, an unconscious, one.' To know the truth, however, and to act on it were two different things. As early as 1877 he had quoted Coleridge's remark: 'Truths, of all others the most awful and interesting, are often considered so true, that they lose all power of truth, and lie bed-ridden in the dormitory of the soul, side by side with the most despised and exploded errors.' Bellamy's mission was to revive these bed-ridden patients, trick them out in new finery, and set them to work again.

He succeeded. *Looking Backward* is a love story as well as a tract. Julian West, engaged in the year 1887 to a Miss Edith Bartlett, retires for the night in his subterranean bedroom, surrenders 'to the manipulations of the mesmerizer,' Dr. Pillsbury (Julian has insomnia), and is put into a deeper sleep than usual. When he awakes 'exactly one hundred and thirteen years, three months, and eleven days' later, Boston and the rest of the world have changed considerably. Julian's introduction to the new society, in which all the problems hitherto plaguing mankind have long been solved, makes up the bulk of the story, but the love affair between the miraculously spared visitor from the nineteenth century and Dr. Leete's advanced and beautiful daughter, also named Edith, is carried on between the Doctor's stupefying revelations, and at the end Julian discovers that his sweetheart is none other than the great-granddaughter of his former fiancée.

Bellamy's trick conclusion, a real touch of genius, must have increased the appeal of his tale and especially beguiled those readers who appreciated it as much for its entertainment value as for its instruction. Julian awakes again in the benighted nineteenth century. The reader as well as the hero believe they have been tricked. Poor Julian, who now knows what the good society is like, berates his friends for their callousness and is just about to be thrown out of Edith Bartlett's dining room by the outraged company when he awakes again and finds that his long sleep was not a dream and that his utopian fiancée is quite real. The last flashback into the horrors of the 1880's gives a final fillip to Bellamy's persuasive book, but Julian's nightmare also dramatizes an early idea of Bellamy's: that no freedom, 'no happiness of the future,' can 'cancel the slavery and sorrow already recorded.'

The style of *Looking Backward* probably had as much to do with its tremendous success as did the plot. He had progressed a long way since the mawkish periods of his early tales and had deliberately prepared himself to write clearly and attractively. It was one of Bellamy's virtues, according to Howells, that he 'never put the simplest and plainest reader to shame by the assumption of those fine-gentlemanly airs which abash and dishearten more than the mere literary swell can think.' That Bellamy himself deplored style for its own sake is borne out by an early entry in his diary:

There is most emphatically such a thing as a too great facility in expression. The taking garb in which this art enables you to invest your ideas deceives you as to their value, conceals their worthlessness. You are in danger of degenerating—till at last gorgeous rhetoric and epigrammatic brilliancy mask mental bankruptcy. . . In exalting eloquence it is too often forgotten how after all she is but the humble handiwork of thought, and otherwise an arrant harlot.

He carefully avoided rhetoric, but his writing, quiet in tone during the long expository passages, takes on an eloquence and fervor when Julian or Dr. Leete is roused by moral considerations. Even the mild-mannered Bellamy cannot entirely remove the rancor and scorn from his words as he expatiates on the ruthlessness, brutality, and waste of cut-throat competition. He rarely employed the oratorical devices of Henry George, who had first produced, said Bellamy, the 'startling demonstration of the readiness of the public for some radical remedy of industrial evils,' but he had George's gift for hitting off striking metaphors and analogies that pleased the fancies and clarified the ethical credos of his audience.

For these reasons, *Looking Backward* was an instantaneous success and began to sell in the hundreds of thousands. Bellamy was besieged with requests for translation rights, and the letters poured in from all over the world hailing him as the new Messiah, the 'Apostle of Humanity,' the prophet of the 'Golden Century.' An English surgeon with the same name received such a flood of correspondence in all languages that he had to publish a card in the *Times* disclaiming the authorship of *Looking Backward*. Bellamy's enemies and critics attributed his popularity to the economic innocence of a public 'just in that twilight of education in which chimeras stalk.' But Howells read it with enthusiasm, and Mark Twain, according to Hamlin Garland, was 'profoundly touched by *Looking Backward*.' Even a saturnine and distrustful man named Thorstein Veblen read it aloud to his wife. Many who started it as a romance found themselves, according to one reviewer, 'unexpectedly haunted by visions of a golden age wherein all the world unites to do the world's work like members of a family.'

Sound economy or not, thousands of Bellamy's readers regarded his reorganized society, not only as a vision of hope but also as a rational plan for social rehabilitation. The smoke of the great strikes of 1885, 1886, and 1887 still hung over the country, but in the society planted some one hundred years in the future, 'a general business partnership' had been established and the affairs of the country carried on by a vast industrial army. Every able-bodied citizen between the ages of twenty-one and forty-five served his stint in the national corps and everyone found himself working at the job for which he or she was most fitted. As in the Fourier phalanx, the unattractive jobs carried with them certain compensations, mainly in the form of shorter hours and greater recognition, and everyone had ample opportunity to cultivate himself, a privilege enjoyed only by a small minority in the nineteenth century. At forty-five, thanks to the immense effectiveness of co-operation, every person retired and spent the rest of his life doing anything he wanted.

No matter how hard or at what occupation an adult worked, he received the same compensation or spending-rights (since there was no money) as everyone else. Each shared alike in the great social fund society had created. 'The citizen,' Bellamy explained to his marveling audience, 'is credited with his annual dividends of the product of the great partnership, and receives vouchers, upon presentation of which at the public stores he obtains what he wants, at such times and in such quantities as he likes.' Would not such a system encourage loafing? No, said Bellamy, for the rewards of honor and prestige and increased authority would satisfy the brilliant and competent citizens in a society where wealth was not a sign of achievement. He had long argued that men sought money 'because it secured power and consequence,' and now in his utopia he elaborated on this early conviction and made it central to his scheme.

While the national authority controlled the industries and businesses managed in the 1880's by the great trusts, considerable opportunities were left to small groups of citizens to work together 'for social, religious, political or other semi-private purposes,' and since crime and fraud and waste (what George had called the 'nonprogressive' activities 'in which mental power is consumed') had been eliminated, the wealth of society had expanded beyond the expectations of man. 'The substitution of scientific methods of an organized and unified industrial system for the wasteful struggle of the present competitive plan with its countless warring and mutually destructive undertakings' released the incalculably potent mental power of the masses and created unparalleled changes in the United States and in the world.

Even if Bellamy's readers had some doubts about the speed with which such a transformation could be carried out (Bellamy maintained that the next generation should surely see it, perhaps even his own), he injected thousands with his own confidence in the possibility of social control and the material benefits that would most certainly result. Because both material comfort and spiritual development figured prominently in his panacea, he could appeal, as George had done, to different tastes and sensibilities. Perhaps, as one critic alleged about *Progress and Poverty,* nine out of every ten readers of *Looking Backward* were incapable of following the arguments of the book and only drank in the 'suggestions of confiscation,' but testimonies of enough men and women remain to measure the inspirational effect of Bellamy's novel. 'Many a man plunging into the political ferment of to-day,' one of his admirers wrote the year of Bellamy's death, 'can look back to some word dropped by some young companion who had been reading *Looking Backward,* or perhaps can remember reading it himself some winter evening on his father's farm.'

Perhaps Bellamy exaggerated a little when he said in 1892 that 'the novel with a sociological motive now sets the literary fashion and a course in political economy has become necessary to write a successful love story,' but in so far as this remark is true, Bellamy must take chief responsibility. *Looking Backward* hatched a brood of replies, criticism, and continuations too numerous to catalogue. Some of these, especially many of the reviews, were abusive in tone and attacked his vision on every conceivable ground, but Bellamy was not perturbed by the opposition. What interested him most was the growing public curiosity about socialism, 'formerly a by-word and a name of reproach,' and the unconscious adoption by publicists and scholars of positions that would ultimately lead them into the camp of Nationalism.

When Nationalist clubs sprang up spontaneously in Boston and elsewhere throughout the country, especially on the Pacific Coast, the naturally sanguine Bellamy interpreted this enthusiasm as a sign of the times, and henceforth devoted himself entirely to the cause. A magazine, *The Nationalist,* established by his Boston friends, became the party organ. By 1890 162 clubs scattered over 27 states were holding their meetings; the Nationalists claimed 6000 organized members and no less than half a million fellow-travelers. *Looking Backward,* with 200,000 copies already sold, was still bought at the rate of 10,000 every week. This was probably the high-water mark of the Nationalist movement.

The adored apostle of thousands refused to be lionized and confined himself to Chicopee and his family circle. Invitations to speak came in sheaves. Editors begged for special articles and books. But Bellamy, never robust and disinclined to expose himself to large crowds, held back as much as he could. Henry Austin, the editor of *The Nationalist,* described Bellamy in those days as a charming, reserved man with 'a curious awkwardness of manner—a sort of country boyishness—which he rarely shook off.' He remarked on his hawk eye and aquiline nose, his voice 'weak and uneven' but 'highly agreeable' in intonation. Austin considered his friend an indifferent speaker with a witty rather than humorous cast of mind. Frances Willard, who interviewed Bellamy about this time, gave more specific details: his medium height, dark-blue eyes, mobile lips, and dark-brown beard and mustache. But her general impression, too, was of a gentle, modest personality.

His life in Chicopee went on as it always had. Bellamy told his intimates no more about his work than before. He spent a good deal of time with his children and his wife, to whom he was completely devoted, shunned publicity, and remained the 'literary recluse.' From the reminiscences of his family, we get the picture of a carelessly dressed man living in a chaotic study, nicknaming his friends, gulping down raw eggs and milk, and reading until very late at night. He could be sentimental over his wedding anniversary and Scotch ballads; 'The Lost Chord' was one of his favorite songs. He loved flowers and all things military, at least in the abstract. The family servants adored him. He usually needed a haircut, hated stiff collars, and had to be forced by his wife to change the blue or black suits he habitually wore. He was no help around the house, having no mechanical skill. He read the Bible, Dickens, Charles Reade, *Alice in Wonderland,* and *The Jungle Books* to his son and daughter. He liked to drink beer.

This was the man, enjoying the light of his study and hating the limelight, who half reluctantly threw himself into a life for which he was not temperamentally suited. He was becoming more and more certain that the principles he established in *Looking Backward* had somehow caught the imagination of the people and so did not regret the time required to answer letters and write articles; but he did not like to play the public leader. 'You are right in inferring,' he wrote to Thomas Wentworth Higginson in 1891, 'that the natural man in me is not socially inclined.'

Bellamy, however, did not entirely approve of the policies of the self-appointed men who ran *The Nationalist*. No central organization of Nationalist clubs existed, and while Bellamy did not object to the flexibility and tolerance of the Nationalist political philosophy—the Nationalists welcomed almost any intransigent group—he wanted a party mouthpiece 'devoted to the discussion of the industrial and social situation, from the moral and economic point of view.' Many of the Nationalists, Bellamy felt, were too nonpolitical. The Theosophists especially, who had been first attracted by Bellamy's psychic tales, now seemed interested in Nationalism only as an avenue toward spiritual development. Madame Blavatsky and her disciples correctly singled out this feature of Bellamy's philosophy as the most significant, and yet short of organizing a number of Bellamy clubs, the Theosophists had no real concern for Nationalism as a practical political movement. Bellamy appreciated their support and friendship, but his more worldly associates now urged him to make an active campaign to 'enlist the middle class who are still the bone and sinew of our people and who are looking around in vague unrest for something.'

So with the advice of some friends and against the warnings of others he decided to establish *The New Nation,* and the second phase of the Nationalist movement began. Henry Austin, editor of the old *Nationalist,* attributed this move to vanity and claimed that Bellamy had written to him afterward regretting that he had ever undertaken the new magazine. If this were true, and it may very well have been, for Bellamy sunk a great deal of money into his enterprise, *The New Nation* was still far more readable than the genteel, amateurish little magazine it supplanted. It admirably fulfilled the requirements of a party sheet, attacking the old perpetual warfare of capitalism but coming out positively for specific reforms: nationalization of the railroads, insurance, telephone, and telegraph; municipalization of utilities; civil-service reform; and equal opportunities for education. Bellamy's new magazine called for the mobilization of a grand army of peace. Extremely optimistic in tone, it welcomed any mildly liberal cause, any faint expression of advanced feeling that confirmed Bellamy's faith in the march of progress.

Critics like Austin accused him of angling for millionaires—a charge that some Nationalists had made against George—and of being too gentle, too all-inclusive. There was probably some truth in the latter criticism. Bellamy tried so hard not to antagonize potential supporters among the middle class that he sometimes appeared overcautious. 'It is not a question,' he once said, 'which side of the subject is the true side—all are true. None can be fully argued without qualification by the others. The question is only which side of the subject is in most danger of neglect and therefore most needs to be proved.' When a man sees all around the problem he is considering, he is not likely to be the best of advocates, but Bellamy never compromised on any important principle. He understood very well the conservative spirit of the people he addressed and deliberately posed as the great conservator of republican institutions against an anarchistic and revolutionary money power. Jefferson had used the same strategy against the Federalist stock-jobbers; but Bellamy went a little further. He would transform American society beyond recognition to make the Declaration of Independence a reality.

As he worked out the plans for this rebuilding in more detail, popular interest in the Nationalist movement began to fall off. The Bureau of Nationalist Literature, organized in Philadelphia in 1893 or 1894, ran steadily in the hole, and *The New Nation,* to the sorrow of its loyal subscribers, folded up in February 1894. Bellamy consoled himself by saying the magazine had fulfilled its intended purpose: 'to state the philosophy of nationalism as a coherent doctrine' and 'to demonstrate its practicality,' and the demise of the journal did not turn him away from the movement. For the remainder of his life he worked on his final testament, the book that would take up the objections of his critics one by one and prove finally that Nationalism was more than a romantic fancy.

He had not tried, he explained, to present the details in his first book, to describe each step in the process toward nationalization, because in doing so he would have concentrated attention and criticism upon the details themselves; the ends would have been overlooked. 'Until we have a clear idea of what we want and are sure that we want it,' he wrote, 'it would be a waste of time to discuss how we are to get it.' It was clear to him, after half a dozen years of propagandizing, that the people wanted a change and believed in his goal. *Equality,* published in 1897 shortly before his death, provided more explicit directions for finding the way to utopia. With its publication, it was at last possible to examine Bellamy's philosophy as a totality.

v] Toward the close of *Looking Backward* Julian West and the Leetes gather in the music room, turn on one of Bellamy's famous gadgets (an early anticipation of the radio), and hear Dr. Barton's Sunday sermon. In describing the remarkable moral transformation of society after the establishment of the new economy, Dr. Barton expresses Bellamy's view of the nature of man, the central point of his ethical system:

that human nature in its essential qualities is good, not bad, that men by their natural intention and structure are generous, not selfish, pitiful, not cruel, sympathetic, not arrogant, godlike in aspirations, instinct with divinest impulses of tenderness and self-sacrifice, images of God indeed, not the travesties upon Him they had seemed.

The new society had not changed human nature, for human nature does not change, but it had created a set of conditions in which 'the anti-social and brutal side' of man found no outlet. A new type of individual emerged, freer and nobler, and the barriers to human initiative weakened and gave way.

Julian's contemporaries had lived in an atmosphere of fear, class isolated from class, and each regarding the other as an alien race. So at least Bellamy saw it. Educational advantages and all the other privileges that went with wealth widened the social barriers between the propertied and the unpropertied until the gulf between them seemed 'almost like that between different natural species, which have no means of communication.' Occupations became increasingly vulgar or honorific, and the 'servant question' agitated republican America. In such circumstances, Julian came to realize from his vantage point of the twenty-first century, it was quite easy to account for the growing distrust and jealousy among the classes and to see why the work of menials degraded the served as well as the server. The unspoken but none the less real assumptions of the closed society not only affronted human dignity but deprived the community of the benefits of collective action.

In the year 2000, Julian discovered, Bostonians justified equal opportunities for education and self-development on three counts: 'first, the right of every man to the completest education the nation can give him on his own account, as necessary to his enjoyment of himself; second, the right of his fellow-citizens to have him educated, as necessary to their enjoyment of his society; third, the right of the unborn to be guaranteed an intelligent and refined parentage.' The principle of equality could thus be vindicated as a natural right and as a social necessity; it made life more beautiful and it made it safer. The system of domestic service under capitalism, of course, glaringly denied this ideal of equality by asking others to do what the masters themselves would not and treating inferiors with contempt for doing so. As Edith the second, Julian's sweetheart, said: 'to accept a service from another which we would be unwilling to return in kind, if need were, is like borrowing without repaying, while to enforce such a service by taking advantage of the poverty or necessity of a person would be an outrage like forcible robbery.' This analogy employed by Bellamy, incidentally, illustrates his habit of using the prejudices of the *bourgeoisie* to unsettle its institutions.

Dr. Leete has no difficulty whatever in demolishing his visitor's feeble defense of inequality in the nineteenth century and the privileges of property, and after the reader has been initiated with Julian into the Nationalist civilization, the doctor's reasons for accepting complete social equality seem unanswerable. All men born on the earth, Dr. Leete tells Julian, inherit the past achievements of the race and are joint heirs of the social machinery that has been developing over the centuries. When the great 'social fund,' created collectively, is siphoned off for the benefit of a minority, it is not only an insult to the God of the human family but also a kind of piracy. Every man, in short, is in debt to society, which offers him the rich heritage, and a 'creditor to society for all he needs.' And the only way in which the debt can be paid and the benefits collected is to nationalize society.

The name 'nationalism' particularly suited the new movement, because, as Dr. Leete explained, it realized 'the idea of a nation with a grandeur and completeness never before conceived.' The older conception of democracy envisaged simply a political arrangement. Nationalism, on the other hand, connoted 'a family, a vital union, a common life, a mighty heaven-touching tree whose leaves are its people, fed from its veins, and feeding it in turn.' It substituted for the vulgar patriotism of the past, with its irrational demands for sacrifice and abasement, a patriotism that instilled a rational love for humanity. The old nationalism set peoples apart; the new nationalism utilized national traditions and sentiments but only as a beginning for a larger brotherhood of peoples.

Just as the new patriotism inspired human solidarity instead of national pride and thereby offered a greater enthusiasm in place of a lesser, so Bellamy intended the industrial army of workers to represent an army of peace, not an instrument of brutal aggression. His critics have made a great deal of his fondness for military display as something unconsciously antidemocratic, but despite the undeniable attraction that all things military held for him, there is no evidence that he ever exalted the military ideal as against the civilian.

Bellamy's fascination with his idea of an army for peace, a 'compact of brotherhood,' becomes more understandable if we remember that he regarded the 'war of existence'—more heartless and bloodthirsty than military war—as a struggle demanding the most complete and effective mobilization of social energies. Nevertheless, the shade of army discipline darkens his utopia. The rhythmic tread of marching soldiers, which seemed to hypnotize him and make him forget, as he remarked in one of his stories, 'that there are individuals,' has a portentous sound to modern ears. We begin to feel the presence of the totalitarian state, unlovely and relentless.

The military metaphor of Bellamy, moreover, drew attention away from Nationalism's objectives and obscured his primary design. Although he believed that war sometimes took men's thoughts away from money-making and although he wanted to gather and preserve 'the tonic air of battlefields' as 'a precious elixir to reinvigorate the atmosphere in times of peace,' he kept the distinction clear in his own mind between the civic and the military, and condemned, for example, the custom of military parades on Columbus Day as being both sinister and in bad taste. The military structure, taken by itself, was nothing more than a technique for welding together an effective working force and making the nation one economic organism. Economic unity prepared the way for moral unity, as Bellamy kept insisting. Nationalism, he wrote to Higginson in 1890,

is, of course, necessarily an economic reform, but its most important aspect is that of a moral movement for uplifting, enlarging, and ennobling the individual life by making every individual contribute his efforts first and directly to the common or national wealth, and himself dependent for his livelihood upon his equal chance in it, so that he is rich as the nation is rich and poor as his fellow citizens are poor and never otherwise. . .

Under the old economic system of the nineteenth century, this fusion and mutual dependence could not possibly develop. The theorists in Bellamy's day taught 'that there were two kinds of science dealing with human conduct—one moral, the other economic; and two lines of reasoning as to conduct—the economic, and the ethical; both right in different ways.' Bellamy, echoing Parker and George and Howells and Lloyd, refused to separate the moral and the economic. 'Any economic proposition which cannot be stated in ethical terms,' he said, 'is false.' And with this affirmation, he repudiated the Spencerians who denied this connection and who created a series of myths that dignified their treason to humanity.

That the moral appeal of Bellamy and his fellow progressives should arouse the religious groups is not remarkable, but Bellamy apparently won over, as George had done, men of property and substance whose ethical idealism had not been quenched by the fight to survive. His respectability must have reassured them, as well as his appreciation of their conservative tastes. Bellamy, as he told his friend Higginson, wanted the social issue taken 'out of the hands of blatant blasphemous demagogues' and placed 'before the sober and morally minded masses of the American people. Not until it is so presented by men whom they trust will they seriously consider it on its merits.' To win over this indispensable group meant, of course, that no hastily proposed changes should be broached, no revolutionary methods adopted. He demonstrated the precarious top-heaviness of present society, pointed out the direction in which world economy seemed to be moving, and showed the middle class how an adjustment into the new economy might be made without precipitating a convulsion. Business trusts and huge labor organizations forecast the future. Under Nationalism these natural tendencies would receive direction and the evolution from private to public capitalism gradually come about.

The phrase 'public capitalism,' which Bellamy used in *Equality*, is an interesting one even though not original with him. It implied the end of the direction of industry and commerce by individuals, but Bellamy very pointedly argued that this did not signify a change in property rights. Nationalism, he said, really insured property rights by converting the government into a large corporation in which everyone had equal stakes. In other words, Nationalism *consolidated* property; it did not abolish it.

But in spite of Bellamy's moderate tone and his middle-class presuppositions, he could not get around the fact that Nationalism was a form of socialism and that the word socialism did not please American ears. Bellamy knew this perfectly well:

> Every sensible man will admit [he told Howells] there is a big deal in a name especially in making first impressions. In the radicalness of the opinions I have expressed I may seem to out-socialize the Socialists, yet the word socialist is one I could never well stomach. In the first place it is a foreign word itself and equally foreign in all its suggestions. It smells to the average American of petroleum, suggests the red flag with all manner of sexual novelties, and an abusive tone about God and religion, which in this country we at least treat with decent respect.

Nationalism, as Bellamy described it, sounded at once more wholesome and domestic than socialism (which seemed to him a loose generic term for any form of collectivism) and a great deal more precise. It defined the process and form of the proposed collective action and the basis on which society shared. But even more important, it personified gradualism and tolerance, and unequivocally rejected the doctrine of class war.

Bellamy possessed only a layman's knowledge of European socialism, he admitted to Howells, but he knew enough to realize that no party calling itself by that name could gain many adherents in America. He feared the extremists who capitalized on mass discontent and raised the cry against all private property, and he deplored socialist efforts to increase the feeling of class consciousness. Like George, he held that no class could gain at the expense of another. 'Forget yourself what class you belong to,' he advised, 'and it will be forgotten by others.'

The Nationalists, unlike the socialists, did not regard themselves as the party of the working class and, in fact, looked upon the unadulterated proletarian with a kind of distaste. Their gingerly if sympathetic interest in the workingman is illustrated by an episode in *Equality*. Dr. Leete and Julian are strolling through the Boston Common and come upon a piece of statuary depicting a group of striking workingmen. The figures are cast in heroic size, suggesting dignity and courage and brawn, but 'The Strikers' (for that is the name of the group) are not idealized like the workingmen in a *New Masses* cartoon. The features of the men are 'coarse and hard in outline,' and their faces stare with a 'scowling intensity.' Julian wonders why these men, whom he knew as ignorant and narrow fellows concerned only with adding a few cents a day to their wages, are honored by the new society as 'the pioneers in the revolt against private capitalism.' Dr. Leete replies (and it is evident that he speaks for Bellamy here) in the following characteristic way: 'Look at those faces,' he bids Julian. 'Has the sculptor idealized them? Are they the faces of philosophers? Do they not bear out your statement that the strikers, like the workingmen generally, were, as a rule, ignorant, narrow-minded men, with no grasp of large questions, and incapable of so great an idea as the overthrow of an immemorial economic order?' Nevertheless, he continues, these strikers are the unwitting instruments of good, furnishing with their 'crude initiative' the brute force required to bring in the new industrial system. The working class, in other words, provides the energy for the 'cultured men and women'

who espouse the workers' cause 'with voice and pen' and lead them
to greener pastures. A book like *Looking Backward* 'will set Cali-
ban thinking.'

In emphasizing the difference between Nationalist philosophy
and the program of the Socialists, Bellamy carefully avoided a
break with the Socialist party. His friend, Cyrus Field Willard, one
of the organizers of the Bellamy movement in Boston and later a
co-worker with Eugene Debs, especially warned him not to alienate the Socialists as Henry George had done and to continue his
policy of co-operating with any cause having the welfare of humanity for its object. Bellamy had no cause to dislike the Socialists, for he had been very well treated by them. Laurence Gronlund, the American Marxian whose book, *The Co-operative Commonwealth* (1884), unquestionably influenced Bellamy's thinking
—not to mention Howells's and Lloyd's—praised *Looking Backward* without stint upon its publication and even withdrew his
own book for a time in order to increase the sales of Bellamy's.
Gronlund later differed with Bellamy in several important respects,
but no rifts developed between the Socialists and the Nationalists.
The Nationalist carried articles praising Lassalle and Marx and a
sympathetic review of *Capital* appeared in *The New Nation* in
1891. Bellamy's habit of regarding any cause tinged with socialism,
whether it was Christian Socialism or the Single Tax or Populism,
as furnishing tributary streams to the Mississippi of Nationalism
may have been unwarranted, but it prevented the kind of sectarian
exclusiveness that weakened other liberal movements.

The public had first to be convinced, Bellamy thought, that socialism or Nationalism can be healthy and democratic, that it
comes about quite naturally, as he wrote in his introduction to the
American edition of *The Fabian Essays,* 'when a people having a
pressing economic problem to deal with become masters of the
democratic method.' Americans had to be shown that their suspicion of collective action under state leadership was short-sighted
and anachronistic. Julian West's contemporaries, always excepting the dyed-in-the-wool individualists, had gone on the theory
that the state should intervene only at that point where individual
enterprise broke down. Bellamy had no strong objections to this

view, although it seemed obvious to him that the state should do what it can do best no matter if individuals could do it or not, but, as his spokesman Dr. Leete pointed out so vehemently, the nineteenth-century state failed to perform adequately even its negative protective function: 'to safeguard the lives of its members.'

Bellamy attributed the failure to live up to this professed principle—for the nineteenth century gave it lip-service—to an archaic holdover from early national beginnings. Democracy had begun in America as a protest against royal authority and lacked, he believed, a new and vital principle of its own. The second phase of democracy, which had obtained advocates early in the century but little mass support, brought with it the sense that the deposing of kings was only a beginning, not an end, and 'merely preliminary to its real programme, which was the use of the collective social machinery for the indefinite promotion of the welfare of the people at large.' And with this second or positive phase, men came to believe that government had to change not only in its external forms but in 'its motives, purposes, and functions' as well. The new democracy, like the old, envisaged government as a protection against popular enemies but saw the chief threat to the nation not in theoretically hostile countries across the water but in the ever-present and unrelenting dangers of hunger and nakedness and cold. It sought, moreover, to supplement its role of protector by guaranteeing, as Bellamy put it before the days of the Beveridge Plan, 'the nurture, education, and comfortable maintenance of every citizen from the cradle to the grave.'

In the pseudo-republic of the late nineteenth century, the shell of democracy (that is to say, suffrage and other so-called political controls) carried little validity, since an entrenched plutocracy controlled the economic citadel and the people were little more than serfs. In the twenty-first century, people assumed that only educated men who had a stake in the society ought to vote, but instead of using this argument to hamstring the democratic process, as the nineteenth-century Tories did, the future Americans drew the opposite corollary—namely, that every man should be educated and have an equal share in the society. Instead of conforming man to things, they followed the Emersonian injunction and reduced things to men.

This realistic and logical application of democratic theory in Dr. Leete's country produced a purer form of democracy than had ever before existed, a government both efficient and humanitarian, which harmonized the welfare of both public and private interests. The rulers of the old democracy, concerned primarily in scrabbling for money, had sacrificed themselves to the commonwealth only during unusual times. Generally, a group of 'designing men and factions' plundered the community at will and thereby transformed American democracy into 'the most corrupt and worthless of all forms of government and the most susceptible to misuse and perversion for selfish, personal, and class purposes.' With the collectivization of the United States, however, the economic motive, formerly so destructive and antisocial, became a unifying influence; under public capitalism each individual citizen acted as the guardian and representative of the majority. Men could then truly say that in following their private interests, they benefited humanity. In such a society, Bellamy said, given mutual dependence and 'universal culture to cap all,' no 'imperfection of administrative machinery could prevent the government from being a good one.' He protected himself somewhat, it is true, by contriving an intricate and effective system of tabulating popular opinion through a telephone poll, which would delight Dr. Gallup, but this change from a representative to a pure democracy—in which legislative duties were relegated to congressional committees and office-holders could be recalled overnight—was merely a refinement. He wished only to emphasize the one key point: that given economic democracy, political democracy would eventually follow as a matter of course.

vi] Between Julian West's profound sleep and his awakening in the twenty-first century, a new democracy had begun to flower. Bellamy at first took advantage of the romancer's license and remained somewhat vague about the events of the intervening century, but in the sequel to *Looking Backward*, goaded on, perhaps, by the jibes of his unfriendly critics and the clichés about visionaries who write glowingly of the future without showing how to get there, Bellamy tried to suggest to his countrymen how the peaceful revolution might come about.

He had written *Looking Backward* during a period of national unrest, and although he did not try to play down the dangers of the present regime, he wanted to reassure the pessimists that humanity was not about 'to take a header into chaos.' Looking beneath the violence of class war, the strikes, the arrogance of corporate wealth, he thought he saw already growing the roots of the new commonwealth nurtured unknowingly by the men who had no conception of the world they were to be instrumental in bringing forth. The ruthless consolidation of the nineteenth century was to end in the Great Trust of the twentieth, and the foundations of utopia would be established.

In *Equality* Bellamy set down in some detail the imaginary events of this earth-shaking epoch and used a rather interesting device to present them. One of the reviewers of *Looking Backward* perhaps suggested it when he wrote in June 1888: 'Could he [Bellamy] not, from that library in which he seems only to have read a little fiction, have withdrawn some book which gave account of the steps in the mighty revolution,—a book of annals, for instance, of the years 1887-1937 during which most of the great work was achieved?' Bellamy took the hint and introduced into *Equality* Storiot's *History of the Revolution,* a mythical text which Dr. Leete read aloud to Julian. The history lesson did not make *Equality* more thrilling as a novel, but the episodes included in Storiot and mentioned elsewhere by Dr. Leete give Bellamy's forecast of the future.

As the nineteenth century drew to a close, Storiot relates, the marvelous technological development of the industrial revolution gave the United States a decided advantage over its competitors. But if wages went up, as government figures attempted to show, popular discontent remained: 'the people,' as one of Bellamy's precocious school children observe, 'were better acquainted with their own condition than the sociologists, and it is certain that it was the growing conviction of the American masses during the closing decades of the nineteenth century that they were losing ground economically and in danger of sinking into the degraded condition of the proletariat and peasantry of the ancient and contemporary European world.' Private capitalism, falsely identified with individual liberty, industrial freedom, and personal initiative, became in fact morally and economically indefensible. Business crises and depressions periodically disrupted economic life and the dreary pattern of high prices and scarcity, mass unemployment, and the further decline of buying power repeated itself again and again. In the words of Dr. Leete:

> The day dream of the nineteenth century producer was to gain absolute control of the supply of some necessity of life, so that he might keep the public at the verge of starvation, and always command famine prices for what he supplied. This, Mr. West, is what was called in the nineteenth century a system of production. I will leave it to you if it does not seem, in some of its aspects, a great deal more like a system for preventing production.

Here and elsewhere Bellamy examined the capitalistic stratagem that Veblen later referred to as 'planned scarcity,' and in his account of the origins of the new society his observations also seem Veblenesque. Nineteenth-century businessmen, Bellamy went on to say, remained oblivious to the weaknesses of their *laisser-faire* economy and imagined they succeeded admirably in producing wealth. 'No reflection,' Dr. Leete tells Julian, 'would have cut the men of your wealth-worshiping century more keenly than the suggestion that they did not know how to make money,' but that is precisely what Bellamy believed. Their system of production was antiquated and wasteful: 'Selfishness was their only science, and in industrial production selfishness is suicide.' Not until 'the idea of increasing the individual hoard' gave way 'to the idea of increasing the common stock' could production be carried out along scientific lines. During the capitalistic 'renaissance,' the 'whole atmosphere of trade was mephitic with chicane,' and the plutocracy indulged in the most vulgar expenditures or, as Veblen called it later, 'conspicuous consumption.' The wealthy class wasted money as a way of demonstrating their shining superiority and hired masses of workers to manufacture 'an infinite variety of articles and appliances of elegance and ostentation which mocked the unsatisfied primary necessities of those who toiled to produce them.'

Even more disastrous was the effect of private capitalism on men and institutions. Nineteenth-century industry not only held back progress by withholding improvements injurious to special interests (a form of industrial sabotage that Bellamy dwelled on at length), but it had an extremely perverting effect on the human personality.

If the relatively few successful giants had simply poisoned themselves and allowed the dependent classes to remain uncontaminated, the results might not have been so bad, but (and this was the most insidious influence) the vested few imposed their values on the community. Parker had recognized this danger, but no one before Veblen pointed out so clearly as Bellamy how 'the vested interests' dominated the culture and institutions of nineteenth-century society. Education prior to the Great Revolution, according to Bellamy's history, was controlled by a learned class—teachers, writers, ministers, professional people—who used the same monopolistic tactics as their economic overlords. As in the case of businessmen and artisans, 'their welfare was absolutely bound up with the demand for the particular sets of ideas and doctrines they represented and the particular sorts of professional services they got their living by rendering. Each man's line of teaching or preaching was his vested interest—the means of his livelihood.' It followed inevitably from this state of affairs that any new thought was not judged on its moral or intellectual merits or on its social utility, 'but how it would immediately and directly affect the set of doctrines, traditions, and institutions, with the prestige of which their own personal interests were identified.'

Julian West's contemporaries never recognized the moral and economic incoherence of their society, although some were disturbed by the frequent breakdowns of the system. The capitalists in fact, right up to the revolution, seemed touched with *hubris:*

They seemed fairly intoxicated with the pride of their achievements, barren of benefit as they had been, and their day dreams were of further discoveries that to a yet more amazing degree should put the forces of the universe at their disposal. . . They appear to have wholly overlooked the fact that until their mighty engines should be devoted to increasing human welfare they were and would continue mere curious scientific toys of no more real worth or utility to the race than so many particularly ingenious jumping-jacks. This craze for more and more and ever greater and wider inventions for economic purposes, coupled with apparent complete indifference as to whether mankind derived any ultimate benefit from them or not, can only be understood by regarding it as one of those strange epidemics of insane excitement which have been known to affect whole populations at certain periods, especially of the middle ages.

And false prophets corroborated and encouraged the capitalists in their insanity, the medicine men of the market, the economists who reared an imposing structure of theory to support the false economy.

How explain the gluts, the crises, the depressions that Bellamy had been speculating about since the early 'seventies? Was it overproduction, as the learned classes maintained? The economists of the pre-revolutionary period, so the account ran, fixed their attention on the market, not on the people. Supply and demand had little connection with human needs and everything to do with the profit system; the market consisted simply 'of those who had money to buy with.' Masses of people might riot for food during a glut, but nothing was permitted to interfere with the artificial movements of the market, and the 'commercial crises' were attributed to sun spots or to a general lack of confidence in the system. In spite of false advertising, 'the only lubricant,' said Bellamy, 'adapted to the machinery of the profit system,' in spite of the cheapening of goods through adulteration and other types of sham reduction in prices made at the expense of wages, the glut of the market persisted and with it the glut of unemployed.

The men who kept reminding the people that an industrial problem existed—a problem they must solve unaided—were not the economists or scholars but the reformers with their protests and the workers with their brute acts of despair. As early as 1873, when the period of agitation began, forces were slowly gathering which ultimately produced the peaceful revolution. Prior to this period, according to Storiot's history, the menace of capitalism had not been clearly discerned. From 1787 to the 1830's, private capital was not yet aggressive. The moneyed class remained small, and an unopened continent 'defied as yet the lust of greed.' Tocqueville's impressions reveal the idyllic tone of the times, 'though not without prescience of the doom that awaited it.' Beginning with the 1830's, however, in the second phase of our history, capitalism emerged more distinctly, and a powerful minority of property holders began to take over the tools and raw materials of the nation. The factory system and the agency of steam accelerated the movement of capitalist domination and 'for the first time in history the capitalist in the subjugation of his fellows had machinery for his ally.'

Already some Americans, the precursors of the latter-day radicals, realized the tendencies of the age and started to think about and experiment with new kinds of co-operative enterprise. But the slavery question prevented any effective action for a new social order, absorbing the reformist impulse and preparing the way for a war that even more firmly entrenched the capitalist system. By 1873, when America had at last freed itself from the incubus of slavery, it 'first began to open its eyes to the irrepressible conflict which the growth of capitalism had forced—a conflict between the power of wealth and the democratic idea of the equal right of all to life, liberty, and happiness.' From 1873 on, the 'pseudo-American Republic' declined.

An era very similar to Fourier's 'incoherent civilization' now unfolded, but Storiot the historian maintained that this incoherent phase ended around 1890. During these few decades there flourished the rank plutocracy, elsewhere described, with the crushing of free men into a proletariat and the hardening of class lines. Supported by a kind of Praetorian Guard, the employers subdued all labor opposition, took full control of the government, and stole what remained of the public lands. Meanwhile strikes and conflicts racked the country as the reformers futilely proposed their remedies to a frustrated people. Jefferson's experiment had apparently failed.

'Nevertheless,' ran the Storiot chronicle, 'no conclusion could possibly have been more mistaken.' Anyone with the power to detect the reality behind the appearance could have seen the slow progress of the masses and the growth of a revolutionary temper intensified by constant failure. The people at last became aware that private capitalism could not be amended and that only a truly radical reformation would suffice:

the innumerable defeats, disappointments, and fiascoes which met their every effort at curbing and reforming the money power during the seventies, eighties, and early nineties, contributed far more than as many victories would have done to the magnitude and completeness of the final triumph of the people.

Plutocratic rapacity, police brutality, and national degradation provided the 'discipline of failure' without which the second or coherent phase of the revolution would not have occurred.

Storiot did not clearly specify the transition point between the first and second phases, but with the year 1890 the dream of the co-ordinated state, as old as Plato, passed into the minds of the population, and the masses gradually realized their own competence to rule. America had been hitherto uninterested in European social theory, but at the close of the 'eighties national conditions forced the people to study carefully all ideas of reform and to recognize that the so-called 'foreign' importation—the nationalization of industry—was nothing more than a continuation of the principles of the 'immortal Declaration,' the 'inalienable equality of all men.' Instead of trying to revive free competition, undermined by the capitalists themselves, the people overcame the giant of private monopoly by creating a greater giant, public monopoly. This was the people's answer to the riddle: 'How shall a state combine the preservation of democratic equality with the increase of wealth?'

The abounding faith coincident with this economic revelation accounted for the dynamics of the revolution. Storiot is naturally a little vaguer here than we should desire, since he is dealing with a spiritual phenomenon, but the point he or Bellamy wishes to make is that the impetus to reform had to be religious in nature. It is significant that a movement Storiot called the Great Revival climaxed the decades of literary protest, and that it was 'essentially a humane movement,' a 'melting and flowing forth of men's hearts toward one another, a rush of contrite, repentant tenderness' which 'contemplated nothing less than a literal fulfillment, on a complete social scale, of Christ's inculcation that all should feel the same solicitude and make the same effort for the welfare of others as for their own.' The organized churches had not dared to foment the movement and had, indeed, branded it as unchristian; but the triumphant people quickly identified their crusade with 'the practical meaning and content of Christ's religion.'

The capitalists, incapable of measuring the moral strength behind the revolution, made no concessions to avert it and offered no resistance when it had been effected. Although a small minority continued to protest, the 'better part' co-operated with the people and no sizable body remained to contest the popular will. Class hostility, while deepening during the incoherent period, never became rooted enough 'to resist the glow of social enthusiasm' engendered by the revival. Minor fracases and 'a considerable amount of violence and bloodshed' marred the transformation, but the organized and sustained class war predicted by some reformers never materialized. Europe faced a longer struggle, but even there the revolution emerged as 'a triumph of moral forces.'

Various schools of revolutionists now offered their plans for the next constructive phase of the Nationalist movement. The trade-union leaders suggested a national federation of the great trades to run the country, with their elected officers substituting for the old bosses. This scheme was dismissed on the grounds that it 'would have brought in a system of group capitalism as divisive and antisocial, in the large sense, as private capitalism itself, and far more dangerous to civil order.' Another school of reformers placed their hopes on co-operative colonies, and still a third on a systematic program of welfare legislation, but the nation did not accept any of these halfway proposals.

Instead, they employed what Bellamy, with his fondness for military analogies, called 'a flanking movement.' The capitalists had expected a direct assault, the sudden and immediate expropriation of private property. The revolutionists chose instead to destroy the old system piecemeal; they 'did not directly attack the

fortress of capitalism at all, but so manoeuvred as to make it untenable and to compel its evacuation.' This was done by national-
izing or municipalizing utilities and other public services, a move
that surprised and alarmed no one, and then by setting up a system of national stores for the five million or so people employed by
the government. As the government expanded the size and varieties
of the public stores and began to manufacture its own products, not
only did the number of people in national employment increase
but thousands more were attracted by the cheapness and over-all
superiority of articles and goods sold in the Federal dispensaries.
The government absorbed empty factories, unused land, and idle
shipping. It imported, duty free, commodities from Europe, and
by using its own script for commercial transactions, it eventually
drove ordinary currency from the market. Meanwhile thousands
enrolled in the industrial army and the program of reconstruction
got under way.

Bellamy does not seem to have thought very profoundly about
the risky procedures involved in the organization of his society,
what modern readers would call its corporate or fascist features.
He saw no threat to popular liberties in the creation of ten great
departments or guilds and a general or president elected by the
veterans of the Industrial Army. He exaggerated the efficiencies of
bigness and apparently had no conception of the realities of bureau-
cratic maladministration. Modern readers may be shocked by the
airy way in which he abandoned judiciary safeguards and by his
preoccupation with the use of power rather than with its possible
abuse. These are serious, if not fatal, shortcomings. And yet his
modern critics, inspired very likely by their horror of the Police
State, have exaggerated the authoritarian aspects of Bellamy's commonwealth and have slighted or failed to mention Bellamy's own
precautions and qualifications.

Bellamy's delight in mass action should not be mistaken as a
love of bigness for its own sake or as an indication that he wished
to obliterate the individual. American economy in the year 2000,
although controlled from Washington, was decentralized, the country divided into a series of self-sufficient areas or 'circles' in each
of which 'all the important arts and occupations' were represented.

Such a system had been established to permit those who did not wish to leave their locality and friends to find congenial work, but, more important, the scheme (perhaps the outgrowth of Bellamy's devotion to Chicopee) reduced centrality and enhanced the responsibility of the individual to his own community. The villager in him loathed the huge metropolitan areas where self-value disappeared and men were absorbed into the rootless life of cities: 'it is a false and unhealthy state of things,' he once wrote, 'breeding incalculable disease in politics, society, and religion.' Bellamy belongs among the first of the planners who wanted to ruralize the city and urbanize the country, to stop the unwholesome exodus from the farms and preserve the regional outlook. The Nationalist society, as he conceived it, did not merit William Morris's conception of it—a vast impersonal organization 'working by a kind of magic for which no one feels himself responsible.'

He would have accepted quite willingly Morris's injunction 'that individual men cannot shuffle off the business of life to the shoulders of an abstraction called the State,' that they must 'deal with it in constant association with each other.' Critics of his communal kitchens and public department stores to the contrary, Bellamy did not advocate a personality-destroying regimentation; in fact he believed that nationalization would revivify the individualistic drives instead of hampering them. 'A government, or a majority,' Dr. Leete tells Julian, 'which should undertake to tell the people, or a minority, what they were to eat, drink, or wear, as I believe governments in America did in your day, would be regarded as a curious anachronism indeed.' And when John Bates Clark, the professor of political economy at Smith College in the early 'nineties, accused Bellamy's movement of crushing individualism, Bellamy wrote to the *Springfield Republican* that if individuality 'be not merely another name for a desire to live on other people, if it be the instinct of a man to be himself and find a free career in the field for which he is adapted, we have in vain set our hands to the mighty undertaking to which we are consecrated.'

The more closely one examines the utopia of Bellamy, the more just and penetrating his criticisms become and the more feasible his recommendations. Compared with the dozens of utopian novels written during the last three decades of the nineteenth century, *Looking Backward* and its sequel are superior in almost every respect. They are less freakish and whimsical, and they are characterized by a kind of controlled idealism, a reined imagination, which distinguishes them from the extravaganzas they helped to inspire. Lewis Mumford remarked that Bellamy's Boston was 'all that a modern city is, exaggerated,' and William Morris shudderingly dismissed it as a Cockney's paradise in *News from Nowhere;* neither observation is fair. The city of the twenty-first century has a leisureliness and sociability, an air of 'quiet happiness,' as David Riesman has pointed out, which contrasts sharply with the glare and frenzy of the modern metropolis. Morris's preference for aristocratic simplicity is understandable, but there is something snobbish about the charming arcadian paradise he conjures up as an uncommercialized alternative to Bellamy's middle-class vision.

Morris attempted less than Bellamy and consequently avoided many of the difficulties that plagued the American. He could write with gay anarchist abandon about a society where all coercion has disappeared and the beneficent instincts are given free play, where lovely women dressed in shimmering silk and handsome men wearing white flannels cut hay along the banks of unpolluted pre-Elizabethan rivers. The simplicity, tastefulness, and elegance of Morris's Nowhere is tremendously appealing, but one feels that his book, with its fine rejection of nineteenth-century materialism and bourgeois values, is far more personal and literary than Bellamy's and that it 'looks backward' whereas Bellamy's book looks forward. This is not so because Morris's utopia consists largely of 'rejuvenated relics,' to borrow Maurice Hewlett's phrase, but because Morris solves too neatly the not-so-easily disposable problems of the industrial age by turning his back upon them. He salvages what he thinks is useful in his society (he retains, for instance, the machinery that can perform the irksome tasks) and retreats to the fourteenth century. He plays God and reverses the time machine.

vii] Upon reflection it will be seen that the final meaning of Bellamy's philosophy, like George's and Parker's, was a plea for individual fulfillment. The ultimate purpose of Nationalism, with all its emphasis on the comforts and conveniences, was to encourage 'the higher and larger activities,' which society will at last be free to undertake. These 'higher' activities are nonmaterial, and we cannot really understand the drift of Bellamy's meaning until we know something about the religious principles underlying his thought. These may be found scattered throughout his private papers, in his early stories and novels, and in his youthful essay, 'The Religion of Solidarity,' which embodied, if somewhat crudely, his philosophy of life.

Bellamy never became a religious man in the conventional sense, despite his clerical antecedents, and neither attended church nor permitted his children to go. His rejection of the organized church, however, did not make him less a follower of Christ—'no lover of his kind,' Bellamy once declared, 'need resent being called by his name'—and his own type of evangelism, although neither sensuous nor sentimental, was heady enough. That there were religious or abstract truths, which could be distinguished from the useful virtues—chastity, honesty, mildness—he strongly believed. 'Men have always been found,' he said, 'who could laugh at chastity and ridicule honesty, but no man ever yet lived who could laugh at self-sacrifice or refuse to respect generosity.' This was natural virtue, the virtue of the soul.

His contemporaries, Bellamy believed, misconceived the reality and the function of the human soul. 'We think the body meant for earth, the soul for heaven, to be kept in a bandbox till death, and then taken out and introduced to the moribund as a part of himself, the only part shortly to be left.' No wonder, he says, 'the poor devil' looks askance. At best Americans accepted the soul on faith, not as a conscious fact, and Bellamy argued that man's potential divinity would never be reached until the soul had been redeemed from its prison. His early tales, in fact, might be described as propaganda for the soul, for it was in these stories, which first attracted the interest of Madame Blavatsky and the Theosophists, that he dealt with the themes of mind-reading and human foresight and the nature of guilt and hinted at man's infinite capacities.

The Emersonian overtones already apparent in Bellamy's

philosophizing become unmistakable in his little treatise on the
nature of man, 'The Religion of Solidarity' (which he composed in
his early thirties). This is nothing less than a transcendentalist
tract deriving directly from Emerson's famous essay 'Nature' and
setting forth Bellamy's own vision of the individual and the Over-
Soul.

Man, Bellamy declares, possesses a dual nature, 'individual' and
'universal.' The first, bound up with everyday life, contends desperately for survival in the world of facts or, to use Emerson's
term, the world of the 'understanding.' The 'universal' in man
transcends space and time, moving freely backward into the past or
forward into the future. Here is the 'Real' world of ideas as contrasted with the 'unreality' or the 'appearances' of mundane existence. During moments of the keenest mental activity, those rare
and infrequent moments of ecstasy, we can establish a rapport with
the impersonal consciousness residing within us and we can link ourselves, if only momentarily, with the great Soul of Solidarity. This
is true individuality, not the pettiness of personality—'an inner
serene and passionless ego' that blends the individual with the All.
And that is why only the Poet—to paraphrase Melville, who had
similar thoughts at one point in his life—can escape the tornadoed
Atlantic of his being and discover the peaceful Pacific within
himself.

Like Emerson, Bellamy made it part of his mission to create a
divine dissatisfaction among his countrymen, who seemed content
with the occasional rays from heaven and remained only half-con-
scious of the god slumbering within them. He sketched for them
the boundless possibilities of movement for the emancipated soul
capable of surmounting the barriers of past and future and pleaded
for the 'universal' in man that is striving to absorb and be absorbed.

The social applications of this transcendental religion are at
last clear, and its bearing on *Looking Backward* and *Equality* substantiated. The first steps for this spiritual enfranchisement must
begin with man's love for man, for nature, and for all other symbols
of solidarity. The spiritual interflowing, the apogee of human experience, is most likely to occur when the physical conditions are
favorable, when the animal wants have been fulfilled and the re-

quirements of the body satisfied. Bellamy does not deny that 'the instincts of universal solidarity also assert themselves quite independently of physical conditions, responding to direct moral appeal, to eloquence of speech or written word, or to the description of beauty or sublimity,' but he goes further than Emerson and gives much more consideration to the desirability of a favorable environment for the masses. Once mankind reaches this stage of spiritual enlightenment and responds, as he says in one of his stories, to the 'divine gravitations ever pulling at the soul,' then truly the salt will disappear from human tears and the tragic sense will disappear.

However one feels about this rather thin and bloodless nirvana, Bellamy's philosophy is not the kind usually associated with regimented and tyrannical societies and explains why Alfred Russel Wallace, the eminent British naturalist, was convinced after reading Bellamy 'that real, not merely delusive, liberty, together with full scope for individualism and complete human privacy, is compatible with the most thorough socialism.'

VIII] In April of the year 1889 Bellamy wrote to his friend Edward Yates on the future of Nationalism. With his customary optimism, he predicted that revolutionary changes would come quickly, almost too quickly 'for the most judicious control,' and sharply disagreed with the experts who saw no likelihood of drastic reforms in the near future. 'Those who talk about centuries being required for the consummation of the process,' he told Yates, 'simply fail to appreciate the portentous rapidity with which the present competitive system, grown topheavy by the enormous modern development of business, is falling to pieces and creating an imperative demand for an adequate substitute.'

He had every reason for confidence at this time. His books were selling fast; the Populist movement, which he was to be influential in directing, had begun to take form; and even his enemies were testifying to the appeal of his dangerous doctrines. As a character in J. W. Roberts's *Looking Within, The Misleading Tendencies of 'Looking Backward' Made Manifest,* declared:

Its Utopian notions have taken root in many minds. Multitudes who never saw the book have received its teachings second hand, and been poisoned by them. Like the upas tree, it is fair to behold, but all who come within its shade are doomed. Its poison is more insidious than that of a rattlesnake, and it does not give warning of its bite until the deadly fangs have struck the fatal blow.

When someone asks this character why he does not combat the noxious influence, he replies: 'Who can fight a dream? Who run a-tilt against the baseless fabric of a vision. While you cannot hurt the fog, it enfolds you and leads you to disaster.'

Roberts's apprehensions were not entirely borne out, but during the great Populist uprising of the 'nineties, copies of *Looking Backward* could have been found in almost every community of the land. 'Probably every village,' an observer wrote in 1893, 'has at least one man who is a thorough nationalist, while hundreds of his neighbors are in sympathy with its principles.' The Chicago *Inter-Ocean,* commenting on the Omaha Convention of 1892, reported that Bellamy's followers 'were the brains of the convention. They were college professors, editors, artists and authors,' concluded the *Inter-Ocean* uncharitably, 'who are infatuated with that socialism which dreams of uniting the nation into a great family, where all shall be dependent children without independence of thought and action.' The fact that there were Nationalist clubs active in fourteen of the middle-western and far-western states might have suggested a more representative make-up of Bellamy's party, but certainly the leadership of the movement remained in the hands of the intellectuals and professional men.

Because Bellamy was temperate and conciliatory and ready to proceed slowly, working for specific objectives of a socialist or semi-socialist character, the Populists found him a congenial partner and far more acceptable to their cause than the more radical partisans of the Socialist-Labor party. The radicalism of the Nationalists did not frighten the farmers and other groups comprising the American middle class, because, as we have seen, Bellamy spoke their language and couched his proposals in terms they could understand and accept. His willingness, however, to pool the energies of his own organization with the Populists and to campaign actively in politics resulted in the absorption of Nationalism into the large and confused united front of the People's party.

He never regarded the free-silver issue as of any importance, even though he recognized the gold standard as part of the modern tendency to centralize the economic forces of the world, and when the Republicans withstood the popular thrust in the election of 1896, he refused to despair. It would turn the attention of the well-meaning but misinformed radicals to the disease itself, not to the symptoms. 'The past campaign,' he wrote to his friend Henry Demarest Lloyd in December 1896, 'has, unless I greatly err, done much to break up the political soil, cause discontent and prepare the people for the radical doctrines.' So Storiot had written, and Bellamy had confidence in his own historian.

At this time Bellamy was slowly dying of tuberculosis and trying desperately to complete his manuscript of *Equality,* which he barely managed to finish. A short stay in Denver did not halt the rapid course of the disease, and he returned to Chicopee, thankful and pleased that he could spend the last months of his life in the surroundings he loved so well. Whether his continuing optimism was simply a characteristic of his illness or further evidence of his incorrigible faith in humanity is difficult to say; other men, Condorcet for instance, wrote the most hopeful books under the most impossible circumstances. But Bellamy kept his tranquillity until his death in the spring of 1898, in spite of the barbarous regimen of creosote and violent exercise prescribed by his doctors. 'My Boston belly has all gone and really I have been in a nervous way,' he confessed to a friend half a year earlier, but he felt better and thought he would 'beat the devil' this time. The great cause did not share 'the debility of its humble servants,' he added, and he hopefully awaited the culmination of the American crusade that would, he told William T. Stead, the English journalist and author of the sensational *If Christ Came to Chicago,* end in the inauguration of socialism by constitutional means: that is, by capturing the legislature and packing the Supreme Court with Nationalists.

Bellamy died before he could become disillusioned. His brother reformers with whom he had worked so ardently mourned his passing—Howells and Eugene Debs and trusty lieutenants like Sylvester Baxter, the Boston journalist and friend of Whitman's, among others.

One man in particular was touched by Bellamy's death, and that was Henry Demarest Lloyd, the Chicago reformer who had corresponded with Bellamy during the hectic days of the Populist movement and had visited him at Chicopee. Although Lloyd had unmistakable reservations about Nationalism ('The movement we are in *is* International Socialism,' he had written to Bellamy in 1896. 'Why not recognize it and say so!'), he admired Bellamy immensely. No other man, he believed, had done more 'to awaken the world to the necessity of justifying the inheritance from the progress of the past by making a little progress of its own along the lines of common brotherhood.' The world had achieved a scientific utopia undreamed of by Aristotle or Bacon or Franklin. 'We must now achieve the social Utopias of Christ, Thomas More, Mazzini, Bellamy, and Howells,' Lloyd concluded, 'or lose the others.'

. . . .

CHAPTER 5

Henry Demarest Lloyd:
The Middle-Class Conscience

1] The writings of Bellamy and Lloyd illustrate, among other things, that progressivism could be a religion as well as a political faith. What they and other consecrated democrats like Gronlund and Howells were preaching was a religion of humanity similar if not identical to the beliefs of Mazzini or Victor Hugo or Henry James senior.

This secular religion, most eloquently set forth by Henry Demarest Lloyd, suggested in part the positive ethics of Comte, but it was less materialistic and actually closer to the views of modern Unitarianism. The religion of progressivism conceived of the mediator between God and man not as an individual Christ but as a universalized Christ, Christ as a symbol of humanity itself. It broke with the orthodox Protestant assumption that 'God's redemptive operation,' to quote Gronlund, is 'confined to the isolated individual bosom' and refused to make religion a private affair between one man and his God. For the progressives, God appeared to man through men and revealed himself in human history and institutions. Men were damned or saved collectively. They entered into communion with God when they shed their selfish personalities and united with one another in a confederation of love. According to this religion, social evil was not confirmed by individual criminal acts but by what the elder Henry James called 'our organized inclemency of man to man.' And in turn, social good could not be attained through individual acts of charity but through the organized clemency of man to man.

These are the sentiments of Lloyd. He taught that men could and would submit to the tremendous gravitational pull of love—an inexhaustible energy lying untapped in the reservoirs of the human spirit—if they stripped off their insulation and permitted its currents to flow through them. Lloyd hoped that the blind and fumbling co-operation, seen in the emergence of an international labor movement, would become organized and extended, and that men would no longer shut themselves 'out of the vast Elysian fields by denying Brotherhood, the People, Equality, Fraternity, Liberty.' 'What we need today,' he wrote, 'is the historian of humanity, the philosopher of the true society, who will discover to men how great is the extent to which they are living love.'

Lloyd became that historian, observing at first hand the social experiments being carried out in various parts of the world, which he believed were bringing the new society a little closer to realization. His standards were severe. Any region where love had not been 'institutionalized' was for him a place 'as yet outside civilisation, an exception to the law of progress, a continent we have not yet surveyed, a No Man's Land.' Like the other progressives, Lloyd never blinked away the social evil, which he had examined more painstakingly than the majority of easy pessimists. But he never gave up the hope that this evil would someday be overwhelmed by love.

II] In 1893, a year of panic and economic depression, the World's Columbian Exposition opened in Chicago. Visitors who scraped up the money to come found a white city pitched on a fringe of lake front, a mélange of architectural styles, and a hodge-podge of instruction and entertainment. The planners of the Fair, according to Louis Sullivan, whose Transportation Building was the only underivative structure on the grounds, had gone on the principle, 'Make it big, make it stunning, knock 'em down,' and they had succeeded admirably. The Fair was grand and phony, from its tasteless official buildings dressed up in elaborate disguises to the franker vulgarity of the Turkish Concert Hall, where 'alluring Nautch girls personifying the poetry of motion' wriggled before appreciative males. To Edward Bellamy the Fair demonstrated the technological advances society had made since the days of medieval serfdom, but it hardly suggested a commensurate moral development.

> At Chicago [he wrote] the exhibits of pomp and luxury and art represent not the enjoyments of the many but of the wealthy few. The wonderful mechanical display presented does not stand for powers used for and by the people for the common welfare, but for devices whereby capitalists enrich themselves and rule their fellow men. The underlying motive of the whole exhibition, under a sham pretense of patriotism is business, advertising with a view to individual money-making.

Bellamy's charge was not simply a piece of Nationalist propaganda. The Fair glowed with commercialism. It gave valuable publicity to the railroads and American manufacturers and furnished abundant testimony, if any were needed, that American capital spoke for America.

Viewed in the spirit of sensitive men like Louis Sullivan and Bellamy, the Fair was the Babel of 'vague and ill-defined and un-related thoughts and half-thoughts and experimental outcries' that Henry Adams described it as being, but even if the Fair set back architecture in the United States for fifty years and resembled a trader's vulgar dream, it had a few promising aspects, which the purists overlooked. Inside the Fair, the parks and lakes and hand-some vistas contrasted favorably with the dingy backyards and the muddy, rotten, ugly look of the city proper. It offered a faint sug-gestion to the people of what they might accomplish in a co-oper-ative society dedicated to the creation of beauty.

Henry Demarest Lloyd, whose social sympathies were more highly developed than his taste in fine arts, took this ground and held that the World's Fair succeeded in revealing to the people the 'possibilities of social beauty, utility, and harmony of which they had not been able even to dream.' Middle-America had never seen anything to match the splendor of Chicago's lake shore, and the popular rapture at the sight of lagoons, domes, columns, and parks again illustrated for him the truth of Motley's remark, 'Give me the luxuries of life; I can do without the necessities.' Lloyd regretted the mercenary and jingoistic accompaniments to the Fair, but he believed its total effect was uplifting and prophetic of the dawning age to come. It encouraged him, in fact, to write the one bit of utopian fancifulness he ever attempted.

'No Mean City,' as he called it, is an imaginative sketch of the Fair's aftermath. The people, caught by the dream of the White City, determine to make the Fair buildings permanent, to rebuild the entire city along similar lines. As in Bellamy's Boston, a religious revival, half moral, half aesthetic, brings out their latent nobility, and all classes join together to beautify the sprawling metropolis. The smoke nuisance is met by passing laws requiring the electrification of all vehicles. Any municipal reform that has proved practicable in Europe or America is adopted in Chicago, and as a result of this social eclecticism, the city is completely transformed. Crime and violence fade away ('as inconceivable as cannibalism had become long before'); women are emancipated and freely enter into business and politics. The last and greatest problem, unemployment, is met by establishing farm communities for the idle workers according to the ideas of the world's most brilliant planners. The new suburb, 'No Mean City,' becomes the Garden City Louis Sullivan had dreamed about; it gradually swallows Chicago itself, which is torn down and rebuilt into a great park housing libraries, universities, churches, and theaters.

It is characteristic of Lloyd in this sketch of a middle-western paradise that he introduced no innovation that had not been worked out satisfactorily somewhere else. What Americans needed to know in their present stage of development was something about the reforms successfully worked out in other countries—experiments in town government, national socialism, voluntary co-operation. Lloyd often said that America could construct a utopia immediately if it would only make use of the social principles already being applied in various parts of the world, and he regarded it as part of his mission to synthesize these uncollected truths.

More than any of the three men already discussed and the others to follow, Lloyd deserved the title of professional reformer, the technical authority most receptive to new theories. Like Emerson, whom he worshipped, Lloyd found something to learn from all varieties of social architects. He knew the works of Ruskin,

Morris, Mazzini, Fourier, and Owen. He kept in touch with the co-operative communities, both religious and secular, of his own day and the leaders of such groups as the Peers of Kosmos Compact-or-Industrial All-Togetherists, as well as with successful officials and public figures like Eugene Debs, Governor Altgeld of Illinois, Samuel 'Golden Rule' Jones of Toledo, Brand Whitlock, and practically every other progressive of note in America and England. No other liberal crusader gave so much attention to the tasks of reform or wrote so extensively about the character and function of the reformer.

Lloyd was really the first of the great reformers to be equally at home among musty business records and court files and in the rarefied atmosphere of transcendental ethics. He was the first progressive technician, the reformer armed at all points, who combined to perfection the roles of preacher, writer, scholar, and agitator.

III] After casting a glance back to Lloyd's adolescence and youth, we find it hard to know at exactly what point his personality emerges with enough distinctness for us to say, 'Here the future author of *Wealth against Commonwealth* reveals himself.' Sensitiveness, passion, intelligence—these qualities he displayed at an early age, but no evidences of extraordinary precocity are noticeable.

His sister, in her two-volume biography of Lloyd, makes a good deal of his revolutionary antecedents (he was a descendant of Goffe, the regicide, and his grandfather, John Lloyd, remained a fiery democrat in a strongly conservative New Jersey community) but such facts are more interesting than significant. Lloyd's father, Aaron Lloyd, seems to have been an honorable but thoroughly undistinguished man, a Dutch Reformed minister by profession, who lost his pulpit some thirteen years after Henry's birth in 1847 and ran 'Ye Old Book Shoppe' in New York City. His mother's people, the Demarests, were several cuts above the Lloyds socially, and it was at grandfather Demarest's house on West Washington Street that the family stayed after their return from Pekin, Illinois, in 1860.

Lloyd and his two brothers must have found the genteel and

impecunious atmosphere in which they lived extremely dreary, nor could they respond very enthusiastically to the bleakness of Dutch Reformed Calvinism. Henry soon repudiated his father's austere faith as well as his politics and apparently managed the break without causing any serious family ruptures. Henry Ward Beecher helped to awaken him, and Columbia College, which he entered in 1863, hastened his intellectual emancipation.

At Columbia, where Lloyd took his undergraduate and law degrees, he studied under Francis Lieber (who converted him into a free-trader and a serious student of the social sciences) and led the fight of the 'barbarians' against the purse-proud, family-conscious scions of the New York rich. After a four-year struggle for recognition, Lloyd won the coveted prize of Class Poet and gave one of the class orations at commencement, in which he traced the connection between the British soap manufacturers and the opening up of the African continent. Two years later, in 1869, he passed his bar examination and left Columbia a poised and confident young man, known already for his facility as a speaker and writer and imbued with an unquenchable idealism.

During the next few years Lloyd distinguished himself in the campaign to open the city library reading rooms on Sunday, but his first real political battle was against Tammany. Allied with a group of young liberals who banded themselves into the Young Men's Municipal Reform Association, Lloyd and his brother Demarest campaigned for good government. Lloyd's little handbook on the election laws, 'Every Man His Own Voter,' won him editorial commendation from *The New York Times,* and he and his friends received a large share of the credit for handing Tammany one of its temporary setbacks.

Lloyd's most important activity at this time, however, was his work in the American Free Trade League, which brought him into contact with such men as Carl Schurz, E. L. Godkin, Samuel J. Tilden, O. B. Frothingham, and William Cullen Bryant. As assistant secretary he helped in preparing several issues of the *Free Trader,* and in 1872, when only twenty-five years old, he attracted a considerable amount of public attention for his losing fight to prevent Horace Greeley, a protectionist, from winning the presidential nomination on the Liberal Republican ticket. The newspapers had a good deal of fun with the 'young agitator nibbling his nearly visible moustache' and carrying the nation's burdens on his shoulders, but he came out of the controversy all the more firmly opposed to 'thimblerigging in politics' and opportunistic compromising. It would not be the last time that the party with whom he identified himself would coquette with its enemies and go under.

A reporter at this time described Lloyd as 'fair-skinned, brown-haired, cool, and good-looking, with more than ordinary aplomb, suavity, and primitive character.' He commented particularly on Lloyd's good manners and even temper, qualities he retained throughout his life and which endeared him to everyone with whom he worked. A photograph taken in 1872 bears out this description, but it reveals in addition heavy-lidded eyes, a sensitive but stubborn mouth, and an arrogant carriage of the head. There is something exotic about his expression. Disdainful, elegant, almost dandyish, he looks more like a poet than a market statistician.

Something of the self-consciousness and theatricality of this portrait appears at this time in his romantic outpourings to his friend Henry F. Keenan. Emotional and immature, they are full of callow speculations on the meaning of life and melancholy doubts as to 'whether happiness is to be mine ever.' Reading a life of Goethe, he despairs of his ability to improve himself and abate his laziness. 'Would that I could transmute this fleeting disgust into some permanent energy.' He is tremendously ambitious and hungers for success. 'I want power,' he wrote to Keenan in July 1872, 'I must have power, I could not live if I did not think that I was in some way to be lifted above and upon the insensate masses who flood the stage of life in their passage to oblivion, but I want power unpoisoned by the presence of obligation.' But he desires even more to become a harmonious individual. 'Sympathies, intellect, the aesthetic faculties, physique, all that is musical, humanitarian, muscular, imaginative, brainy, poetic, powerful with man and material I would develop to the highest point.'

Lloyd's yearning for power and recognition did not incline him toward the money-making occupations. The law repelled him, as it did Bellamy; it was too traditional, too technical. He dismissed his father's profession with the remark: 'I am too unconventionally and unaffectedly pious to be a minister, I can do what ministers can't do, I can be right without being religious.' As for 'mere literary culture,' he found it irksome and not 'sufficiently practical.' Only politics, which had attracted him since boyhood, and journalism really interested him. Journalism seemed to offer the best solution, since one could obtain great power without the obligations incurred in other occupations, and Lloyd confessed to Keenan that he would rather be Samuel Bowles, editor of the famous *Springfield Republican* (whose son was to become a close friend), or Greeley or Bennett 'than the most successful lawyer or richest merchant or most brilliant author in America.' Journalism, he declared, would provide the hard, vigorous training necessary for the successful agitator. While Lloyd was in this frame of mind, Horace White, co-worker in the Free Trade League and editor of the *Chicago Tribune,* offered him a job, and Lloyd took it. In September 1872, he left the east for Chicago.

IV] Immediately after his arrival in Chicago, Lloyd threw himself into his work with his usual eagerness, as if he knew that he would die young and leave years of work incompleted. As literary and night editor, he found much to keep him occupied— writing furiously, gorging himself on new books, and doing everything he could to show Horace White (whom he sometimes found overly critical) 'how to write and run a newspaper.' On his own time he helped to organize a literary club, a free-trade league, and a Sunday Lecture Society. He also met and married a girl named Jessie Bross.

His marriage was a particularly important step not only because Jessie Bross turned out to be a devoted and sagacious wife, but also because her father, William Bross, was a pioneer of the city and a quarter owner of the *Chicago Tribune.* Lloyd eventually broke with his father-in-law over the question of social reform, but the ten shares of *Tribune* stock he had been permitted to buy enabled him to do the work he wanted to do without having to worry about steady employment. Lloyd never had as much money as his friends sometimes thought, for William Bross refused to pass on his property to a radical, but during these early years his social position was high. Had he not followed the dangerous and unsound principles he so recklessly espoused, he would certainly have lived longer and died richer.

The longer he stayed in Chicago, however, and the more he studied the practices and attitudes of men like his father-in-law, the angrier he became at their moral obtuseness. After taking on the financial editorship of the *Tribune* in 1875, he watched the machinations of the speculators with growing distaste and began to gather evidence for his attack upon the Lords of Industry. It is possible that his economic heresies and his undisguised disrespect for monopolists had something to do with his promotion or demotion from financial editor to editorial writer in 1882, but this new assignment gave him freer scope to unmask the boodlers, to speak out against Vanderbiltism and the misdeeds of the railroads.

He felt informed and confident enough by this time to air his notions before a larger audience than the *Tribune* subscribers, and in 1881 there appeared the first of the witty and eloquent essays on the practices of businessmen and corporations, 'The Story of a Great Monopoly,' which struck a new note in American journalism and brilliantly anticipated the less literate contributions of the muckrakers. Similar articles that followed, all solid and vibrant and written with style and dash, impressed reformers and literary men alike, from eccentric John Swinton (editor of *John Swinton's Paper*) to Howells and Robert Louis Stevenson.

When Lloyd, overworked from his long stint on the *Tribune,* resigned in 1885 and took his first trip to Europe, he had become a prominent figure and well known to the men he associated with in England during that year. In London he met Parnell and James Bryce and Thorold Rogers of Oxford, William Morris, 'a Norse god style of fellow, big, broad, hairy, loud, and kind,' Stepniak, the Russian nihilist who so impressed Howells, and William Clarke, the Fabian journalist, with whom Lloyd began an extended and fascinating correspondence. By the time he returned to the States, he had recovered from his near breakdown, but the insomnia and headaches which had troubled him before his departure continued. He never thereafter completely regained his health. His thirteen-year connection with the *Tribune* ended (William Bross, for reasons that are not hard to guess, thought it best that Lloyd not return), and Lloyd had to content himself with his stock and the privilege of writing letters to the editor.

v] In August 1898 Lloyd wrote to his friend Samuel Bowles about the scandalous administration of McKinley's Secretary of War, Russell A. Alger. 'The iniquity is undoubtedly as great as you believe and represent,' Bowles replied. 'You are a reformer, and it is right and desirable that you should take an exaggerated view of the evil you are trying to reform.' Lloyd's rage over the Alger affair does seem a little exaggerated (Alger had been assailed for his blundering attempts to reorganize the army and prepare for war), but Bowles's answer suggests that Lloyd habitually overstated, if he did not misrepresent, the facts in his exposés and that all of his works, including *Wealth against Commonwealth,* his masterpiece of exposure, must be read with this in mind.

Critics of Lloyd, mistaking passion and indignation for irrational bias, have seized upon this supposed failing to minimize the force of his accusations. They are unfair. Even if Lloyd might have displayed on some occasions greater coolness and objectivity, he never permitted his bias to alter the facts he exhumed from the record. A reformer is by nature un-neutral. Excessive zeal for a cause can make him careless, but if he is honest, as Lloyd was honest, he passes judgment after the evidence has been gathered. Lloyd hit hard, but he never perjured himself, and he followed to the letter the advice he gave to a newspaper man on the technique of preparing a story. 'Make it,' he said, 'full, detailed, precise, and state nothing that cannot be backed up, but state all that can be, even if it unveils private indecency.'

Events educated Lloyd into this position. Like his great contemporaries, George and Bellamy, he too had a gift for observation and a conscience that made him oversensitive, perhaps, to the injustices taken for granted by the average man, but he took part in a series of episodes between 1885, when he left the *Tribune,* and 1894, when he published *Wealth against Commonwealth,* that would have warped and killed a smaller man.

Lloyd early appreciated the power of organized wealth. He found it was one thing to snipe from newspaper columns and something else again to fight as an unprotected individual. When Chicago's gentry arraigned and hanged the Haymarket anarchists and Lloyd protested, he not only estranged himself from William Bross and lost a fortune, but he also experienced the meanness of social ostracism. And after he had taken up the cause of the miners of Spring Valley, Illinois, locked out by their employers, and written *A Strike of Millionaires against Miners* (1890) ('the Iliad of the industrial revolution,' as General Weaver called it), he learned an important lesson: that his revelations about the miners' working conditions had no influence upon the employers except to make them bitter, and that it was not enough merely to expose, to photo-graph unsavory conditions; it was necessary to map out a solution as well.

After the Haymarket martyrs were hanged in 1887, Lloyd pledged himself to work for the weak and unrepresented. 'I am on the side of the underdog,' he wrote to his father. 'The agitators on that side make mistakes, commit crimes, no doubt, but for all that theirs is the right side. I will try to avoid the mistakes and the crimes but I will stay by the cause.' The gallantry of the miners at Spring Valley, their laughter, their acceptance 'of the inevitable ill fortune of life' astonished and touched him. 'It seemed to me,' he wrote, 'that, had I been thus made the victim of inhuman greed for "more," had I and my home and my life been butchered—not "to make a Roman holiday," but an American dividend—I would have thought a lifetime too little to give to a crusade of retribution.' But it suddenly occurred to him 'that there is a sanctification which comes, however unconsciously, to the victims of wrong and in-justice, and that it is the master, not the slave, who receives the double curse of oppression.'

Lloyd's sympathy for laborers, great as it was, and his firsthand knowledge of their exploitation, did not make him an uncritical tribune of the working-class movement. He spoke for labor, con-tributed his money and his time, and wrote the history of labor's fight from the 'eighties until his death in 1903, but he refused to convert the cause of labor into a crusade for a single class. Lloyd preferred to fight against the possibility of class war, which Marx said was inevitable, and to abolish those conditions that split society. His countrymen may have been wrong in denying the existence of classes in the United States, but this claim, he decided, 'at least shows that the people feel that the spirit of our institutions demands that there should be no class.' The great rebels he read and respected—Mirabeau, Phillips, Lassalle, Marx, Bebel, Singer, Liebknecht—all preached the abolition of classes; as a middle-class liberal, Lloyd repudiated the two-class, rich-poor, either-or classification of society as undemocratic. Neither side alone represented the people or looked after the true interests of the commonwealth. He called for a 'sovereign umpire,' begotten by the people and subject to their wishes. 'We cannot leave it to class conferences to enforce the responsibilities of this power; they can be enforced by a power only, stronger than both of them. There is one such power —the State.'

Lloyd developed and qualified this notion during the next decade, in addition to clarifying his ideas on class, privilege, property, and kindred subjects, but if we take his work collectively before the publication of *Wealth against Commonwealth,* one large theme stands out above all the rest and indeed comprehends them—the capitalist ethos and the character and conduct of the entrepreneur. This is the phase of Lloyd's thinking that is of necessity the most negative and destructive and yet the one that he had to work out before he could begin his constructive formulations. It resembles in part the comparable reflections of Parker and George and Bellamy, and yet it is done with a thoroughness and authority, with a concreteness and deftness that were new in American reformist literature. Robert Louis Stevenson discerned this quality in Lloyd's mordant appraisal of the capitalist and his code when he remarked to a friend: 'he writes the most workmanlike article of any man known to me in America, unless it should be Parkman. Not a touch in Lloyd of the amateur.'

VI] Lloyd's case against capitalism rested mainly on two charges: that it was immoral and socially destructive and that it was anachronistic and impractical. Put another way, capitalism corrupted its beneficiaries as well as its victims and failed to accomplish what its supporters claimed it did. This is really one of the underlying themes of *Wealth against Commonwealth,* but although stated there with the greatest dramatic power and profusion of detail, its genesis can be traced in most of Lloyd's previous writings.

Now the gospelers of business preached the antithetical doctrine of self-interest, a primitive conception that worked, so Lloyd wrote in *Wealth against Commonwealth,* when 'a society was not highly developed enough to organize the exploration and subjugation of worlds of new things and ideas on any broader basis than private enterprise, personal adventure,' but which was clearly unsuitable to modern conditions. The 'picnic centuries' had passed; the social could no longer be made subordinate to the individual. Modern capitalists had yet to learn that 'the music of the spheres is not to be played on one string,' that 'Nature does nothing individually.'

He knew well the explanations of the Social Darwinists, those 'professors of the tomahawk and scalping knife,' and resented their distortions of evolution. Lloyd admired Darwin and profited from him, but he drew from Darwinism a different set of deductions than the fatalists did. The theory of evolution smashed once and for all the myth of an earlier golden age and taught men to look ahead instead of behind. Sometimes, Lloyd thought, Darwin argued like a Malthusian, writing 'into science the philosophy of selfish competition which he saw at work in the social world about him' and making natural selection in biology the equivalent of *laisser-faire* in economics. But the truths of evolution surpassed the claims of its discoverer. The examples Darwin cited to illustrate the struggle for survival also taught the lessons of co-operation (for instance, the plants that exterminated weaker varieties were fertilized by the pollen of different plants carried by the winds and insects); the Darwinian exegesis of evolution by no means justified the conclusions of the pseudo-scientists who borrowed from him. Rightly understood, Darwinism gave scientific sanction to the processes of reform and revolution, but 'the first effects of Darwinism,' Lloyd wrote later to Alfred Russel Wallace, 'have I think been depressing and destructive. Huxley and Spencer have measured its doctrines and terminology shamefully, and made science the spokesman of reaction.'

Lloyd strongly objected to what he called 'the cant of science,' even more disgusting to him than religious cant, and he took occasion to explode whenever he could the much publicized error, which men like Rockefeller accepted, that survival meant superiority and that evolution was a synonym for 'progress.' The most useful and the best frequently succumbed to the bestial, and atavism, degeneration, and atrophy were not unknown in the natural world. When the Social Darwinists harped upon the futility of interfering with the natural processes of struggle and survival, Lloyd reminded them that social intervention often opens careers to talent and leaves 'the king-like Lincoln, who is hidden in the body of the people, free to emerge and rise.

> The fact is [he wrote in an early essay] these hypothetical economists have done for the industrial descent of man what Haeckel and his evolutionists have done for the theory of his physical descent. They have substituted assumption and dogma for a Darwinian patience in accumulating facts and reserve in generalization. They deserve the same rebuke that Virchow administered to Haeckel. . . Virchow . . . warned Haeckel that he and his school were treating as dogma proved, that which was only a problem to be investigated; and uttered these wise words, which should be branded into the mental cubicle of every disciple of the closet economists: We who support science, we who live in science, are all the more called upon to abstain from carrying into the heads of men, and most of all into the heads of teachers, that which we only suppose.

It was not scientific to say, in a world of industrial savagery, that the fittest survived, Lloyd said—only the 'fightingest.'

The business classes, however, did not take their cue from Lloyd but from the political economists skilled in 'shifting responsibility for injustice and legal selfishness from human shoulders upon the back of Nature.' His resentment of orthodox economics grew out of his conviction that it was abstract and unrealistic, divorced from humanity and built of 'syllogistic brick on imaginary foundations.' It was taught as 'a body of settled truths, revealed by teachers, and to be applied as a universal solvent. It is what nothing can be,—an apostolic science,' and it was incomplete:

Laissez-faire theories of politics and political economy are useless in the treatment of the labor question, or the regulation of railroads, sanitary and educational government. It is not to be denied that competition is an industrial force, and a mighty one, but it is only one. By neglecting the other forces, from sympathy to monopoly the abstract political economist deduces principles which fit no realities and has to neglect those realities for which we need principles most. When combination comes in at the door, the political economy of competition flies out of the window. It is a political economy of persons, not of the people.

William Graham Sumner and his predecessors relied more upon hypothesis than observation, because, as Sumner said, history furnished too few facts. Lloyd, familiar with the strategy of monopoly, the magic of the stock-market wizards, and the devices of the financiers, saw no dearth of facts for the economist to interpret. Depressions and corners and artificial scarcity had to be explained, not to mention the phenomenon of the modern exchange. While the textbook writers prattled about 'the imaginary trade of prehistoric trout for Pre-Adamite venison between the "first hunter" and the "first fisherman," ' Lloyd said, the machinery of the exchanges determined the actual prices of wheat and hogs:

The honest industry that builds up our greatest fortunes is raising wheat and pork on the Chicago Board of Trade, mining on the San Francisco Stock Exchange, building railroads in Wall Street, sinking oil wells in Williams Street, and picking cotton in Hanover Square.

In their efforts to be scientific, the political economists averted their gaze from the by-products of capitalist enterprise, but in doing so they distorted the entire picture. The moral and cultural consequences of an economic system mattered more to Lloyd than its technical achievements or failures and could not be discounted in any final estimate. If competition robbed a worker of his security and destroyed his pride of workmanship; if it took a man, used up his good part and left 'the bad parts of him to be healed, upheld, and buried, by the mass of society; that is, by those not "smart" or "strong" enough to outwit their brothers and secure this sinister advantage,' these costs had to ᵗᵒ reckoned with. And if the business code demoralized and corrupted and if it stood for the rule of force, this seemed an evil thing to Lloyd, whether the power resided in the rulers or among the working class who emulated their superiors.

What he objected to in competition was not the natural inclination for one man to exchange his goods with another; he admitted that in the early days of capitalism 'there was a certain rough justice in the maxim, The devil take the hindmost.' But when competition countenanced cruelty and falsehood and idiocy and the victors turned out to be 'the kind of men the devil wants,' then it was clear, as he wrote in his account of the Spring Valley strike, that American industry was 'passing out of the control of business men into that of business animals, whose prototypes must be sought for among the carnivora that go on all fours, and who need, as Emerson said of similar men of his time, to be educated out of the quadruped state.'

Lloyd questioned on practical as well as on ethical grounds capital's divine right to rule and to distribute largesse. Businessmen, he knew, claimed their privilege to be free from supervision or interference as a reward for their superior abilities, but like Veblen, who analyzed these claims in a similar spirit, Lloyd concluded that they had no validity.

> A study of the facts would easily show [he wrote in his notebook in 1888] that business success is won by a sort of predatory over-reaching, down-trading quality. Others invent the machines, plan the enterprises, discover the countries, chemicals and forces, perfect the currencies, educate the labor, which the business man seizes on and works, and tries to 'hog down' all the benefits of. Business men have always resisted change, whether a reform for the people, or themselves.

Lloyd distinguished, as Veblen was to do, the 'tool-makers' from what he mockingly referred to as the 'antediluvian captains of industry who call themselves masters, walk on Market Street or on Wall Street as if it were Mount Ararat, and they were just landed from the ark.' The technicians joined 'the melancholy procession of two thousand years of scouts, inventors, pioneers, capitalists, and toilers who march behind the successful men.'

When the industrial captains pursued their policy of restraint, scarcity, and high prices unchecked by governmental interference, 'free enterprise' ended in monopoly. Lloyd was not fooled by the cant of 'free men,' 'free markets,' 'my business,' and 'no dictator.' He knew all the arguments made for trusts and the reasons given for the so-called irresistible momentum toward concentration. All of his knowledge and insight he packed into *Wealth against Commonwealth,* conceived in the early 'seventies when the Standard Oil Company was no bigger than a man's hand and completed when the Standard was probably the most powerful industrial corporation in the world. Howells had been influential in publishing Lloyd's first exposure, 'A Story of a Great Monopoly,' in the *Atlantic Monthly* in 1881; fifteen years later the full-blown history, replete with facts and figures and fired with vehemence, made its appearance.

VII] The photograph of Lloyd which prefaced a feature article on him in *The Arena* (October 1894) reveals a prematurely aged man with white hair combed back in pompadour fashion, a drooping mustache, and a lined, tired-looking face. The shoulders sag a little, and there is a melancholy cast to his expression.

Although the writing of *Wealth against Commonwealth,* published in September 1894, had taxed his energies severely, and although he was depressed by the meaning of his own revelations, the last three or four years of research and composition had been pleasant ones. Surrounded by his family and dividing his time between a summer home in Sakonnet, Rhode Island, and his own house in Winnetka, Illinois, he could prepare his great book in an atmosphere far more congenial for literary work than George or Bellamy enjoyed. Reformers and social workers came to Sakonnet or Winnetka (the latter, as Jane Addams said, was practically an annex to Hull House) and so did political figures like Governor Altgeld and Clarence Darrow. English celebrities mingled with callow girls, charmed by Lloyd's quiet courtesy and gentleness, and the visitor never knew whom he would find at the household: an invalid factory girl nursed by Jessie Lloyd or a crowd of women

from Marshall Field's department store or a scholar looking for
the kind of information only Lloyd could provide.

In the attic of the Sakonnet house and in his Winnetka study,
Lloyd began about 1889 the serious work of putting his book together. An extensive library and an elaborate collection of periodicals, pamphlets, and documents, amassed and catalogued over a
period of twenty years, were ready to be consulted whenever necessary, and portraits of Lincoln, Morris, Ruskin, and Emerson looked
down upon him from the walls to inspire him when the burden of
his task seemed too great to bear.

Emerson remained not only his moral and intellectual guide but
his literary model as well. All of Lloyd's published and unpublished
writings are studded with quotations from Emerson and allusions
to his essays, and the very rhythm of his gnomic style, epigrammatic and terse, and the concrete, homely diction suggest the
Concord sage. Lloyd's vivid use of metaphor and his amazing facility for dramatizing the technical and reporting the most complex
operations in swift, clear prose made him unique among his contemporaries. He had Emerson to thank for this talent. For if Emerson could not have written the kind of popular article that Lloyd
turned out so superbly, he taught him (as one can see from reading Lloyd's piece on Emerson) how wit could be used effectively
to puncture pretension and hypocrisy.

Lloyd learned from Emerson to write as elegantly as he dressed.
There is a polish to his work that makes him one of the most literate of the reformers and, with the exception of Veblen or John
Jay Chapman, the most quotable. He is invariably well-bred even
when bitter and sarcastic; he can write cool and masterly exposition, and he can 'set the facts on fire,' as Lyman Beecher used to
say about himself. Witty, stinging, persuasive, and keenly sensitive
to the dramatic, he framed his charges with the greatest of care,
well aware of the reformer's penchant for exaggeration, which his
friend Bowles remarked upon, and of the value of irony and under-
statement.

Lloyd could be blunt, but he usually gave a wry twist to his
comments and a pithiness that raised them above the common-

place. 'The Standard has done everything with the Pennsylvania Legislature,' he said, 'except to refine it,' and the Pennsylvania Railroad ran the State Supreme Court 'as if it were one of its limited trains.' The rebate employed by the trusts was the 'golden rule' of the 'gospel of wealth.' In describing the difficulties of gathering evidence on the Standard Oil Company's business policies, he found that 'all had vanished into the bottomless darkness in which the monopoly of light loves to dwell.' The coal owners were 'the vaudevillists of the world of values' and the swollen capitalization of their companies 'was obtained by adding the dropsical mining stocks to the dropsical railroad stocks. This is one of the cases in w ich like has not cured like.' When the casket-makers joined forces, Lloyd observed that 'their action to keep up prices and to keep down the numbers of coffins was secret, lest mortality should be discouraged.'

He understood and used with skill the literary devices of anticlimax as well as the dramatic, clinching summary: 'A work of money is needed that shall generalize the multitudinous facts from wampam to confidence in terms intelligible to common people, business men, other economists—and the author.' His account of Jay Gould's corporation-wrecking technique is a longer and more sustained illustration of his art. Here is a part of it:

The hidden hand pulled another wire, and the editor of the *New York World* began to launch forth through its columns startling exhibits of the financial rottenness of the company, and editorial, that is virtuous, indignation at its abuse of the public and its franchises. Then came another can-can in the courts, led by lawyers, who danced long and well, according to the New York code of legal ethics that if a lawyer is not a judge he need not be a gentleman, and if he is a judge, he need not be investigated. Receivers were appointed, more stockwatering was authorized by the courts, and affidavits poured forth from insiders that the company was hopelessly and irretrievably bankrupt. . . Manhattan stockholders flung their certificates away for what they could get. The price sank to fifteen and one fourth. Suddenly what had seemed a mass of ruin crystallized into the symmetrical structure of a monopoly, and on its peak, but a few days after he had sworn that Manhattan was hopelessly and irretrievably insolvent, sat the manufacturer of mouse-traps, master of the rapid transit of the greatest city of America. The prentice hand that had fashioned the

Erie trap had become the perfect instrument of an artist in the science
of exchange.

The dramatic structure of this passage, the quality of suspense it
evokes, is its most striking feature. Language and sentence rhythm
and imagery (the figure of the can-can dance) become increasingly
agitated (note the force of 'poured,' 'flung,' 'sank') until with the
sentence beginning 'Suddenly. . .' Jay Gould and monopoly slowly
materialize out of the ruins of the Manhattan. A long periodic sentence filled with latinate words follows the short choppy phrases,
and the passage ends with the appropriate coda.

Lloyd thought epigrammatically, trying always to rephrase the
familiar; he is at his best in the sententious Emersonian statement
that so frequently concludes an argument: 'We must degrade Christ
into the ranks of common humanity; we must discrown God.' 'A
single privilege like a single leak will founder the ship.' 'Corporations have no souls, but they can love each other.' All of Lloyd's
works were filled with similar expressions of wit and wisdom, but
in *Wealth against Commonwealth* especially, they formed a corus-
cating background for his somber presentation of facts.

VIII] The idea of Lloyd's powerful book, according
to his sister, occurred to him in 1876 when a modest corporation
known as the South Improvement Company first attracted his
notice. Over the next decade he painstakingly accumulated a dos-
sier on Mr. Rockefeller's venture, and in 1889 he began to write
his saga of the company whose progress he regarded as 'the most
characteristic thing in our business civilization—the most illus-
trative of the past—the most threatening for the future.' He had
originally planned to make *Wealth against Commonwealth* one volume in the 'Bad Wealth' series; other experts would cover such controversial subjects as the spoliation of public lands by the land-
grant railroads, the facts unearthed in the investigation of railroads
by the various state committees, the coal industry, the moral and
social significance of poverty, and others. Such a series, he hoped,
would 'put into popular form the mine of information, of the highest value, which is now buried in official reports, investigations,

lawsuits.' Certainly this was one of the important purposes of his own contribution.

His book was not an easy one to write. The facts he dug up depressed him, and he found the work distasteful. 'It keeps me poking about and scavenging in piles of filthy human greed and cruelty almost too nauseous to handle,' he wrote to his mother in 1891. 'Nothing but the sternest sense of duty and the conviction that men must understand the vices of our present system before they will be able to rise to a better, drives me back to my desk every day. When I get this book done, I am going to write one to suit myself. The subject will be The Commonwealth of Nations.' Lloyd loved his fellow men, but he saw them as dupes, 'dear fools,' who had to be awakened to the menace of monopoly.

The naming of the book bothered him. He wanted something popular and expressive, and he played with such titles as *The New Brotherhood, Marketing Mankind, This Ends an Era, The Rule of Gold and the Golden Rule, Barbarians of Business, The Age of Monopoly, The Civilization of Industry, U.S.A. United Syndicates of America,* before finally deciding to use the simpler and more forceful *Wealth against Commonwealth.*

After he had finished the book in the spring of 1893, he sent the manuscript to Harper's, who informed Lloyd that neither he nor they would find it profitable to publish it. Their readers found it too long and too embittered. Lloyd ought to have let the facts speak for themselves and omitted the hortatory asides. They complained about his gratuitous insults to living people, the arrangement of his book into topics instead of a chronological history. Lloyd defended the length of his book and the plethora of facts it contained and scouted the company's fear of libel. The manuscript had been checked and double-checked by lawyers and authorities on the oil industry. But Harper's turned it down and Houghton Mifflin followed suit. Lloyd then cut down his manuscript to 250,000 words, and finally, after Appleton's had sent it back and he had recast it four times, Howells took a hand and Harper's finally risked it. Even so, Lloyd put up five hundred dollars.

Lloyd had deliberately sacrificed some of the book's readability (although less than he feared), but he hoped his ransacking of the musty pigeonholes of business would reveal 'the keys of the present and clues to the future.' One purpose would be fulfilled, he wrote a few months after the publication of his book, 'if it succeeds in giving our novelists, dramatists, poets, and historians some hint of the treasures of new material that lie waiting for them in real life. Here are whole continents of romance, adventure and ungathered gold which have been terrae incognitae to our explorers of the pen.' This hope was realized. Dreiser, Frank Norris, Harold Frederic, Henry B. Fuller, and others scavenged for themselves, and a new generation of investigators, following his lead, stirred up the slime again with their muck rakes.

But *Wealth against Commonwealth,* despite its sensational chapter headings, its rhetorical asides, its startling accusations, was more than clever journalism, and to emphasize these features, as some historians have done, is to misconstrue its real intention. Actually it was a polemic against Spencerian economics and the claims of Social Darwinism. It proclaimed the immanence of social disintegration if the present tendencies continued and it made a plea for survival. Finally, it attacked monopoly and demonstrated through hundreds of closely packed pages why monopoly was not inevitable or cheap or efficient.

Lloyd had been trying for many years to make these points clear to his contemporaries, who were impressed by size and deceived by the propaganda of the trusts. Words like 'cheapness' and 'efficiency,' he realized, were relative terms. A monopoly might cheapen the cost of a product to the consumer, and yet the product would not be cheap. It was not always easy to determine, moreover, whether the combination or other less publicized factors produced the economies. There was always the question, too, of the social cost of cheapness. Did cheapness justify the ends used to make things cheap? Such a claim seemed to Lloyd uneconomic and unethical. *Coups d'état* were simpler and cheaper than national elections, but that made them no more desirable. Even if it were true that monopoly brought about vast benefits to the consumer, it would still be monstrous, and anyone who participated in the spoils would share in its complicity; piracy was no less villainous when all shared in the proceeds. His 'adulterous generation' did not have the moral insight to see this, and that is why *Wealth against Commonwealth* must be read as a prophet's cry to a sinful people just as much as an attack on Standard Oil. The Americans had fashioned and worshipped a golden calf that embodied their own ideals.

Unchecked power, particularly industrial power, corrupted. Monopoly not only stole the property of others, but like all other tyrannies, it had to extend its domain over non-economic areas, 'government, art, literature, even private conversation.' In short, it was the idea of monopoly rather than a particular form of economic exploitation that Lloyd opposed. Public opinion blamed the corporation, the railroad, the landlord for the social ills.

> But [said Lloyd] the corporation is merely a cover, the combination of corporations an advantage, the private ownership of public highways an opportunity, and the rebate its perfect tool. The real actors are men; the real instrument, the control of their fellows by wealth, and the mainspring of the evil is the morals and economics which cipher that brothers produce wealth when they are only cheating each other out of birthrights.

Any society in which a man could start with nothing and end up owning hundreds of millions of dollars while hard-working competent men had difficulty making expenses was 'over-ripe' and headed toward destruction.

Wealth against Commonwealth, opening with the familiar announcement, 'Nature is rich; but everywhere man, the heir of nature, is poor,' ends with a solution, a plan to overthrow the entrenched few who manipulate the Congress, the press, the school, and who corrupt the national life. Lloyd traces the rise of monopoly's archetype, the Standard, in a chronicle of human predation, which starts with plans of a group of determined men to achieve power by any device, fair or foul, favorable to their advancement. He describes melodramatically but factually how a gang of business sappers, working under cover of darkness, make their corrupt bargains with the railroads and introduce the 'secret weapon' of the rebate, 'soundless, noiseless, invisible, of extraordinary range, and the deadliest gun known to commercial warfare.' Corporations like the Standard, which received rebates on the

freight of its competitors as well as on its own, no longer needed
to build and dig and create:

> They need only get control of the roads. All that they want of the
> wealth of others can be switched off the highways into their hands. To
> succeed, ambitious men must make themselves refiners of freight rates,
> distillers of discrimination, owners, not of lands, mines, and forests—
> not in the first place, at least,—but of the railway officials through
> whose hands the produce must go to market; builders, not of manufac-
> tories, but of privileges; inventors only of schemes to keep for them-
> selves the middle of the road and both sides of it; contrivers, not of
> competition, but of ways to tax the property of their competitors into
> their own pockets. They need not make money; they can take it from
> those who have made it.

He relates with gusto the conspiracies, briberies, and subversions,
the corruption of petty officials and senators, and the entire devious
course of the Standard from oil to politics to philanthropy. All the
operations are laid bare and all the important trials and investigations and personal testimony, before Lloyd is ready for his final
indictment and his resolution.

His solution contained nothing startling, for he had been preaching it for many years: 'When capitalists combine irresistibly against
the people, the government, which is the people's combination,
must take them in hand.' Popular co-operation in the interests of
the many, he knew, would not come until enough people were imbued with the 'new conscience' and had purged themselves of
those qualities most successfully incorporated in the business captains, the incarnations of their ideals. But if public virtue rested
on private virtue, private virtue came to nothing unless it was organized. The 'citizens of industry' without association remained as
helpless as the unaffiliated 'citizens of government.' Only men in
combination could 'get and keep freedom' and become truly civilized. The irresponsible merchant-trader, 'the cruelest fanatic in
history,' who upset the delicate reciprocities of economics, had to
go and with him the ethics of power and greed. Lloyd believed the
American people would act when they learned the facts and saw
through the 'ordinary stupidity of the vested mind.'

Did he expect too much? Louis D. Brandeis doubted whether

Lloyd's book would have the desired effect of arousing popular opinion, and he disagreed with Edward Everett Hale's designation of *Wealth against Commonwealth* as the *'Uncle Tom's Cabin* of industrial times.' It was far too removed from the ordinary experiences of the people, he wrote to Edwin Mead, and would hardly lessen their admiration for the industrial captains. Lloyd, Brandeis thought, should have printed the names of the malefactors and shown them as the convicted criminals they were.

Aside from the fact that no publisher would have dared to print the book Brandeis had in mind (Harper's was frightened to death as it was), Lloyd had never intended to write a personal assault against specific individuals. He wanted 'to unfold a realistic picture of modern business,' as he said, and to show how American society became an unwitting accomplice to the villainies of its overlords. 'We are waiting for some genius of good who will generalize into one body of doctrine our partial truths of reform, and will help us to live the generalization,' he had written at the end of *Wealth against Commonwealth,* and in saying this he explained himself and his purpose.

In the years that have followed the publication of *Wealth against Commonwealth,* critics have assailed him on every conceivable score and damned his book as dishonest, slanderous, overemotional, inaccurate, and prejudiced. Lloyd's defenders, on the other hand, have maintained that in the great majority of instances Lloyd was a careful and accurate historian and not the vindictive liar he has been made out to be.

But it is not important now to revive the old battles and decide whether or not the Standard must be held responsible for blowing up a rival's refinery or whether its officers were more or less unscrupulous than their piratical adversaries. Presumably the Standard does not use such tactics today, if it used them then. The significance of Lloyd's book does not depend upon the accuracy of any single indictment, although Lloyd's mistakes are surprisingly few. Lloyd introduced overt examples of fraud, which no one today condones, as crude illustrations of a deeper malaise extending beyond the business community and infecting the entire nation;

business malpractice was simply one symptom of that sickness that the balm of 'political Christianity' or 'industrial religion' might heal.

               IX] The key to *Wealth against Commonwealth*, and indeed to all his philosophy, is a book compiled from his manuscripts and fragments of published material by his friends Jane Addams and Anne Withington. *Man, the Social Creator*, as it was called, was published posthumously in 1906. For many years before his death in 1903, Lloyd had been gathering material for a book on his religion, a book that would bring together the philosophical notations he had been inscribing regularly in his notebooks and synthesize the conclusions of the trips to England, New Zealand, Australia, France, and Switzerland he had taken during the 'nineties in search of new political and economic strategies. The residue of these experiences boiled down to the Emersonian maxim: love is the foundation of the state.

Man, the social creator, the maker of his own institutions, advances according to his success in controlling the force of love, 'a natural force which the science of society proves to develop as certainly by the contact of men with each other as heat or electricity by the friction of matter.' Love provides the energy for the social movement and lies ready for the wise engineers who care to exploit its vast and unused reservoirs. Somewhat akin to Whitman's all-dissolving *Spirita Sanctis*, it crumbles the walls isolating brother from brother, ends the tyranny of hate and fear, and re-establishes the union of the community on the true principles of social harmony.

Lloyd conceived it to be the real task of the labor movement to counteract the separating tactics of capital. He therefore affiliated himself with the only body powerful enough to oppose business anarchy. From the Spring Valley strike to the great coal strike of 1902, he spoke and wrote and fought for labor's rights. He made himself an authority on factory conditions and savagely attacked the employers who manufactured slums and proletarians along with their sweated products.

But Lloyd was pro-labor not because he hated its oppressors;

just as the trust symbolized for him a principle more fundamentally wicked than its brute manifestations, so the labor movement represented an idea more noble than the practices of its members. It belonged to 'the great upward movement of humanity' as capital belonged to the downward. Its ultimate mission, as Lloyd saw it, was 'to extend into industry the brotherhood already recognized in politics and religion, and to teach men as workers the love and equality which they profess as citizens and worshippers.' In a business civilization, aggressive and ferocious, labor set 'its sternest face against certain materialist and atheistical aspects of modern thought' (note the echo of Parker here) when the church was silent. Labor was the party of peace, the embodiment of rights painfully won by past martyrs.

Lloyd's apologia for labor may strike some people as uncritical if not sentimental, but Lloyd had no illusions about labor's mistakes and weaknesses. The workers were often wrong, he admitted on many occasions, *'but theirs is always the right side.'* The flare-ups of labor violence he blamed on the provocations of the employers, on their stubborn refusal to arbitrate, and on their inflexible hostility to unionism. For Lloyd, organization was a law of life, and the union-breaking policies of management he regarded as an 'attempt to dehumanize the workman, and de-civilize the world.' Management invariably fell back on the court injunction, the yellow-dog contract, the lockout, and the scab. When these devices failed, the soldiers and the Pinkertons could be called upon. No wonder the workingmen were sometimes tempted into violence.

Lloyd argued persuasively that industrial peace would never come until capital accepted the trade-union, 'the precursor of the union of all men.' He placed too much faith, perhaps, in the New Zealand plan of compulsory arbitration, which he explained in his book, *A Country without Strikes* (1900), but he was one of the first of the labor specialists to sense the importance of good public relations and the value of winning public support. He disapproved of secret agreements in the settling of industrial disputes as much as he did of secret agreements between corporations, and he constantly tried to make labor see that its future influence would depend on the degree to which it stood as a bulwark between the people and monopoly. In this he took the view of George and Bellamy. Labor, he believed, had no more divine right to rule than capital, and although he approved of the co-partnership of employer and employee as preferable to their traditional enmity, it was mainly because such experiments would help to train the leaders for the future democracy of socialistic industry. He did not overlook the possibility of a labor-capital conspiracy against the public, and he spoke against it.

If labor furnished the shock troops for the co-operative commonwealth against the 'Money Brotherhood,' it was the mission of the enlightened middle class to provide the leadership and direction for the new democracy. 'The middle class,' Lloyd wrote in *Newest England* (1900), an account of his New Zealand and Australian trips, 'is not to be exterminated, but is to absorb the other classes.' This was the ideal of all the progressives, the absorption of the extremes by the middle. Lloyd hoped that a moderate and progressive middle class would prevent the necessity of choosing 'between the catastrophes of state socialism and trust socialism' by instituting its own brand of democratic socialism. His interest in the International Labor Congress at the World's Columbian Exposition may have been prompted, as Laurence Gronlund intimated in a letter to Lloyd, by the possibility of forming 'a worldwide Fellowship of a few hundred enlightened persons to lead Socialism into its beneficent channels.' Gronlund continued, in words that partly expressed Lloyd's own feelings:

> For this is my contention: that Socialism is not so much the cause of the poor and the weak as of the *capable, gifted,* and *cultured;* that it appeals not alone to the self-sacrificing but even now to the *nobly ambitious.* If Socialism be inevitable (and the Trusts prove that to me), then surely it is desirable, that it come here under the auspices of the Enlightenment, and it is important to us, that in Europe such may control the violent and coarse elements.

Lloyd, as we shall see, questioned some of the implications of Gronlund's letter, but he fully agreed that the cause of labor and socialism ought to appeal to the 'nobly ambitious,' and he looked upon the alliance of the middle class with the plutocracy as disastrous. He pointed out repeatedly to his middle-class audiences that although the agitator might be 'jailed or hanged' first, the middle-class writer will be next to feel 'the lariat of the law'; that while the farmers and the white-collar workers cheered the prosecuting attorneys who tied down 'the struggling Samsons of labour,' their rights would disappear soon after. The middle class had a choice to make. The issues were black and white. Both morality and expediency made only one course possible.

x] 'The essence of Democracy,' Lloyd wrote in 1903, 'is that the Democrat submits to no power of which he is not a constituent part and partner.' Obviously, then, any man with good sense and a conscience had to disassociate himself from a government that responded only to the will of plutocrats. If democracy meant 'the use of all the resources of nature by all the faculties of men, for the good of all the people,' then clearly America was a very imperfect democracy and needed drastic overhauling.

Lloyd knew that many attributed democracy's failures to human weakness and the imperfection of democratic institutions. He had no illusions about the incorruptible nature of man, no exaggerated ideas about the morals and intelligence of the electorate, but the remedy he thought lay in more, not less, democracy. Liberty needed new liberties more than it did new markets. No government could call itself democratic, regardless of its fine pretensions, when it denied security and justice and leisure to its citizens. Real democracy, industrial as well as political, had yet to be tried.

In the United States, the people entrusted the resources and machinery of government to men who converted the country into a private preserve. They had been seduced by the values of their gold-hunting masters and now they sanctioned the lie that 'the scramble for profit is the best method of administering the riches of the earth and the exchange of services.' The mores of business permeated their songs, catchwords, and customs, and they had gladly given 'the prize of power to the strong, the cunning, the arithmetical.' The way out was to withdraw this spiritual allegiance and to act in a manner consistent with democracy's assumptions: that government be operated in the interests of the majority of the people who compose it. As Lloyd wrote in *Wealth against Commonwealth:*

> The time must come in social evolution when the people can organize the free-will to choose salvation which the individual has been cultivating for 1900 years, and can adopt a policy more dignified and more effective than leaving themselves to be kicked along the path of reform by the recoil of their own vices. We must bring the size of our morality up to the size of our cities, corporations, and combinations, or these will be brought down to fit our half-grown virtue.

Such a course—the establishment of a genuine democratic society—carried with it certain dangers of which Lloyd was perfectly aware. Nonconformists did not always get fair treatment in majoritarian-minded societies, and 'the greatest happiness of the greatest number' principle often made the 'convenience of the public' an excuse for tyranny. Democracies, he felt, had to be especially zealous to encourage independence and leadership and to remain progressive, lest their own flexible theories harden into dogma. 'Man,' he once wrote, 'is always harmonizing liberty in organizations, and breaking up organizations to get liberty.' Democracies had to be most scrupulous about permitting the dissatisfied to air their destructive views. 'The community,' he said, quoting Wendell Phillips, 'which does not protect its humblest and most hated member in the free utterance of his opinions, no matter how false and hateful, is only a gang of slaves.'

Individualism of this sort, the individual free to think and speak as he chooses, meant everything to Lloyd, for it alone provided the real dynamic for democratic evolution. This was not the kind of individualism that permitted a person or faction to run rough-shod over the community and commit depredations in the name of liberty. Men only developed a true individualism when they met in friendly association with their brothers on terms of equality. It took free men and good men to run a democracy; despotisms got along very well with the mindless masses. Lloyd believed that democracy was doomed when liberty became a privilege, not a principle, and the right to be a person—the opportunity for self-fulfillment—was restricted to the rich.

Even the well-ordered society, especially as it approached collectivism, threatened to submerge the individual's identity, and Lloyd was always thinking of ways to balance or limit the tendency toward centralization. He believed in a large measure of government control and authority—although never so much as Bellamy —but, as he wrote in his book on Switzerland, *The Sovereign People,* 'we can have centralisation safely only if, at the same moment as we aggrandize and develop the centre, we aggrandize and develop the individual in himself and in his control of the centre.' All his experience made him suspicious of power imposed and controlled from above. At a time when many socialists and Nationalists blithely recommended entrusting all to a national bureaucracy, Lloyd urged that America model itself after the small countries 'in which the citizens know one another, in which their affairs are within their comprehension, imagination, and control; in which the centre is not out of reach of those on the circumference; in which the machinery is not so massive that the mind and the hand of the common people cannot grasp it.' A large country like the United States could not achieve decentralization so easily as Switzerland or New Zealand, but it had to approximate a purer form of democracy, a larger degree of direct popular participation in government if it were to survive.

'All social problems,' Lloyd wrote in this connection, 'are problems of union. The significance of the social settlement is in its essay to re-establish union in communities grown so large that all social connections are endangered, domestic as well as civic.' He appreciated the tragedy of a rootless, aimless populace, unidentified and placeless. Such people had no stake in the society and no feeling of responsibility. They were the real victims of the industrial revolution, the alienated people who had been removed from the neighborhood, with its censorship, its regulations, its loyalties. The neighborhood, which related family life to 'the larger associations of state and nation,' had to be strengthened and the love of family and locality extended to the nation and to the world.

Neighborhoods not only gave a man a sense of his own personality, but they provided a training ground for democracy. Hence Lloyd's constant agitation for home rule and local prerogative and his often expressed fear that everything had become too large, that the breach between the people and the government constantly widened. Government had already become monopolized by 'experts' who made a business of politics; and the people were too ready to delegate their authority to disloyal representatives and turn their energies to what they considered more practical business. In doing so they renounced their sovereignty.

No greater fallacy existed, in Lloyd's opinion, than the idea that the citizenry did not need to be trained to run a democracy, that all we had to do was to let 'everything drift into the hands of the trusts with the idea that we can then by a coup d'économie change masters from monopolist to democracy.' Many socialists thought so, but they were mistaken. 'Just as we are about to shake ourselves for this grand transformation,' he said, 'we may find, too late, that the process of preparation has annihilated us.' The trusts were neither scientific nor useful, and the socialists, in condoning their development as inevitable and in planning to absorb them after the social damage had been done, were in effect allowing the ends to justify the means. Rather than permit these monstrosities to mushroom, Lloyd wanted the government to keep hacking them down to manageable size.

XI] Critical of the Socialists as he was and always qualifying his support, Lloyd nevertheless moved closer and closer to the party and tentatively decided to join it in 1903. Why he considered this step and why he did not go through with it will become clear after we have reviewed his major activities during the 1890's.

Between his trips to Europe and the Antipodes, Lloyd participated in the formation of the People's party, a movement already assuming formidable proportions by 1892. His success in organizing the World's Fair Labor Congress in 1893 and the immense popularity of his speech to the American Federation of Labor convention in December of that year established his reputation as a labor statesman. Already plans were being made for an international labor conference in 1900 to bring together widely assorted groups of unionists and theorists and to lay the foundations for the collectivist society. Then came Coxey's army and the flare-up at

Pullman, which culminated, Lloyd believed, in the railroad oper-
ators' instigation of the car-burnings 'as the surest way to bring
the Federal troops and defeat the strike.'

By this time, too, Lloyd had involved himself in the People's
party and was closely watching the development of the movement
he had helped to supervise during the days of its inception in 1890.
He attended the important conferences in 1891 and 1892, and
after the Populists had succeeded in pulling a million votes in the
'92 election, he began to hope that at last a new party had arisen
to challenge the two corrupt established ones. 'A country in which
the people have at the elections only the right to be crucified between two thieves—who are not crucified'—he had remarked in a
Washington Day speech, 'is not the Republic of Washington.' It
looked now as if 1856 would repeat itself, for the people, driven
on by hard times, seemed to be on the march.

Lloyd saw in this spontaneous revolt of the Mississippi Valley
a chance to unite laborers with farmers in a true people's movement, a movement that might induce the highly self-conscious
minority parties—Socialists, Single Taxers, Nationalists, and Anarchists—to join forces with the radical Democrats behind one
candidate for the People's party. Between 1894 and 1896, it
seemed that he might succeed in realizing his dream. Largely owing
to his tact and shrewdness and to the trust he inspired among the
divergent groups brought together in this uneasy allegiance, Lloyd
helped to keep the People's party in Illinois a genuinely popular
movement and to limit the influence of the men, out of sympathy
with its radical features, who wished to make it the party of the
silver interests. But in the end his intelligent and practical com-
promises failed. The conservatives in the party disliked and feared
their reluctant socialist allies; the Single Taxers constantly made
trouble; and the Socialists, never entirely in sympathy with Lloyd's
and Bellamy's modified collectivism (Lloyd wanted to submit all
socialistic proposals to the initiative and referendum), pulled out.
This setback, together with other disappointments that followed in
quick succession, made him less optimistic about the immediate
prospects of the people's cause.

It was not the failure of his one venture into national politics that disturbed him. He had not expected to win a congressional seat after his nomination to Congress in 1894, for he was running in a heavily Republican district, but the People's party, with its semisocialist platform, still approached the goals he was working for. The events occurring between 1894 and 1896 soon proved him wrong. Lloyd had to watch the sickening spectacle of a great popular movement disintegrating, weakened by inside fights between splinter groups and sold out by the fakirs who subordinated all the strong features of the Omaha platform to the folly of free silver.

After the fiasco of the 'gagged, clique-ridden, and machine ruled' St. Louis Convention of the People's party, where the Populist leaders 'were forever only too happy to respond to the voice of the siren of Fusion and slip out of the straight and narrow way of principle into the sweet fields of dalliance for office,' Lloyd had just about enough. Free Silver he likened to 'the cowbird of the Reform movement':

> It waited until the nest had been built by the sacrifices and labour of others, and then it laid its eggs in it, pushing out the others which lie smashed on the ground. It is now flying around while we are expected to do the incubating. I for one decline to sit on the nest to help any such game.

It infuriated him to see such a delusive issue take pre-eminence over so many more important ones and at the same time provide Hanna's men with such perfect propaganda materials. No honest reformer could give his whole-hearted support to a party that made currency its chief concern and chose a temporizer like Bryan for its candidate:

> It is preposterous [Lloyd commented after the St. Louis trip] for an intelligent people to hold themselves dependent on the freaks of the bonanzas and placers for their means of exchange. This is to substitute the accidents of nature for the creative powers of the people as the arbiter in one of the most vital of our social functions. A people that is a people will *create* its money, and keep it responsive with the accuracy of its other machinery to the task it is invested to attend to.

When the scales had fallen from Lloyd's eyes, and he saw the People's party for what it actually was, 'an imperfectly-formed and half-understood revolt against the money power, with vague tendencies that might, in a general way, be described as socialistic,' he knew that McKinley would win the election. He had begun to suspect by the summer of 1895 that 'the political motives of our people are as rotten with selfishness and greed as their industrial morals,' and by the time the convention days were at hand, he was able to guess the outcome in the battle between 'a fortuitous collection of the dissatisfied' and the well-heeled 'broad-cloth mob' who opposed them. Whatever one might say about the gold-bugs, they were united; they knew what they wanted.

The People's party failed, he concluded, partly on account of its vacillating and dishonest leadership. A group of 'moderates' were strongly entrenched, the kind of men who habitually affiliate with reform movements only to destroy them, who profess to be liberals and yet are suspicious of any minister 'whom they find wandering towards economic Christianity.' After the election, Lloyd was sick to death of these people and their talk of 'moderation.'

There is no moderation [he wrote in 1897] on the part of the syndicates and plutocrats. A policy of 'moderation' proposes to fight the devil without fire. When moderately cold ice and moderately hot boiling water, moderately pious Christs and moderately honest 'Old Abes' count for anything, the policy of moderation in fighting the immoderate aggressors will deserve more success than it can possibly have now.

Lloyd blamed the people of this stamp for corrupting the People's party and making it the 'boss-ridden, ring-ruled, gang-gangrened' thing that it turned out to be.

Only one group during the campaign period emerged with any kind of distinction—the Socialists. 'They are the most intelligent, most energetic, most reliable workers we have,' Lloyd had written to Clarence Darrow in 1894, and he felt that Henry George had made his greatest mistake in deserting them to escape 'the odium of "socialistic" affiliations.' After the betrayal of the People's party in 1896 and the nomination of Bryan, Lloyd, in spite of his reservations, voted Socialist-Labor, a ticket he felt obliged to support until some new and truly representative party had been formed.

In the biography of her brother, Lloyd's sister says that Lloyd fully intended to join up with the Socialists officially, even though he squirmed, as he said, when he heard the 'everlasting "proletariat" and "class conscious" slang' of the more sectarian members. With the two old parties controlled by monopolists and the Populist party 'Bryanized,' the Socialists seemed to be the only party through which a reformer might work. It alone refused to shy away from the bogy of public ownership and to present, at the same time, an intelligent policy for international peace. The war with Spain, which in a burst of irrational patriotism he had at first interpreted as a struggle between two irreconcilable civilizations, he soon recognized as a manifestation of an expanding imperialism. Only the Socialist party offered a constructive corrective to capitalistic mismanagement in the Orient and Europe and an alternative of internationalism to the vicious jingoism becoming alarmingly prevalent in the United States.

His opinions had changed a little on this subject after the Spanish war. As an idealistic nationalist of the Mazzini or Whitman stripe, he had envisaged the spread of the American idea of democratic brotherhood, starting in the neighborhood and spreading beneficently across all national boundaries. His travels abroad, however, showed him that the American system was only one among many and that other countries had been more successful in solving certain political and economic problems than America. No nation, he came to realize, particularly a new one, 'may safely and conveniently go its own gait, working out a free destiny in the void of history.' Such an attitude was 'indeed a fatuous form of insolence, involving a heavy penalty in waste of progress if not in tragical disaster.' He desperately hoped that Americans would have the wit 'to make a salad' of all the good ideas of the outside world—co-operation, socialism, trades-unionism, land resumption —and develop them, but the imperialistic ventures of the 'nineties worried him. 'I sometimes think I see chilling intimations that our whole destiny is to exhaust ourselves in creating another of the vast unities called empires,' he wrote in 1901, 'which by bringing the people together in masses promote universal brotherhood tho at the expense of the promoters.'

Socialism, he believed, counteracted this tendency. By 1903 he was ready to apply for membership, after having been assured that the party was tolerant enough to permit a certain latitude in the opinions of its members. According to his sister, Lloyd did not join the party then because he felt that such a move would impair his value as an advocate for municipal ownership of the Chicago traction system. Certainly his friends agreed. John Mitchell, with whom Lloyd had labored so arduously to win the epoch-making coal strike a few months before, advised against his joining. Richard T. Ely, the economist, and John R. Commons, the labor historian, concurred after Lloyd had asked their advice. But still other reasons may have had something to do with his decision to hold back.

As we have seen, Lloyd identified himself with the democratic wing of the Socialist party, with those who 'rallied precisely to prevent this proletarianization' regarded by the Marxians as necessary and who wished to unite all classes in the building of the new society. He could not see the logic of making 'a class movement of an agitation to abolish class.' He was a social reformer before he was a socialist, and the ideas of the doctrinaire socialist leaders discouraged him even as he was about to join them. In his last great crusade, for which he quite deliberately and consciously gave his life—the traction fight in Chicago—he had expected the Socialist party to take the leadership. Here, said Lloyd, was a cause that would educate the people in the techniques of public ownership and prepare them for the ultimate job of taking over the means of production. If it were successful, democracy would strike a hard blow against monopoly, remedy the working conditions of the employees, improve and cheapen the transit service, remove corrupt officials, and encourage the movement for public ownership of other utilities. But the Socialists held back on the grounds that the agitation would save the workingmen only a few cents. One of them even charged Lloyd with thinking like a professional reformer instead of like a wage earner.

Lloyd died before he could re-think his position on Socialism, and it is impossible to say whether or not he would have eventually joined the party. He had expended what little strength remained to him in trying to help the people reclaim their stolen privileges. In 1903 he died the way his predecessors had died, in harness, and like them was spared the pain of seeing a cherished measure go down once more beneath the concerted attack of money. Had Lloyd lived to see this defeat, he would not have despaired. He was used to defeat and preferred hard actualities to pleasant delusions.

I am actually frightened [he wrote in 1898] by the acceleration already begun of all the corruptions, scoundrelisms, privileges, tyrannies, growing so rapidly before. But I believe I can still see a greater sweep of good than of evil in the Titanic convulsions obviously ahead of us, and in that faith I rest with what security I can. It was an idle dream that *we* could progress from perfection to perfection while the Chinese ossified and the Cubans and Philippine people were disembowelled and the Africans continued to eat each other, and I am content to wake from it.

Lloyd remained an optimist, 'but not,' he said, 'for today—for some tomorrow.'

XII] Lloyd's career followed closely the lines laid down by Emerson in his famous remarks on the American Scholar. This was not an accidental parallel. 'I believe his to be the greatest mind of our times,' he had written to a friend in 1895, '—perhaps of all times. He seems to have absorbed all prior learning, and with this to have seen deeper into the mind of man and nature, and farther into the future than any other poet, or philosopher. . .' Emerson described Lloyd when he spoke of the Scholar as one 'who raises himself from private considerations and breathes and lives on public and illustrious thoughts.' From earliest manhood, Lloyd led a dedicated life, instinctively veering to the unpopular, unrepresented sides and expounding a secular religion of love and service.

He has no counterpart today, no one who can command the same respect, almost the adoration, of labor leaders, reformers, statesmen, and writers or who can show a record so utterly devoid of equivocation or moral weakness. He is probably the finest product of the middle-class conscience in our history, a hater of cant, a man of great passion, a believer in equality. What he said is of particular importance for us today, because he demonstrated so impressively how a middle position—gradualist, pragmatic, tolerant—can be vital and deeply radical at the same time. He rejected authority and absolutism whether it be socialistic or plutocratic. He reconciled association with individualism and showed that democracy and collectivism need not be contradictory conceptions. Patriotic as he was, he welcomed dissent and feared the subversive flag-waver more than the radical foreign-born.

The red, white and blue of the American flag [he said] has a hospitable democracy in its mingling of the signs of the classes which is good enough for me. But if any one wants to fly the ancient red cap of the slave as a banner I would prevent the proudest government on earth from interfering with him. Discontent has a better right to a hearing than content. Every new civilization began as discontent, and we can afford to tolerate the wildest dissents from everlasting to everlasting in the chance of hearing the voice of a Christ or an Emerson at intervals of a thousand years or so.

Thus spoke the genuine evangelical progressive.

CHAPTER 6

. . . .

William Dean Howells:
The Gentleman from Altruria

1] It is only a short jump from the journalism of exposure to the literature of exposure, from the social gospel of the
sermon to the social gospel of the novel. The works of William
Dean Howells simply embody in fiction the ethics and the economics of the progressive reformers. He, like them, expressed the
middle-class radicalism whose roots were not in some 'alien' literary
socialism but deeply implanted in the American experience.

The first blasts at both the genteel and vulgar scoundrelism of
the Gilded Age were not made by Marxists but by men who
measured civilization by agrarian standards. 'The depravity of the
business classes of our country,' Whitman wrote in 1871, 'is not
less than has been supposed, but infinitely greater.' As he turned
his 'moral microscope' upon the splendid new America, upon this
'mighty, many-threaded wealth and industry,' he saw 'a sort of dry
and flat Sahara . . . cities, crowded with petty grotesques, mal-
formations, phantoms, playing meaningless antics.' And Mark
Twain, who also carried with him a vision of 'a great moral and
religious civilization,' was forced to modify his expectations and to
admit, as Mr. DeVoto has said, 'that something must be wrong
with the whole process.' What had started out so gloriously in the
Hannibals of America was to end, Mark Twain believed, in 'stu-
pendous wealth' and 'moral blight.'

William Dean Howells agreed with his friend's opinions about
the plutocracy, but he refused to believe that mankind was irretrievably damned. Without entertaining any exalted ideas about

172

human capacities, he felt that it was possible to construct a society in which the jungle attributes would be refined, if not entirely eliminated, and in which men, without harm to themselves, could be kind to one another. His novels and writings are, in one sense, an expression of that hope as well as a repudiation of the state of affairs reported in the investigations of his close friend, Henry Demarest Lloyd.

II] 'I am reading your great book as I get the nervous strength for it,' Howells wrote to Lloyd in November 1894, 'and I find that it takes a good deal of nervous strength.' Stories of business thuggery and sordid anecdotes that dirtied the pages of *Wealth against Commonwealth* revolted Howells even more than they did his sensitive Chicago friend, but Howells, with the literary man's appreciation for skillfully presented dramatic incident, was tremendously excited about Lloyd's 'kinetoscopic impression' of business corruption and congratulated him for relating so powerfully his repulsive truths.

Some fourteen years earlier Howells had accepted Lloyd's first article on the Standard Oil monopoly for the *Atlantic*. Ever since that time the two men had become close and understanding friends, working for the same neglected causes and sending each other encouraging notes of appreciation.

Despite their similarity in taste and temperament, however, Howells and Lloyd were fundamentally different sorts of men. Howells was not a professional reformer and he never could have used the methods and tactics of Lloyd. More covert and circumspect, less impetuous, scrupulous to observe the decorums, Howells at first glance seems out of place among the colorful reformers, or at least outshone. There is a deceptive placidity about his long and honorable life, so respectable and apparently so unruffled, which contrasts strongly with the tumultuous careers of the others; and in confining themselves to his solidly Victorian attributes, his critics and friends have succeeded in hardening the conception of a polite, mousy, dun-colored man who carefully excluded unladylike details from his books and embroidered the commonplace.

Now there is a large amount of truth in this view. Howells

tended to transmogrify immorality into mental aberration, as James observed, and to avoid the strange and perverse as unsuitable themes for the chaste American muse. All of this is so obvious that one is tempted to ticket Howells once for all and to accept the often witty appraisals of his limitations as final. But if Howells is a fuddy-duddy, he is a complicated one, and he is by no means all of a piece or invariably predictable. Beneath the often tame and genteel surface of his work there runs a troubled and complex intelligence; the polite, whimsical, ironic tone of the genial editor is occasionally drowned out by accents of anger and despair. Reading his mellow commemorations of a wholesome America, those stories of kindly, well-fed people who take trips on their wedding anniversaries and fall into the most unhazardous predicaments, it is hard to remember that this same man could be chilly and bleak at times and express the most 'un-Howellsian' sentiments to his friends. The mystic who awoke at night in a room 'dense with spirits,' who made a religion of equality and sought out men like George, Bellamy, Gronlund, and Lloyd, who attended Socialist meetings and exploded to Mark Twain about American imperialism, merged with the decorous editor, the uneasily conventional citizen, the devotee of cultivated society.

This was no Jekyll-Hyde dichotomy, as we shall see, for Howells conceived of himself as both critic and apologist of the social order. The intensity of his social criticism grew in direct proportion to the popular deviation from his dream of material and spiritual sufficiency he evoked in his novels. He appreciated comfort, charm, good conversation, quiet elegance, simplicity, but he could not enjoy these amenities knowing that they were restricted to a privileged group. All of his social writing hinges on the problem of humanizing the rich and the poor alike and creating a carefully measured average out of the repulsive extremes—a middle-class 'Altruria.'

III] His idea of the civilized community, refined and democratic, must have originated in the Ohio days when, as a young man of nineteen with no family connections and little formal education, he was admitted freely to the best houses in Columbus and dined with the Governor. No one questioned his antecedents or the size of his bankroll. The ladies whom he found so attractive and attentive were much too interested in Thackeray or Heine or the latest poem in the *Atlantic Monthly*. It is true, as Howells later recalled with pain, that the Columbus of 1858 would not have welcomed the young poet-reporter if he had still been a typesetter, but Columbus, at any rate, was not New York City. 'There was an evener sky-line, with scarcely a sky-scraping millionaire breaking it anywhere.'

Men of leisure were rare in Columbus as elsewhere in America during this time, and their example, as Howells wrote later, was 'not one to make the Republic pine for that leisure class which the Old World finds indispensable to its government and refinement.' Hard work at a daily occupation seemed as natural to the young Howells as studying five languages at the same time. His father, William Cooper Howells, believed in the Swedenborgian principle that any person ought to have some useful job, and it is possible that Howells—who sat in a printing office before he was ten—derived his distaste for loafers and parasites from his unsuccessfully successful father.

Howells senior, an impractical son of an impractical father, never got very far in his long and somewhat feckless life, but his many failures, journalistic and commercial, did not sour him or poison the atmosphere of his household. Howells never received any material benefits from his family, but his mother gave him sympathy, and the winning example of his father, eager 'to get upon the common ground with every person and every thing,' provided him with a living embodiment of the model Christian Democrat. A gentle, good-humored man and a most understanding parent, he stood up to his libertarian principles before the Civil War, when it took courage to be an antislavery man in certain parts of Ohio, and after the war, when most of the abolitionists had lost their zeal for crusading. 'He could not look with content upon the present outcome of our social and political experiment,' Howells wrote in 1895, 'and he hoped, as I do, for a true commonwealth, in which those who work shall rule, and all shall work, in the spirit of liberty, equality, and fraternity.'

Howells never lost touch with his family beyond the Alleghenies, but after his New England pilgrimage in 1860 and his departure for Venice the next year, he had little desire to revisit the scenes of his boyhood, where he had been more miserable than happy. In *A Boy's Town* and *Years of My Youth,* the terror and anguish of his foreshortened boyhood are recounted with fidelity and feeling. The most striking quality of these ostensibly mellow evocations of village life in Ohio is not the occasional nostalgia for the simpler golden days, which intermittently shines through the sunnier portions of his reminiscences, but the steady undercurrent of fear and gloom that darkened his adolescence and youth.

Boyhood was a nightmare time, and the boys he wrote about were not the appealing barefoot urchins sentimentally reproduced by most forgetful adults, but unblinking little barbarians—cold, unformed, humorless, and cruel—who preferred a dead horse to a rose and who reveled in dirt. Howells's boys had no courage, no decency, no manliness. 'They lived in a state of outlawry, in the midst of invisible terrors, and they knew no rule but that of might.' To a sensitive and precocious boy, hag-ridden with guilt and subject to a thousand fears, the company of these venturesome savages must have been extremely unpleasant. Howells hurried himself out of his childhood as fast as he could and never pretended in later life to yearn for the primordial days long past. Even as a youth he longed for what he called 'the cleanly respectabilities,' and the 'worship of girlhood and womanhood,' he afterwards confessed, was probably stimulated by his revulsion from masculine brutalities. After he had become a reporter in the late 'fifties, he much preferred to write up a female seminary graduation or a Sunday sermon than to attend a police court. He gravitated instinctively toward those circles where the 'mumps and whooping coughs' of the world, as Emerson called them, were not so unbearably evident.

Howells left the West with a hunger for the genteel amenities and an unquestioned if untested faith in democracy. The curse of boyhood and the shadowy demonic world of his imagination lay behind him. Ahead lay the tolerant East, the four golden years in the Venetian consulate, and the pleasant New England interlude, during which the young editor found himself, as James A. Garfield reported to the elder Howells, in 'the centre of all that is best and brightest of the thought of Cambridge and Boston.'

IV] After completing the Boston-Cambridge-Concord circuit in 1860 and meeting the immortals—Lowell, Hawthorne, Holmes, Thoreau, and Emerson—in their own hallowed sitting rooms, Howells got his consulship in payment for his well-received campaign biography of Lincoln and spent the war years in Venice, conscientiously absorbing the culture around him for future use and yet retaining all the while the image of a 'cleaner, sweeter land' where people ate better and lived 'much purer and nobler and truer' lives than in any other place on the globe. The class distinctions of England and on the Continent affronted his ideas of village equality, and the 'filthy frankness' with which the Europeans indulged their vices disgusted him. A short time before, Hawthorne had told Howells that he would like to visit a part of America where 'the damned shadow' of Europe had not fallen; it was possibly with this conversation in mind that he wrote to his sister Victoria, 'The less we know of Europe, the better for our civilization.' He returned to the States in 1865 with a knowledge of Italian language and literature, and a strengthened urge to become a famous writer. The war, which had not seemed very important among the Titians and the Tintorettos, was over, and Howells now confronted a new industrial America, neither Ohioan nor Venetian, which would gradually impress itself upon his plastic mentality.

Until his thirties Howells had been living in a pre-industrial, a pre-evolutionary world. Cervantes, Pope, Goldsmith, Scott, and Irving molded his literary tastes, and eighteenth-century assumptions about man and his place in the universe, eighteenth-century ideas about unity, fraternity, and civilization cushioned his consciousness against the shocks of the new science. Darwinian ideas had not yet risen to plague him, and the blemishes of the factory age did not disturb his sensibilities. The momentary glimpse of industrial life he caught at Lowell while on his way to sacred Concord did not chill his raptures or disturb the blissful anticipations of his coming interviews. He had read *Walden* two years before, but it was not until he looked back upon the book after a lifetime of experience that he appreciated Thoreau's attack against 'industrial slavery, and the infinitely crueler and stupider vanity and luxury bred of it.' Certainly the sight of the Lowell factory girls walking home from work did not remind him of Thoreau's reflections on the business enterprise, 'protracted and unwearied,' which robbed the factory operative of 'the leisure for a true integrity' and rubbed away the finest qualities of his nature.

> In the cool of the evening [he afterwards wrote] I sat at the door of my hotel, and watched the long files of work-worn factory-girls stream by, with no concern for them but to see which was pretty and which was plain, and with no dream of a truer order than that which gave them ten hours' work a day in those hideous mills and lodged them in the barracks where they rested from their toil.

During the next twenty years, from 1866, when he took on the assistant editorship of the *Atlantic,* until 1885, when he moved to New York, Howells slowly made his way out of his clipped and hedged garden into the nineteenth-century jungle where the business carnivora prowled amidst a vast and purposeless disorder. He made his adjustment with greater ease and less soul-searching than his friend Samuel Clemens, but he too bore the scars of his struggle; his temper, prevailingly optimistic, was henceforth shot through with a gentle pessimism—despair would be too strong a word—and his manner became increasingly ironic. Clemens, whose violence and lack of discipline only aggravated his spiritual plight, never acquired Howells's balance and detachment; he was at once too much a part of his age and too much the alienated rebel. Howells, whose entire career seems at first glance to be a classic illustration of a man's cozy rapport with his times, always remained a critic, sometimes friendly, sometimes hostile, but slightly removed from his contemporaries. However timidly he capitulated to their conventions—indeed, capitulation is hardly the word, since it would probably not have occurred to him to do otherwise—the materialism, the appetites, and the morals of his generation never seduced him. He began his introduction to the new America a political and social innocent, but he had crossed the mountains eastward already indoctrinated with a village ethic that the Gilded Age could not corrupt. In 1866 Howells was an incipient rebel; his later radicalism had a kind of inevitability.

The liberal views of his father on all political and economic subjects certainly influenced the young Howells before he went East. John Brown was one of his boyhood heroes (and forever after a symbol of courage and indomitable will); Parker and Wendell Phillips he read in the columns of his father's *Ashtabula Sentinel*. During the winter of 1856 in Columbus, Howells became friendly with some of the German 'forty-eighters,' one of whom he later honored in the character of the revolutionary Lindau in *A Hazard of New Fortunes*. In fact most of the issues and themes he later discussed in his novels and essays—the immorality of capital punishment, the cruelty of class distinctions, the attractiveness of community life—were all ideas familiar to him before the war; and when the social problems of the post-bellum years began to concern him, he was able to draw upon his earlier experiences and associations and to apply the Swedenborgian injunctions of his father.

His continued interest in Swedenborg is revealing not only as another indication of his mystical bent but also as a clue to the religious basis of his socialism. Swedenborg's theology repelled him as he came to know a little more about it—all theology did for that matter—but Swedenborgian ethics, as they were distilled through the mind of the benignant William Cooper Howells, taught him to neglect forms and to do right 'from a love of doing right.' Swedenborg's God, whatever one might think of his angels and devils, was the great equalizer, and his books, according to Henry James senior, whom Howells read with profit and enjoyment, vindicated 'an intimate Divine presence' in all men's souls which would eventually 'obliterate all those superficial differences in human character upon which our social legislation has been based.' In an early review of James's *The Secret of Swedenborg* Howells praised the equalitarian doctrine of salvation through love and described hell not in terms of the Calvinist torture chamber but as a state in which the guilty are blind 'to the divine natural humanity.' This firmly fixed conviction of man's absolute equality before God Howells acquired early and retained even during the periods of religious doubt which followed.

Thus in tracing the gradual process of Howells's social awakening—an awakening variously attributed to his reading of Tolstoy, Gronlund, Björnson, George, Bellamy, and Richard T. Ely, or to the impact of the Haymarket riot and the subsequent industrial turmoil—one should not minimize his early and unconscious absorption of democratic notions. Howells came to Boston a bit of a prig and with no well-defined social philosophy, and yet under his editorship, especially during the 'seventies and early 'eighties, the *Atlantic* featured articles on Owenism, monopoly, labor unions, the Single Tax, and co-operatives in addition to the standard essays and stories. There seems to be no evidence, it is true, that the Bostonian pundits attempted to repress the young Westerner; the circle of acquaintances who now gathered about him encouraged him to be even bolder and more realistic in his work. But Howells's cautious animadversions on Boston snobbery, which began to appear in the early novels, reveal an underlying democratic bias that was pre-Boston, a bias implanted in Ohio and soon to become increasingly assertive.

It was during the 'eighties that Howells discovered the men who confirmed his vaguely thought-out, half-articulated ideals. In contrast to the other reformers taken up thus far, it is plain that Howells depended more upon the opinions and utterances of others. Some of these intellectual debts he publicly confessed; others he acknowledged in private letters or by the casual admissions in his reviews. We know, for instance, that he likened his discovery of Tolstoy 'to the old-fashioned religious experience of people converted at revivals,' and that his reading of the Russian novelist made him more fiercely equalitarian than ever. But what of the other influences? Laurence Gronlund, the gifted Dane whom Lloyd named a little exaggeratedly as 'one of the greatest thinkers of our time' and a person of a 'Goetheian grasp,' furnished Howells with many important suggestions when Howells was constructing his own co-operative commonwealth, *The Traveler from Altruria*, and Gronlund's influential books, some of which Howells reviewed, introduced him to Marxian ideas with their proletarian and revolutionary brambles carefully pruned. Henry George, whose *Progress and Poverty* had been favorably and unfavorably discussed in the

December 1880 issue of the *Atlantic Monthly,* offered no convincing solution to the American dilemma as far as Howells was concerned, but he respected George exceedingly (he knew him personally and visited him on occasion) and brought his land theories into several of his novels and essays. The experience of reading George, and more particularly Edward Bellamy, to whom he was deeply drawn, as we have seen, and whose gentleness and unaffectedness touched him sincerely, stirred him out of his lassitude and lingering complacence.

He found it difficult, however, to ally himself with a cause or an organized movement after he had brought himself around to a practical acceptance of its fundamental principles. He attended socialist meetings, 'quiet and orderly as a Sunday school,' where 'poorly dressed, well behaved' people listened patiently to hard facts, and he accepted the socialist platform in principle. But his support was always qualified. Certain fears about the dangers of intellectual repression under socialism possibly held him back. One would have thought that the Christian Socialists, many of whose ideas he sustained in his novels, would appeal to him particularly, but he told his father that he could not associate himself with a group so 'loaded up with the creed of the church, the very terms of which revolt me.' The Nationalists and the Single Taxers also appealed to him strongly, but he saw no reason to pin his hopes on the dream of either of their prophets. Anarchism, of course, except in the Emersonian sense, he rejected without reservation, even though he called the Haymarket affair 'an atrocious piece of frenzy and cruelty for which we must stand ashamed forever before history.' It became a significant incident in his development toward political maturity, but it made him no less critical of anarchism.

After an analysis of Howells's social philosophy during the years immediately preceding and following his move to New York in 1885, it can be seen that it was an essentially private and uncertainly held faith in equality and justice, tinctured with misgivings about the human material that had to work out the new society and yet optimistic about man's ultimate prospects. He had no doubts at all about the inadequacies of capitalist society and little patience with the defenders of the competitive order who scoffed at the

visions of the dreamers. He noted with amusement how some
people who shuddered at the very name of socialism found
Bellamy's collectivized world, safely catapulted into the next century, completely charming, and he later took pleasure in reminding hysterical conservatives who wrote sentimentally about the
Brook Farm Eden that the radicals of former days were no more
amiable than their present counterparts. 'There were then red-
mouthed abolitionists,' he told them, 'just as now there are red-
mouthed socialists; and the agitators of that period were not
shorter-haired, less incendiary, or less malevolent, in the general
eye, than the agitators of this.' And yet none of his theories or
criticisms, taken by themselves, showed much originality or audacity; indeed they were simply a mixture of humanitarian and
socialist sentiments, intuited and felt rather than painstakingly
thought out, which cast greater credit on his heart than his head.

What prevented Howell's from being merely derivative, a pale
literary echo of more forceful voices, was his skill and success in
serving the truisms of progressivism in palatable forms for his
family of middle-class readers. Howells belonged to this family by
birth and preference, articulating its highest aspirations and condemning its apostasy. He wanted to cure his erring brothers and
sisters and rid them of their false illusions, not to kill them; he
wanted them to share the satisfactions that had come with his own
emancipation and to make them conscious of their respectable
vices. His novels stood like a series of mirrors in which the middle
class beheld its comeliness and its deformity. Howells dwelt lov-
ingly on the kindness, the generosity, the homely decencies of the
middle-class men and women who talk and travel and love through
his long American chronicle; he was their poet as well as their historian. But their meannesses, their insensitivity to the misery of
the distant poor, their complacency and their unreflective materialism did not escape him. Ferocious satire and polemics, he knew,
would not cajole them out of sin; elegance, irony, good temper,
simplicity, moral fervor might prove more successful. He performed his delicate decapitations of pretense and snobbery with
'the weapon of contempt,' more to his taste than a bludgeon, and
avoided as much as possible the blunt and the shocking. In con-

trast to the Naturalists, Howells never enjoyed describing a beggar rooting around in a garbage can, even if he very occasionally introduced such unsavory episodes into his novels and sketches, but he dearly loved the edged remark casually dropped in the parlor, and he had a real facility for making snobbery and injustice appear hopelessly vulgar.

As a novelist and a psychologist, he was particularly concerned with the blighting effects of the capitalist ethic on the American personality, and he humanized and objectified the broader moral generalizations of the non-literary reformers. In effect, Howells documented the assumptions of Bellamy and George and of Theodore Parker, that 'brave, devoted friend of mankind,' as Howells described him. He preferred the vehicle of the novel to record the story of his social awakening rather than the conventional autobiography, because, as he said in *Years of My Youth,* 'No man, unless he puts on the mask of fiction, can show his real face or the will behind it. For this reason the only real biographies are the novels and every novel, if it is honest, will be the autobiography of the author and the biography of the reader.' His so-called economic novels (*The Minister's Charge,* 1887; *Annie Kilburn,* 1888; *A Hazard of New Fortunes,* 1890; *The World of Chance,* 1893; *A Traveler from Altruria,* 1894; *Through the Eye of the Needle,* 1907) are in part dramatic representations of his conversion to the progressive faith.

v] All of these novels were written after his departure from Boston, a fact of some interest but not so crucial as it might appear to be. Only three novels in the above-mentioned list have a New York locale, and two other novels of the later period, which show a strong social strain, *The Landlord at Lion's Head* (1897) and *The Son of Royal Langbrith* (1904), have New England settings. It simply happened that Howells's move to New York occurred at a time when social issues were becoming increasingly important to him, and that living in New York seemed to bring these issues—of which, to be sure, he was already aware—into a clearer and more terrifying focus. The big garish city with its extremes of wealth and want, its unlivableness, and its icy impersonality seemed to symbolize all that was hateful and ugly in capitalistic industrial civilization.

Some inkling of Howells's first reactions to New York may be gathered from the experiences of Basil March, his alter ego in *A Hazard of New Fortunes,* whose feelings about the monstrous purposelessness of the city paralleled those of his creator. 'The whole at moments seemed to him lawless, godless,' Howells writes; 'the absence of intelligent, comprehensive purpose in the huge disorder, and the violent struggle to subordinate the result to the greater good, penetrated with its dumb appeal the consciousness of a man who had always been too self-enwrapt to perceive the chaos to which the individual selfishness must always lead.' Here, spread out before his eyes, were the shocking illustrations of the Georgian paradox, Fifth Avenue luxury and East Side squalor, the *nouveaux riches* driving through Central Park in their four-in-hands and shiny landaus and the unemployed workingman lurking in the foliage 'like some forlorn wild beast.' In New York, Howells inhaled the smell of poverty, a smell he could never forget. He visited the tenements of the Irish and Jews on his East and West Side rambles, loathing the foulness and dirt and hideousness of the scene and yet struck, as he confessed after a trip through the Jewish quarter, 'by men's heroic superiority to their fate.'

His Tolstoyan attitude toward the poor and miserable revealed in his sadly humorous, ironic and compassionate pictures of New York slum life contrasts with the brilliantly aloof and unconsciously snobbish impressions of Henry James, who toured the same area several decades later. After Howells had spent a little time on the East Side, conditions in the teeming ghetto seemed less loathsome than he had first supposed. The humor, the 'decent tidiness,' the courage of the Jewish proletariat appealed to him, and he knew, as Henry James did not, something about the life in Russia from which many of them had recently escaped. 'They are then so like other human beings,' he told his readers, most of whom had never bothered to investigate for themselves, 'and really so little different from the best, except in their environment, that I had to get away from this before I could regard them as wild beasts.' Henry James did not regard them as wild beasts; he saw them rather as a frightening portent of the ethnic invasion, the swarming army that was fated to destroy the American identity and pervert American looks and language. The East Side Jews were not people to James, as they were for Howells, but some dark, alien, exotic force, a savage racial energy. He felt as if he had been dumped into 'some vast sallow aquarium in which innumerable fish, of overdeveloped proboscis' bumped together 'amid heaped spoils of the sea.' Howells, who had no curious notions of racial purity and could not understand the seaboard aristocracy's fear of contamination, saw the same swarming ghetto for what it was, a part of the fascination and horror of New York. The great city, rank with life for his realist's pen, continuously offended his village sensibilities.

A Hazard of New Fortunes is, in part, a journal of these New York years, an expression of his sympathy for the men and women trapped in the city's gigantic maze. Howells must have been pleased with its reception (everyone from Henry James to Rutherford B. Hayes went into ecstasies over it), for its episodes of violence, poverty, and martyrdom were not usually the sort he enjoyed writing. The novel, which centered around the affairs of Mr. and Mrs. Basil March and the operation of a magazine owned by a pathetic and corrupted millionaire and managed by a brazen entrepreneur, was in still another respect a vision of big-city life by a man who had never dared look directly at the misery and unhappiness around him. March's aestheticism gradually dissolved before the realities of the drab squeezed-out humanity dumbly pressing against him, and it suddenly came to him, as it did to Howells, that the happy never see unhappiness because they never feel obliged or inclined to look for it.

Howells tried to show at the same time how capitalist values corrupt painlessly and quietly without the victims' being aware of the disease eating away their better nature. It was not simply old Dryfoos who underwent what Howells called 'a moral deterioration, an atrophy of the generous instincts,' his sagacity 'turned into suspicion, his caution to meanness, his courage to ferocity.' Millions of young Americans, those fated to succeed and the unsuccessful aspirants, made his career their 'ideal and ambition,' all of them driven by the same fear of insecurity for themselves and their families. 'And so we go on,' March continued,

pushing and pulling, climbing and crawling, thrusting aside and trampling underfoot; lying, cheating, stealing; and when we get to the end, covered with blood and dirt and sin and shame, and look back over the way we've come to a palace of our own, or the poor-house, which is about the only possession we can claim in common with our brother-men, I don't think the retrospect can be pleasing.

No matter where one looked in New York, in Wall Street or among the push-cart capitalists of the East Side, the blood-thirsty game continued, each contender haunted by the prospect of failure, which, Howells believed, 'every man has in his secret soul, and which the man who has known want must have in greater measure than the man who has never known want.' But the common danger of poverty did not unite the competitors or make the rich love the poor. The majority simply accepted the rule of chance and did not bother to understand why they succeeded or failed or why an economy ought to continue 'which perpetuates their inequality, and makes a mock out of the polity which assures them their liberty.' To Howells's astonishment and annoyance, the Americans submitted themselves to the cash nexus as fatalistically as they did to the weather and to all of the capitalistic ritual and folklore of which it was a part. And Howells was sure that as long as false standards endured and 'having and shining' were dignified as the highest ends by our business civilization, men would go on encouraging their children to perform the traditional dirty stratagems until, as March said, 'some heroic few of us, who did not wish our children to rise above their fellows—though we could not bear to have them fall below—might trust them with the truth.'

New York had quickened him in spite of the fact that it was no place for a man to live, and Howells's novels began to show a growth and maturity, in substance if not in form, which delighted his good friend William James. 'You couldn't possibly have done so solid a piece of work as that ten years ago, could you?' James asked after reading *A Hazard of New Fortunes*. William's brother Henry, who had for some years been urging Howells to exorcize the 'romantic phantoms' still plaguing his fancies and to become the American Balzac, took particular pleasure in Howells's steady progress toward realism, and although he evidently did not care for most of the American types displaying themselves in his friend's crowded streets, he enormously appreciated the view from Howells's luminous window. 'It's because,' he told him, 'you open so well and are hung so close over the street that I could hang out of it all day long.' *A Hazard of New Fortunes* succeeded, James wrote to Howells, 'as a triumph of *communication*.' The novels of Howells after 1885 were probably no more 'solid' or vivid than the earlier ones, but they dealt with live and controversial issues and probed into areas, previously skirted, about which there was an increasing popular interest. Bellamy, along with Henry and William James, sensed this when he wrote to Howells in 1888: 'You are writing of what everybody is thinking and all the rest will have to follow your example or lose their readers.'

Whether or not the sights and scenes of New York were chiefly responsible for his sharpened awareness of the world about him, it is apparent by the middle 'nineties that Howells's loosely thought-out social views had hardened into something resembling a philosophy of society. In the novels already mentioned and in the essays he contributed to the periodicals, his ideas on plutocracy, equality, and government emerged with greater distinctness than they had before; it could at last be seen where he was heading and how far he would go, what aspects of American life disturbed him the most, and what he thought could be done to remove their offensive presences. Howells always remained a bit of the 'amiable and sentimental dreamer' Victor Yarros made him out to be (he half recognized the symptoms himself), but he was intelligent and sensitive too, and his diagnoses of the plutocratic age are valuable in the same way that Whitman's or Mark Twain's are.

The comments of Howells on wealth and its ugly manifestations are less violent than Mark Twain's eruptions and less satisfying, too, in certain respects, because we miss in them the honest rage, the blurted-out truthfulness of the unpremeditated outburst. But if Howells's strictures were more discreet than those of his friend in Hartford, he was less confused by the duplicities and beguilements of the enemy and never unconsciously identified himself with the forces he criticized; he had less of the capitalist ethos in himself to combat, and he had a better knowledge of his own moral limitations.

Who are the plutocracy? Howells asked. In his many answers he described the plutocracy as a vast body of people comprising not only the businessmen who 'made' money as contrasted with the workers who 'earned' it, but any person, bloated or lean, with the millionaire psychology, any person who burned to be rich, whether he failed in business or succeeded, whether he owned a factory or worked in the shops. Plutocracy, in short, was a state of mind. Howells had some rather naïve things to say about the absurdity of the wage-earner's zeal to perpetuate an injurious economic system, but he saw with particular astuteness how the values of capitalism corrupted democracy and destroyed national solidarity, and he understood the part played by the plutocracy in this demoralizing process.

The causes of the rise of the plutocratic class, Howells believed, lay embedded in our history. From the very beginnings of American national life 'the business spirit' assumed its dominion. No rival traditions, no established classes, blocked the way of the trader, and it required only a little time before the manufacturer and the businessman filled in the democratic vacuum and became the bona fide aristocracy. During the supercharged ante-bellum days when the slavery question raised politics to a high theoretical and moral level and the national crisis diverted the minds of most men from purely materialistic considerations, the business spirit had been somewhat checked. Howells remembered this period 'before the era of our immense material prosperity,' when the noble and civic-minded type was not such a rarity and the millionaire had not yet been canonized. After the war, according to Howells, the motives that had carried politics 'upward and onward' disappeared.

They became, in a sense, business affairs, with no question but the minor question of civil-service reform to engage the idealist's fancy or the moralist's conscience. After the war we had, as no other people had in the world, the chance of devoting ourselves strictly to business, of buying cheap and selling dear, and of marketing our wares at home and abroad.

The country's natural richness allowed for a standard of living that made possible the 'smiling realities' Howells so dearly loved to picture, but it also produced the terrible paradoxes he had read about in *Progress and Poverty* and had seen for himself in New York. He began to think more about 'the defects of our advantages.' Thus he could write in the vein of Bellamy and Lloyd during the 1894 depression:

If we have built many railroads, we have wrecked many; and those vast continental lines which, with such a tremendous expenditure of competitive force, we placed in control of the monopolies, have passed into the hands of receivers, the agents of an unconscious state socialism. The tramps walk the land like the squalid spectres of the laborers who once tilled it. The miners have swarmed up out of their pits, to starve in the open air. In our paradise of toil, myriads of workingmen want work. . . The public domain, where in some sort the poor might have provided for themselves, has been lavished upon corporations, and its millions of acres have melted away as if they had been a like area of summer clouds.

Capitalism split American society 'financially, industrially, economically' into congeries of 'infinitely repellent particles' and actually produced the state of nature described by Hobbes.

The moralist in Howells was outraged by a system that not only encouraged erring men to sin by holding up a vicious standard for success but allowed the innocent to suffer with the guilty money-chasers. He by no means discounted human responsibility—he was too much of a realist and a psychologist for that. But Howells placed the blame for the brutishness of man on the conditions in which he found himself and could not escape. 'We can't put it all on the conditions; we must put some of the blame on character,' Basil March declared, but he added that 'conditions make character.' Howells was not struck so much by the amount of human degeneration he saw about him—how could it be otherwise?—as he was by the 'kindliness and good-nature,' the 'symmetry and proportion' that could be faintly discerned even among the most depraved and wretched.

Capitalism drew out and nurtured human vices like a malevolent sun, ripening moral weaklings like the embezzler J. M. Northwick

in *The Quality of Mercy* and ranker specimens like Royal Langbrith, who lived a lie all of his life and almost had it enshrined
after his death. Capitalism brought security and comfort to many,
but 'the holiday expression of the vast prosperous commercial
class, with unlimited money, and no ideals that money could not
realise,' did not begin to compensate for the slums the well-to-do
never bothered to find out about.

Nobody understood better than Howells the little dodges and
stratagems practiced by the *bourgeoisie* to rationalize away their
sense of guilt; it was a form of self-deception he had used too often
himself to be deceived when he saw it tried by others. He knew
precisely the emotions of the dunned pedestrian who realizes perfectly well that street beggars ought not to be encouraged and fin-
gers desperately for a coin small enough to protect the supplicant
from being debauched and large enough to appease his own conscience. He was a master of the ironic and amusing homily in
which he said bitter things with an air of whimsy.

In many of his novels, Howells dealt extensively with the amiable
and self-indulgent sentimentalists, 'so easily moved to any cheap
sympathy,' but his most careful treatment of charity and the rich-
poor relation appears in *Annie Kilburn,* a story of what happens
in a small New England community when some well-intentioned
and obtuse Lady and Gentleman Bountifuls try to impose their
charity on a village yeomanry that will not be patronized. Annie,
soon revolted by the attitude and methods of her equals, switches
to the party of the stubborn poor led by a radical minister and
supported by a caustic but high-minded alcoholic lawyer. Annie's
shift to the left occurs fairly early in the book. The Reverend Mr.
Peck, a more countrified and active Conrad Dryfoos (the millionaire's martyred son in *A Hazard of New Fortunes*), is responsible for her first misgivings when he assures her that money 'can't
create sympathy between rich and poor,' only common experience
can do that. Peck shows her, as Putney the lawyer rephrases it,
that instead of being the kindly benefactress she first imagined
herself to be, 'she was a moral Cave-Dweller, and that she was
living in a Stone Age of social brutalities.' Chided by Hamlin
Garland for not demanding justice instead of alms, Howells re-

torted with every right that 'from first to last' *Annie Kilburn* was 'a cry for *justice,*' and although his book was not the Single Tax tract Garland would have liked it to be, it indicated Howells's dissatisfaction with a society that substituted a face-saving charity for true fellowship.

The letters he wrote during 1888, the year of *Annie Kilburn's* publication, show a preoccupation with this question. He was convinced, he wrote to Henry James, that everything would turn out badly unless civilization based 'itself anew on a real equality,' and he was no longer sure, he told Edward Everett Hale, that America offered the same chance for every man to develop the best within him. Hayes saw that this was what Howells was implying in *Annie Kilburn* and wondered if there were a word that would describe 'the doctrine of true equality of rights. Its foes call it nihilism, communism, socialism and the like,' he noted in his journal. 'Howells would perhaps call it justice. It is a doctrine of the Declaration of Independence, and of the Sermon on the Mount. But what is a proper and favorable word or phrase to designate it?'

Howells preferred the simple word 'equality' to describe the theme of *Annie Kilburn* and, indeed, the philosophy behind most of his other social novels. The poor and the excluded wanted brotherhood, to be related in a broad spiritual kinship which would 'enlarge itself to the bounds of humanity as fast as people learn that in likeness there is the only rest and comfort and pleasure that man can know.' Likeness united; difference divided. Men sought out their fellows with kindred interests, the patrician mingling with his equals because inferiors made him uneasy, the plebeian staying with his own kind because his superiors made him uncomfortable. Equality seemed to obtain only during crises or in new civilizations where personal worth commanded a special value; it had long disappeared in America.

In contrast to Europe, to be sure, America was an equalitarian society, as yet unsullied by the heritage of old ancestral wrongs and blessed or cursed (depending upon one's perspective) by a burgher nobility which both inspired and depressed writers like Stendhal or Henry James. Even our inequality lacked the picturesqueness of the European, because everyone in America looked alike and dressed alike, the difference merely being in the quantity, quality, cleanliness, or newness of the dress. No matter how hard the would-be American aristocrat tried to emulate his authentic European cousin, he could not catch that 'last wicked grace of the aristocracy.' He could assert his wealth, but wealth was a transitory thing and conspicuous display did not impress as inherited elegance did. For James, the flatness and anonymity of America, its apparent classlessness and general dead-levelness were uncongenial or at least unsuitable for the novelist, and by implication for the sensitive intellectual. The American landscape did not seem so flat and barren to Howells, perhaps because his post of observation was closer than James, and he completely rejected the Jamesian contention as a kind of unconscious justification, even if on aesthetic grounds, for social inequality. He had to protest, pleasantly but firmly, that James was wrong.

Ethically speaking, James's artistic predilection meant that the inferior, who never enjoyed his picturesque inequality in real life, would be ignored or patronized, and artistically speaking, Howells would not admit that equality ruled out the picturesque. Bellamy's utopia corroborated his feeling that variety and individuality flourished when men lived in terms of social and economic democracy, and he saw the ridiculousness as well as the cruelty in the American plutocracy's efforts to establish a native aristocracy. The great leaders produced in the United States who towered over their contemporaries—the Franklins and the Lincolns—soared from their common origins precisely because there were no Jamesian paraphernalia, no aristocracy, court, sovereign, church, to keep them down. Our great men, Howells wrote,

are notable for their likeness to their fellow-men, and not for their unlikeness; democracy has subtly but surely done its work; our professions of belief in equality have had their effect in our life; and whatever else we lack in homogeneity, we have in the involuntary recognition of their common humanity by our great men something that appears to be peculiarly American, and that we think more valuable than the involuntary assumption of superiority, than the distinction possible to greatness, among peoples accustomed to cringe before greatness.

Americans would never tolerate a society based upon European distinctions, that he knew, but a plutocracy was, if anything, worse, and the American people above all others had to watch lest they succumb to the lure of the material, which Emerson, the philosopher of equalitarianism, had warned against. Howells looked upon his countrymen as 'a practical, patient, straightforward people, vulgarized as all commercial peoples must be by the war of interests, but lifting themselves above them when there is a supreme need.' He hoped that they would somehow become dematerialized and respond to their better natures, and he looked upon the middle-class intellectuals to provide a persuasive example for both the 'Plutes' and the masses. 'Have the inventions, the good books, the beautiful pictures and statues, the just laws, the animal comforts, even,' he asked, 'come from the uppermost or the lowermost classes? They have mostly come from the middle classes, from the community lifted above want, but not above work, from the inexhaustible and generous vitality of the widest level of life.' Howells called upon the middle-class leaders to remember and respect their trust: 'They must never forget that they are the best company, or suffer themselves in their meekest moments as individuals to relax the collective consciousness of their social primacy.'

vi] Howells's belief in social equality, his hatred of distinctions and his devotion to the great average determined his aesthetic as well as his political theory, an identification Henry James did not really approve of. Indeed, it would not be too far-fetched to say that his well-known arguments in behalf of realism in literature grew directly out of his equalitarian postulates. As James noted, Howells glorified the simple and the plebeian. What he praised most in a man like Franklin, for example, who seems to have attracted Howells on many scores, was not his genius or his success. Franklin, he wrote, 'was rather a blackguardedly newspaper man, a pitiless rival, a pretty selfish liberal politician, and at times (occasionally the wrong times) a trivial humorist.' He really loved Franklin's commonness, which prevented him from assuming 'any superiority of bearing, and the unconscious hauteur which comes of aristocratic breeding.' Washington bore the stamp of the patrician; Hamilton had it, and even Jefferson, who tried hard not to have it; but Franklin, their great antitype, touched the masses in a way that the glittering aristocrats never could. Howells found more literary inspiration, as an artist, in the commonness of a Franklin or a Lincoln than in all the man-made hierarchies of the world. In America, he wrote,

such beauty and such grandeur as we have is common beauty, common grandeur, or the beauty and grandeur in which the quality of solidarity so prevails that neither distinguishes itself to the disadvantage of anything else . . . these conditions invite the artist to the study and appreciation of the common, and to the portrayal in every art of those finer and higher aspects which unite rather than sever humanity. . . The arts must become democratic, and then we shall have the expression of America in art.

The bearing of this sentiment on the doctrine of Realism is plain, for what is Realism, in the Howellsian sense, but a mean or average between a meretricious and glittering romanticism (the literary equivalent of the plutocracy) and a sordid, Zolaesque, and repulsive Naturalism (the literary equivalent of the proletariat)? Howells saw the stock hero of the popular romance, with 'his vain posturings and ridiculous splendor,' very much in the same light as he sees one of Ward McAllister's' New York nabobs, 'a painted barbarian, the prey of his passions and his delusions, full of obsolete ideals, and the motives and ethics of a savage.' The writers who exalt such pasteboard personages and who glorify the cheap sentiments of a synthetic nobility really encourage the divisive tendencies in society, the 'folly and insanity, egotism and prejudice' that freeze human sympathies and hide the real world with a gaudy curtain of lies.

He had little more sympathy for romanticism's dirt-besmeared polar opposite, Naturalism, which likewise (he felt) distorted the truth under the guise of a false scientism and which discouraged fraternity by its undue emphasis on men's brutish nature. The Naturalist's fondness for violent contrasts and exaggeration (really an unconscious romantic urge, he once noted in discussing Zola) necessarily led to distortion when the American scene was under consideration, because American conditions did not lend themselves to the Naturalist's sensational vision any more than they did to the romanticist's. The frankness of a Zola or a Norris or a

Dreiser appalled him, he candidly admitted, but he tried (although not always successfully) to keep his objections on non-personal grounds and to criticize the extreme realists for offending against truth rather than against his squeamish sensibilities. Certain themes and subjects he neither cared nor dared to write about, and he did not like to have them treated by others; he was neurotically fastidious. And yet Zola, whom he had ferociously damned in 1877 for 'diving down into unutterable defilement,' he defended in 1902, for by this time Howells belonged to the radical camp and had somewhat modified his views on what constituted the American average. He retained, however, the Realist's passion for the neutral, his hatred of excess, and created his own kind of idealized society—gentle, humane, genial, polite, and intelligent—which he had once assumed was characteristically American and which he still thought possible to attain.

In the writings of Gronlund and especially in the books of Edward Bellamy, whose ideas and style, from Howells's point of view, were eminently democratic, he found support for his realistic position. Bellamy illustrated the truth, as his predecessor Hawthorne did, 'that the fancy does not play less freely over our democratic levels than the picturesque inequalities of other civilizations,' and he never patronized his readers. Like Emerson, Bellamy did not hesitate to use 'a phrase or a word that was common to vulgarity, if it said what he meant,' and he held forth the same Howellsian hope that an Altruria where 'every man is a gentleman, and every woman a lady' might develop out of the American experiment.

Howells's own little socialist pastoral, *A Traveler from Altruria,* and its sequel, *Through the Eye of the Needle,* most certainly derived from *Looking Backward* as well as from William Morris, Mazzini, Campanella, Ruskin, and Plato. The descriptions of the Altrurian commonwealth read like nostalgic recollections of Brook Farm and the innocent fabrications of Arthur Brisbane.

The account of the Altrurian emissary's experiences in the United States, his romance, and his return to his homeland with his American wife makes up the story of these two earnest if not artful books. In the first, Mr. Homos, the Altrurian, engages in a series of informal conversations with representative Americans during a few weeks' sojourn in a New England summer resort. A candid, perceptive banker, a narrow and opinionated professor, a blunt but well-meaning manufacturer entirely devoted to his own self-interest, a humane doctor (very briefly presented), a cool objective lawyer, and a timid and wishy-washy minister speak for America and betray their country's hollowness under the questioning of the devastatingly naïve Altrurian. Mr. Homos, taking the protestations of American democracy quite literally, is startled to discover by ear and by eye that America is a plutocracy crisscrossed with class barriers, a country where freedom of opportunity is a carefully cultivated myth and the values of business are unquestioned by the majority. In the United States the community is systematically despoiled in the name of individualism, and the exploiters, faced with the disparity between what they affirm and what they do or see, either resort to euphemisms (workers are 'laid off,' not 'left to starve') or fall back upon a cynical indifference.

The contrasting picture of Altruria, as described by Mr. Homos in *A Traveler from Altruria* and by his American wife in the sequel, is a genteel vision of America *in posse,* for it is made clear that Altruria emerged from a similar sort of plutocracy. Altruria turns out to be a kind of superextension of the White City at the World's Columbian Exposition (that is the only analogy Mrs. Homos can think of when she tries to describe her new home to her friends in America!), a place of sanity and peace, where people dress sensibly and attractively, eat various varieties of edible mushrooms, and have a good deal of time to cultivate themselves. No unsightly megalopolis like New York City, makeshift and hideous, mars the Altrurian landscape. The continent is regionalized, decentralized, electrified, spanned by magnificent highways, and converted into a harmony of grass and trees and white marble; even the factories nestle in bosky nooks. The external beauty of Altruria, however—rather tepidly presented by Howells, as heavenly bliss must always be—is really secondary; it is only a pale reflection of an inner beauty and purity that are to him far more important.

Altruria is the neighborly village on a grand scale. Odious class distinctions and the frenzied struggle for survival have passed away like a nightmare, and a man can be a gentleman unashamedly, knowing that his good fortune does not rest upon the misfortune of others. Advances in machine techniques have ended the necessity of back-breaking tasks and long hours, and the archaic pleasures in artistic craftsmanship, the delight in work for its own sake, are recovered. Men live for each other rather than on each other; the co-operative ideal permeates all of the Altrurian institutions. There are no police courts where the victims of capitalist society are publicly humiliated, no cruel ostentation, no parasitical leisured minority.

In this dream-world full of healthy, happy, and intelligent people, Howells reconciled his fondness for cultivated society and the high-toned amenities he enjoyed so much with his passion for justice. A theoretical socialist, he was at the same time, as he told Mark Twain, a practical aristocrat, and he suffered all the guilty emotions that such a paradoxical position compels. When Howells was a young man, he had some of the qualities of his narrator in *A Traveler from Altruria,* the snobbish, narrow Mr. Twelvemough, who listened to the Altrurian's criticisms of American society with an annoyance all the more intense because he recognized their validity. Mr. Homos put him in an uncomfortable position. Plutocracy put Howells also in an uncomfortable position, and he somehow felt bound to needle the class he described and represented, the class whose good impulses he trusted in so implicitly and whose stupidity and callousness he believed it was his duty to expose.

The middle class showed up best in those communities not entirely given up to money-making and worst in the business metropolis. Altruria, therefore, had to avoid the ennui of the country town, shut off from the advantages as well as from many of the evils of the great world, and to introduce some of the bucolic restfulness of the village into the city, 'getting,' as Howells said, 'the good of the city and the country out of the one into the other.' Community experiments like Brook Farm and New Harmony, and religious groups like the Shakers at Shirley had partially solved the problem on a small scale, but, said Howells, speaking through one of his characters, 'the community saved itself from chance by shutting out the rest of the world. It was selfish too. The Family must include the whole world.' World salvation would be possible only under a democratic socialism where the public could not be battered, insulted, and degraded by the 'corporate collectivities' in the name of individualism.

Howells never shared Bellamy's faith that the peaceful revolution would occur in his own or his children's lifetime, nor did he expect either of the two great parties, as they were then constituted, to legislate his utopia, but he wrote to his father in 1890 that he anticipated the rise of a new party 'that will mean true equality and real freedom, and not the images we have been mocked with hitherto. The poor Negroes,' he went on to say, 'whom we laughed at for expecting the government to give them each "forty acres and a mule," have a truer ideal of a civilized state than the manufacturers who want more and more tariff but won't raise their workmen's wages a cent.' He already detected a decline in national complacency during the 'nineties and welcomed the American people's healthy awareness that their economy was sick; they would continue to grope, he predicted, 'in the unexplored regions beyond the republic for some yet more vital democracy, or equality, or fraternity, to save us from the ruin into which our own recreancy may have plunged us.'

During the last years of the Austrian oppression, when Howells occupied the Venetian consulship, he had sympathized with the Italians in their struggle for political liberty, and yet, as he admitted later, he would have scoffed at their unconscious expectation of economic security. He later abandoned what he considered his callow and thoughtless prejudice and came to realize that safety or security from want is as much a part of real liberty as the opportunity to cast a ballot every few years. Only a person assured of his livelihood could be called free, and only a free man was truly responsible. A democratic society in fact and not merely in name would see to it that this kind of freedom was the privilege of all and not merely the few, for in its restricted form, liberty might lapse into tyranny. As the Reverend Mr. Peck told his Hatboro congregation, 'In the political world we have striven forward to liberty as to the final good, but with this achieved we find that liberty is only a means and not an end, and that we shall abuse it as a means if we do not use it, even sacrifice it, to promote equality.' If, in the name of liberty, an individual could and did jeopardize the rights of others, Howells concluded that 'we can enjoy liberty only in its ultimate form of safety, and we can not any one of us, or any part of us, be safe, unless all the rest are safe, for the insecurity of others is the perpetual menace of our own security. We must somehow be equals in opportunity and in safety or we cannot be free.'

The savagery in American life, the remorseless ethics of trade, which ruled out any mercy for the weak or the unlucky, Howells attributed, as the other reformers did, to an all-pervasive fear of want—that sacred incentive of the *bourgeoisie* 'worthy of as much veneration as capital punishment.' Only the rich and the safe could afford the luxury of generosity in a capitalist society; self-sacrifice, the freedom to accept an obligation, was the prerogative of the wealthy alone. If this was true, as Howells believed it was, society had no right to demand an equal sacrifice from those who were denied the freedom of choice and whose very existence depended upon the terms and duration of their employment. When all men were sure of their livelihood, then they too would begin to exhibit the generosity and self-sacrifice, the Altrurian civility, which is characteristic of freemen and gentlemen.

These ideas about equality and security bore an obvious relation to the whole question of labor, which had weighed on Howells's mind since the beginning of the great strikes in the middle 'eighties. He never approved of strikes and labor violence in themselves, but he appreciated, he once wrote, the 'savage necessity of self-assertion, in the warfare which manifests itself in strikes, riots, mutinies, murders.' The workers naturally enough wanted the same liberties enjoyed by their employers, not more; and although the ostensible issues of labor disputes hinged on wages and hours, at bottom Howells saw the 'question of more power, more ease, more freedom.' For the individual workingman trying to sell himself in an employer's market, alienated from his co-workers and alone in an impersonal world of chance, the only way to preserve his identity was to join a union and to apply what Howells called 'the principle of simultaneity,' or the pressing forward 'toward a common point from every side at the same moment.'

The working class, trapped in 'the underworld of overwork,' had never taken this lesson to heart, Howells frequently remarked, and he counseled a reliance upon the ballot rather than the strike. As Mr. Bullion, the canny banker, observed to Mr. Homos:

> Those fellows throw away their strength whenever they begin to fight, and they've been so badly generaled, up to the present time, that they have wanted to fight at the outset of every quarrel . . . when they have learned enough to begin by voting, then we shall have to look out.

Howells openly and privately criticized the high-handed methods of the bosses who refused to arbitrate and manipulated public opinion through a kept press, but he believed with his fire-eating lawyer in *Annie Kilburn* that the working class could escape its thralldom any time it wished. Unfortunately, 'workingmen *as* workingmen' were 'no better or wiser than the rich *as* the rich,' and 'quite as likely to be false and foolish.' The tactics they employed were just as much a part of the system of competition as the lockout and the shutdown of the employer. Their only salvation lay in a people's socialism voted in accordance with democratic procedures, operated in the interests of the majority, and inspired by the scholars, artists, and humanitarians. These were the free people whose passion and indignation had prompted most of the great reforms, who had first dreamed 'the vision of the soft-handed scholar Plato' and the 'English gentleman, Sir Thomas More,' and who were alone qualified by character and intelligence to redeem a trapped civilization.

In the Altruria of Mr. Homos, the people regarded the man who had given 'the greatest happiness to the greatest number—some artist, or poet, or inventor, or physician' as the national hero; in the America of William Dean Howells, the rich businessman was the cynosure of the less successful as well as the national oracle, ready to make announcements or give opinions on any issue. Howells in his gentle and ironic way tried to show his countrymen the triviality of their ideal, not by portraying the business elite as a set of ogres (that would have dignified and denigrated them more than he intended) but by quietly contradicting their assumptions and by demonstrating how they were being corrupted by their own values. He held up for examination not only the Dryfooses and the Langbriths but also their petty reflections such as Mr. Gerrish, the unshrinking self-made merchant in *Annie Kilburn,* who proclaimed to the Hatboro ladies:

> I have always made it a rule, as far as business went, to keep my own affairs entirely in my own hands. I fix the hours, and I fix the wages, and I fix all the other conditions, and I say plainly, 'If you don't like them, don't come,' or 'don't stay,' and I never have any difficulty.

Howells's own feeling toward such men was curiously complicated if his literary protagonists or his sensitive young heroes are in part reflections of his own personality. Apparently he resented the average American male's contempt for the man of literature; he resented being patronized by insensitive automatons who looked upon novels as playthings for their wives. No one glorified the American female more than Howells or delineated with more devotion her charm and brightness and sympathy, but he saw perfectly well the implications of her cultural dominance, and they were not flattering to him or his profession. At the same time, if we can judge from his books, he must have been uneasy, almost afraid, of the businessmen who provided the leisure for the women; his counterparts are always made to feel their inadequacy when confronted by these strong, coarse-grained and sometimes vulgar money-getters.

This ambivalent feeling toward the businessman resembled Emerson's in the sense that Howells also admired power and strength; he, too, dignified aggressiveness and enterprise. But both men, having acknowledged the vulgar vitality of business and the self-reliance of its devotees, gave the palm to the scholar-artists, the passive doers, the utopian planners. It was their way of telling the mercenary generations that intelligence and spirit were more basic than cash, and for Howells, at any rate, it made up for the rebuffs he felt as a western outsider never quite at home in the *beau monde* of Boston and New York, where lineage and wealth counted for so much and natural abilities for so little.

His own brilliant success in both cities would seem to contradict such a conclusion; as far as Lowell or Oliver Wendell Holmes were concerned, he had fit in beautifully with his new surroundings. But just as Howells's roly-poly figure—in spite of his inveterate correctness and the care he lavished on his clothes—seemed almost incongruous when contrasted with the elegant and graceful appearances of his high-born heroes, so his imported young men from the provinces, who seem so completely easternized or urbanized, are nevertheless detached and separated; they feel and are made to feel their difference. Jeff Durgin, the virile and engaging hero of *The Landlord at Lion's Head,* who comes as close to the primitive as Howells ever dared go, never quite looks right in his clothes, although they are identical with those worn by the young aristocrats in the Harvard Yard, and he remains a 'Jay,' snubbed by his betters and excluded from the charmed circle. And Howells too, despite his protective coloration, his almost excessive good breeding and gentility, never really belonged in Boston or New York, though he was happier in those places than he ever could have been in Jefferson. He could not live in the West, that intolerant region haunted by 'terrible water drinkers' and topers, by saints and sinners, but it remained for him a kind of spawning ground for the vigorous and the talented, the men and women destined to dissolve the artificial barriers of the seaboard.

Did this feeling of alienation, this hunger for acceptance he so cleverly concealed, help to strengthen his more or less theoretical socialism? The almost stern way in which he rules out variations in food and dress in his utopia and prohibits any manifestation of the private and the exclusive would seem to show that he felt more deeply about the slights experienced by his characters and the amusing arrogance of the socially and economically secure than he let out. We know, for instance, from his essay 'I Talk of Dreams' (more revealing than he supposed) that he dreamed more than once 'of being slighted or snubbed in society.' In one of these dreams, he relates how he attended a fashionable gathering and felt quite at home. He was modishly dressed, talked brilliantly, and was pleasantly conscious of his own aristocratic manner. Turning away from the group of ladies he had been entertaining, he heard one of them say to the rest 'in a tone of killing condescension and patronage, "I don't see why that person isn't as well as another." ' Howells interpreted this dream as an illustration of his inherent snobbery. 'If I am,' he concluded, 'I cannot help hoping that it will not be found out; and in my dreams I am always less sorry for the misdeeds I commit than for their possible discovery.' Howells always tried to be honest about himself, and the fact that he deprived his Altrurians of every vestige of private opulence—rich foods, lavish clothes, of anything, in short, that smacked of the luxurious —is significant, because Howells enjoyed the good things of the plutocracy and must have given them up with a certain reluctance.

Furthermore, he was turning over the management of the state to the masses whose good sense he was forced to assume as part of his democratic logic but whose failings he both deliberately and inadvertently chronicled. Sometimes his remarks on the state carried a Thoreauvian or Emersonian ring, which clashed discordantly with his socialism:

> The State is still, after individual despots have been largely modified or eliminated, a collective despot, mostly inexorable, almost irresponsible, and entirely inaccessible to those personal appeals which have sometimes moved the obsolete or obsolescent tyrants to pity. In its selfishness and meanness, it is largely the legislated and organized ideal of the lowest and stupidest of its citizens, whose daily life is nearest the level of barbarism.

Howells, to be sure, was writing about the capitalist state and added that the 'lowest' and the 'stupidest' might very well 'be occupying a very high place socially, politically and financially,' but his observations applied just as well to the socialist state. He was too highly trained in the art of ferreting out human frailties not to suspect in his more cynical moments (which occurred more frequently than the casual reader might think) that men, individually and collectively, were the most unreliable of animals and capable of the basest as well as of the noblest actions.

Howells the socialist sometimes disagreed with Howells the novelist, but then his characters and conversations emerged from observation and direct experience; his socialism rested on faith. He knew perfectly well that his countrymen behaved at times like knaves and hypocrites, that they concealed their own and their nation's greed behind high-sounding platitudes, that they railroaded anarchists to death on the flimsiest of pretexts and 'civilized' Philippine insurrectionists with Krag rifles. He spent a good many years of his life recounting the old story of man's inhumanity to man and acknowledged 'the black truth, which we all know of ourselves in our hearts.' But he believed all the while that a society might be established in which men lived together as brothers and did not need to be ashamed or humiliated in each other's presences. He knew this sounded like utopian nonsense to practical people, but he stubbornly clutched his faith. Ever since More wrote his *Utopia,* Howells remarked in 1903, 'anything too good to be anywhere true has been called Utopian; but every fruitful and hopeful scheme of modern civilization,' he decided, 'is based upon what were once Utopian ideas.' It was not accidental that his Altrurian novel stimulated more correspondence from all classes of people than any of his other books. 'There never was a dream that was so perennially dear to the heart of humanity as the dream of Utopia.'

vii] After Howells's last private crusade, the anti-imperialist agitation, which absorbed his attention between 1896 and 1902, he settled down for the next eighteen years and paid less notice to the social problems that had formerly touched him so deeply. His opinions did not change in any important respect, but the first World War absorbed all of his interest. The war was a just war, of that he was sure, and although he protested publicly against the execution of Sir Roger Casement by the British as a stupid and brutal act of *Schrecklichkeit,* he believed wholeheartedly in the Allied cause as against a ruthless German militarism.

In 1896 Howells had angrily criticized the smug expansionists who instigated wars that poor men fought and paid for, and he was scathing on the subject of professional patriotism. Was it always the fine emotion we thought it was, he asked at that time. One could never be sure. The rage that filled American hearts during the Venezuela crisis 'may have been merely a vindictive impulse, the explosion of a shabby desire to humiliate and abuse an ancient enemy.' As far as Howells was concerned, the Spanish War of 1898 simply provided an excuse for America to grab coaling stations. 'After the war,' he wrote to his sister, 'will come the piling up of big fortunes again; the craze for wealth will fill all brains, and every good cause will be set back. We shall have an era of blood-bought prosperity, and the chains of capitalism will be welded on the nation more firmly than ever.'

Three years before his death and on the eve of a new period of plutocracy and blood-bought prosperity, Howells accused the Germans, 'who seem the worst people in history,' of trying to rule the world, but by this time he was content to play his role of the grand old man of American letters and the beneficiary of testimonial dinners.

His last years were not particularly noteworthy. He had tidied up his life and solved his problems, religious and political, long before. Alfred Russel Wallace had ironed out Howells's religious doubts when he published in 1903 *Man's Place in the Universe.* Wallace in this book denied the existence of human life on the planets and thereby rescued man, in the words of Howells, 'from a humiliating sense of his infinitesimality in a boundless and myriad-peopled universe.' By depicting an earth 'islanded in a measureless solitude' and by suggesting that man 'is really the masterpiece of the Creator,' Wallace carried Howells back to his eighteenth-century security. Science had taken away 'those props on which the fainting soul relies' and made him half believe the Social Darwinists' views of the world, a world of caprice and accident. It seemed at one time to Howells, as it did to Basil March, that 'accident and then exigency' were the only forces at work, 'the play of energies as free and planless as those that force the forest from the soil to the sky; and then the fierce struggle for survival, with the stronger life persisting over the deformity, the mutilation, the destruction, the decay of the weaker.' Wallace provided new props for Howells's tenuously held faith in Providence; he restored the beliefs of his boyhood, Howells wrote to Mark Twain, by making man once more the center of things and re-establishing the sense of his own importance.

After Howells died in 1920 the memory of the honorable and conventional literary dean persisted, and the younger and more militant Howells—the champion of underdogs, rebellious young authors, and progressive ideas—became dim. Two days after his death *The New York Times* published a long editorial praising the venerable author for his charm, geniality, and versatility ('the most distinguished purely American literary figure of his time'), but the editorial writer did not mention socialism, anti-imperialism, or the Haymarket Riot. Since an editorial a few days before had fulminated against the Socialists and denounced Eugene Debs as a criminal, a eulogy of Howells's radicalism in this Mitchell Palmer era would have been too much to expect, but one might have assumed that a newspaper allegedly printing all the printable news would have made at least a passing reference to Howells's non-literary activities in the long obituary on the next page.

But what would Americans in 1920 have made of Howells's sermonizings about the slavery of competition, the solidarity of men of all classes 'marching abreast, to the music of our own heartbeats,' or his dream of a great American family, 'a natural growth from indigenous stocks, which will gradually displace individual and corporate enterprises by pushing its roots and its branches out under and over them, till they have no longer earth or air to live in'? What writers spoke now of 'a whole heaven of mercy and loving-kindness in human nature waiting to open itself'? Was it appropriate, moreover, to remind Americans of Howells's contempt for the business intelligence at a time when the businessman was approaching his apogee? Or to quote his message to the school children of America, written only eight years before his death?

> While I would wish you to love America because it is your home, I would have you love the whole world and think of all the people in it as your countrymen. You will hear people more foolish than wicked say, 'our country, right or wrong,' but that is a false patriotism and bad Americanism. When our country is wrong she is worse than other countries when they are wrong, for she has more light than other countries, and we ought somehow to make her feel that we are sorry and ashamed for her.

Things were once more in the saddle, and the commercial spirit began to infect even those few areas in American life which had miraculously escaped contamination. Eugene Debs and Robert La-Follette, the last of the progressive standard-bearers, were marching out of the American picture, and the face of one of Howells's fellow Ohioans, handsome and characterless, would soon be plastered all over the newspapers. The friend of Hayes and Garfield and Taft was spared that sight. Even his optimism might have been shaken by an administration that made Grant's lamentable regime seem almost respectable.

. . . .

CHAPTER 7

Thorstein Veblen:
Moralist and Rhetorician

i] The coming upswing of American business had already been presaged several months before Howells's death by a man whom he had joyously praised in 1899 but whom he had apparently never continued to read.

At home in America [this man had written in the 1919 *Dial*] for the transient time being, the war administration has under pressure of necessity somewhat loosened the strangle-hold of the vested interests on the country's industry; and in so doing it has shocked the safe and sane business men into a state of indignant trepidation and has at the same time doubled the country's industrial output. But all that has avowedly been only for the transient time being, 'for the period of the war,' as a distasteful concession to demands that would not wait. So that the country now faces a return to the precarious conditions of the *status quo ante*. Already the vested interests are again tightening their hold and are busily arranging for a return to business as usual; which means working at cross-purposes as usual, waste of work and materials as usual, restriction of output as usual, unemployment as usual, labor quarrels as usual, competitive selling as usual, mendacious advertising as usual, waste of superfluities as usual by the kept classes, and privation as usual for the common man.

The writer of these words, an expert on the morphology of the middle class, managed to finish the decade and to complete his analysis of the still rising patriciate—but with none of Howells's benignity. His name was Thorstein Veblen.

ii] Howells had never heard of Thorstein Veblen until he reviewed *The Theory of the Leisure Class* in 1899. Before that year only the readers of the learned journals could have been familiar with Veblen's name, and Howells, whose acquaintance with academic theorists was very slight (he knew something about Richard T. Ely's safe and sane generalizations) approached this new sociologist of the leisure class almost apologetically. 'His name is newer to me than it should be,' he wrote, 'or than it will hereafter be to any student of our status; but it must be already well known to those whose interests or pleasures have led them into the same field of inquiry. To others, like myself, the clear method, the graphic and easy style, and the delightful accuracy of characterisation will be part of the surprise which the book has to offer.' The two articles Howells based on *The Theory of the Leisure Class*—one could hardly call them reviews—undoubtedly helped to launch Veblen's book, as Veblen's biographers have pointed out, and to introduce him to a class of readers who ordinarily might have passed him up, but they have a further significance not very generally appreciated. They are the comments of a man responding to a congenial philosophy as well as to a provocative style.

If Howells missed the profundities and regarded the book too literally as a satire on aristocratic prejudices (his two notices were neither searching nor brilliantly interpretive), he had studied pecuniary culture closely enough to catch the Veblenian drift and to recognize the similarity between the American middle-class elite 'and any aristocracy in the traits of piety, predacity, courage, prowess, luxury, conservatism, authority, and other virtues and vices which have characterised the patricians in all times.' Howells enjoyed Veblen's humor and irony, which some of Veblen's disciples in their efforts to emphasize his seriousness have played down, but he regarded *The Theory of the Leisure Class* as more than a clever and funny tract. It was for Howells just as much a chapter in the American story as *Wealth against Commonwealth* and just as useful to the unborn writer who would some day incorporate its observations into the great American novel. Here too one could read of 'the relentless will, the tireless force, the vague ideal, the inexorable destiny, the often bewildered acquiescence' of the struggling contestants in the battle of business. Howells had attentively examined the well-to-do 'barbarians.' He had moralized about conspicuous display and invidious expenditure, the niceties and ritual of status, and the role of emulation in a plutocratic society. He also wrote about the significance of business ideals, ubiquitous and all-pervasive, in determining the American social outlook. He was not deceived by Veblen's apparent objectivity or by the solemn latinities of the Veblen prose.

It would be hard to conceive of two people more unlike, physically and mentally, than the gentle, monogamous Howells and the owlish, indecorous troglodyte, Thorstein Veblen, long-legged and spare like the frontier rascals of The Tall Tales; and yet both were outlanders (Veblen—the more uncouth and, from the leisure-class point of view, the more disreputable one—the self-conscious renegade Howells was clearly not) and both drank out of the same progressive well. Veblen, it is true, belonged to a different generation. He was twenty years younger than Howells, too young for John Brown and Phillips and Parker, but the Middle West in which he grew up was still a region of protest and rebellion, and the agrarian revolts erupting during the 'seventies and 'eighties were if anything more fierce and widespread in the West than ante-bellum dissent had been. During his undergraduate years at Carleton College Veblen championed Henry George, and as a young man he read Bellamy at about the same time Howells did. He read Björnson, too, who exercised such an important influence over Howells, and English socialists like William Morris and Ruskin. Veblen's admirers have been so struck by his genius that they have romanticized his strangeness and made him more unique and detached from tradition than the facts would warrant. But Veblen, as we shall see, did not spring fully armed from the earth; he sometimes wrote as if he had dragonish antecedents, but actually he belonged to the same family as the earlier progressives. William Dean Howells was his womanish cousin.

Veblen never acknowledged his relationship; in fact he quite consciously encouraged the legend of his remoteness and intellectual orphanhood, scoffing at the humanitarians who tried to change petrified institutions and shunning moral exhortation. Born into a Norwegian-American community in 1857, the son of a successful and highly intelligent father, Thorstein Veblen remained, in a spiritual sense at least, a hyphenate and a renegade, separated from the place of his origin physically and mentally and yet not at home in the world of the gentile. He describes his own predicament when he wrote of the renegade Jew:

For him as for other men in like case, the skepticism that goes to make him an effectual factor in the increase and diffusion of knowledge among men involves a loss of that peace of mind that is the birthright of the safe and sane quietist. He becomes a disturber of the intellectual peace, but only at the cost of becoming an intellectual wayfaring man, a wanderer in the intellectual no-man's land, seeking another place to rest, farther along the road, somewhere over the horizon. They are neither a complaisant nor a contented lot, these aliens of the uneasy feet.

From the time of his boyhood, when he wrote Greek curses on the fence of a neighboring farmer, until his death, he lived strangely and unpredictably. Classmates at Carleton College (where all the Veblen children were educated) found it difficult to understand or to like this derisive and arrogant iconoclast who seemed to know everything already. He in turn liked few people himself and was not gracious even to his best friends. He remained aloof and laconic, preferring to be misunderstood than to explain himself and rather enjoying the fear and respect of his uneasy colleagues.

Veblen never relented, never 'opened up' to a society that had rebuffed him or had never taken the trouble to comprehend him. His books, despite the excellent reviews most of them received, enjoyed the scantiest sales. He died as unobtrusively as he had lived, and lest the world, which had never fussed about him when he was alive, discover any more about his private self, he ordered all of his letters and papers to be burned, thus making it extremely difficult for any friendly or invidious investigator to peer behind the Veblenian curtain.

Even today it can hardly be said that Veblen's name is a byword in the United States. Although he enjoys a considerable vogue among students and malcontents, especially among those who share his views and relish his malicious wit, he is certainly not an American hero. Economists suspect him. He is still unclassified, still *sui generis*. His 'predilection for shifty iconoclasm' (to use one of his own epithets) distinguishes him from other social philosophers who instinctively make use of the idioms and the values of the middle class.

Irascible, dour, and sardonic, living precariously along the fringes of the American university world he anatomized so mercilessly, Veblen remained during his lifetime a kind of academic rogue, admired by an increasing number of discriminating disciples but never winning the kudos handed out to his less able but more circumspect colleagues. Academic recognition was slow and half-hearted. A belated attempt to press upon him the presidency of the American Economic Association was blocked in 1924 by a group of conservative elder members, men out of sympathy with his personal habits, his intellectual arrogance, and his economic beliefs.

Almost from the beginning of his career, however, the virus of Veblen's thought infected a handful of scholars and writers, and during the ensuing years these ideas were introduced into ever widening circles. Events themselves seemed to justify his most heretical opinions and to confirm his seemingly far-fetched prognostications, and it was natural for men watching the fascinating convolutions of American business during the late 'twenties and early 'thirties to discover new insights in Veblen's caustic reflections.

Why has Veblen's influence been so pervasive and far-reaching? He was by no means the first American to find fault with business enterprise and its cultural ramifications; the criticism of money-makers and money-making is as old as the country. Radicals of every description assailed the activities of the entrepreneur with greater fury and eloquence. There is nothing in Veblen, for instance, to match the invective of Theodore Parker's tirade against the merchants, or Thoreau's cutting references to the slaves of property. Other investigators, such as Henry Demarest Lloyd, dealt more exhaustively with specific examples of capitalistic chicanery; socio-religious writers, muckrakers, and progressives exposed the gross inequalities of our society with greater passion.

Veblen's current popularity must be attributed in part to the relevance of his social and economic ideas (his views on war, religion, education, business, and manners are as pertinent today as when he first expressed them), but his general and more enduring appeal lies in his power as a moralist, satirist, and rhetorician. Critics of Veblen have pointed out, and with justification, that he was careless in acknowledging his intellectual debts and given too much to unsupported generalizations. Such accusations are becoming less and less important as Veblen's contemporaries fade into the past. It was Veblen's talent for making the usual unusual and illuminating the commonplace, his gift for stating thinly veiled value-judgments in a startling and provocative manner that make his writing perennially interesting. In spite of his academic trappings, his conspicuous erudition, and his ostensibly scientific predisposition, it is Veblen the moralist setting out quite deliberately to destroy national myths and unsettle time-honored conventions who will continue to delight and to exasperate future readers.

Veblen's writings must therefore not be judged simply as a critical appraisal of a particular economic system or as a detached and informative analysis of a culture. Had this been true, he might never have inspired his assiduous cult. Far from being an aloof and disembodied intelligence benignly contemplating the antics of earth-dwellers, he was, like most great satirists, a fierce hater who tried but failed to conceal his ethical preconceptions. 'We are interested in what is, not what ought to be,' he would tell his students, but the venom and anger frequently discernible in his works belied his feigned neutrality. America, in Veblen's eyes, was a land full of Yahoos, and the beneficiaries of our business civilization, the 'kept classes,' became for him the quintessence of all the human ineptness, stupidity, cruelty, self-delusion, and credulity that satirists have jeered at for centuries.

This critical spirit, this inability to adjust himself to the views of the workaday world have been attributed in part to his Norwegian family background and in part to his personal idiosyncrasies. Had he been a more normal person, more at ease in Zion, his enemies have charged, he would have been less disgruntled with what he saw. But the *ad hominem* argument which imputes Veblen's bitterness to his poverty and dismisses him as a crank whose 'sense of inferiority caused him to withdraw within himself . . . and sneer at American life and American business' is beside the point. By the same kind of logic college professors would be less radical if their salaries were higher and Jews would never be communists if they were not snubbed at summer resorts. No matter what prompted Veblen to become a renegade, immune, as he described another kind of renegade, 'from the inhibitions of intellectual quietism,' it does not lessen the accuracy of his observations or blur the truths that his biased perspective enabled him to discern. All radicals, in one sense, are out of step with their times. The psycho-neurotic or racial factors that alienate a man from the majority will sometimes clarify his vision. Veblen's characterization of Marx as 'a theoretician busied with the analysis of economic phenomena' while 'at the same time, consistently and tenaciously alert to the bearing which each step in the process of this theoretical work has upon the propaganda,' might just as well apply to himself.

By setting himself, as it were, upon another planet, Veblen saw an America that differed sharply from the picture in the eyes of the uncritical majority. It was a deluded topsy-turvy America, illogical, irrational, vainglorious, superstitious. Veblen was realistic enough to see that this state of affairs could not be attributed solely to the machinations of an unscrupulous elite, and he had no formula to bring about the Golden Day. The perpetuation of decrepit institutions, whose only function was to keep a parasite class in the ascendancy, simply illustrated man's reluctance to forsake outmoded ideas and adjust himself to new ones.

He made much of the ludicrous paradox of deluded men cheerfully acting against their own best interests, bolstered in their irrationality by the resurgence of old superstitions, clannishness, and national conceit. The common man, swayed by 'imponderables' (by 'imponderable' he meant 'an article of make-believe which has become axiomatic by force of settled habit'), was forever befuddled by his 'picturesque hallucinations.' The retention of obsolescent beliefs in the workings of business enterprise, education, and politics, beliefs 'so at variance with the continued life-interests of the community,' tended to enhance Veblen's instinctive skepticism about the possibility of a future millennium. Sometimes, he admitted, the instincts of workmanship and efficiency were powerful enough to break through the dams of prescription and precedent and permit 'the current of life and cultural growth' to flow again. But episodes of this kind were rare. In general, he concluded, 'history records more frequent and more spectacular instances of the triumph of imbecile institutions over life and culture than of peoples who have by force of instinctive insight saved themselves alive out of a desperately precarious institutional situation, such, for instance, as now faces the peoples of Christendom.'

But because Veblen's belief in the thickheadedness of the human race existed side by side with a generous awareness of man's potentialities, he could never maintain the godlike scorn that marks the true misanthrope. The possibilities of human progress were as evident to him as the failure thus far to achieve them. One might almost say that the intense bitterness with which he analyzed human error revealed an inner concern for his fellow men that all his icy disdain could not conceal.

His conception of human nature was essentially utopian and very similar to the notions of the other progressive reformers, despite the anthropological vocabulary with which he encased his sometimes unscientific assumptions. Even if he did not sentimentalize about an ideal state of nature, he expressly repudiated the naïve ideas about primitive society espoused by nineteenth-century ethnologists and denied the political and social conclusions of the Hobbists. If the selfishness and egotism everywhere present in pecuniary society rested on deep-seated human traits, so did the ideals of friendliness and brotherly love, the 'Christian morals,' as Veblen called them, which actually antedated the Christian era and were not vouchsafed to man through divine grace. 'And in an obscure and dubious fashion,' Veblen wrote of brotherly love, 'perhaps sporadically, it recurs throughout the life of human society with such an air of ubiquity as would argue that it is an elemental trait of the species, rather than a cultural product of Christendom.'

One can detect behind Veblen's scientific pose a view of man and society which links him with the middle-class reformers he patronizingly disregarded. Thus he could speak of institutions diverting the 'genius of the race from its natural bent' and anticipate the time when human nature, no longer savagely repressed, would once more take on its mild and pacific character. The competitive way of life, of comparatively recent out-growth and coinciding with radical economic transformations, did not encourage Christian forbearance, mutual aid, or 'the ties of group solidarity.' In the competitive society all 'social and civil relations' are formed 'for pecuniary ends, and enforced by pecuniary standards.' Yet, Veblen observed, even in a business-minded society, the 'savage spiritual heritage' of brotherly love could not be extinguished: 'this principle is forever reasserting itself in economic matters, in the impulsive approval of whatever conduct is serviceable to the common good and in the disapproval of disserviceable conduct even within the limits of legality and natural right.' In the fight between business as 'an impersonal, dispassionate, not to say graceless, investment for profit' and 'the impulsive bias of brotherly love,' he believed that ultimate victory lay with the latter.

The ideas of Veblen, then, despite their outmoded and mechanistic features, were not merely destructive and negative. He was no reformer with a systematic program, to be sure, but he at least held forth the prospect of a rational and orderly economic life once mankind had freed itself from 'prehensile ideas.' Less evangelical than most American nineteenth-century reformers, more dubious about the inevitability of a foreordained progress, he kept his eyes fixed on the world around him and on the problems of the men who inhabited it.

There was something comforting in Veblen's serene naturalism, even though it explains some of his shortcomings. He too was aware of the failure of nerve that followed in the wake of the First World War, the 'maggoty conceits' of the supernaturalists, and he scornfully assailed the 'same fearsome credulity. . . running free and large through secular affairs as well.' He offered no positive remedy, only suggestions. He remained honestly skeptical. But if he did not encourage his readers to dream visions, at least he rid their minds of cant.

III] *The Theory of the Leisure Class* comes as close as any single book of Veblen's to explaining his social dynamics—most of his important ideas are at least touched upon here—but his configuration of society emerges distinctly only after reading some of his lesser-known articles and books: *The Theory of Business Enterprise* (1904), *The Instinct of Workmanship* (1914), *Imperial Germany and the Industrial Revolution* (1915), *The Higher Learning in America* (1918), *Absentee Ownership* (1923), and the essays gathered in a volume called *The Place of Science in Modern Civilization* (1919). Taken collectively, these books not only present clearly Veblen's principal premises, but also constitute a kind of saga of American society, a socio-economic record that starts in prehistorical times, fluid and plastic, and ends with a picture of the institution-hardened present. Veblen tells this story unemotionally, but actually it is quite as colored and slanted in its use of contrasts, in its occasionally dubious conjectures, and in its highly arbitrary selection of facts as anything written by his reformist predecessors. It is a melancholy story, wry and humorous. It has a melodramatic cast of characters, heroes and villains, exploiters and exploited, crafty dupers and guileless dupes. Although it is not told with the muckraker's passionate abandon, it is lighted up here and there with flashes of rage and irony and comedy.

Parker used the sermon and the lecture as vehicles for his progressive philosophy; George wrote his masterpiece as a dramatic prose-poem; Bellamy composed sociological romances and Howells realistic novels, while Lloyd embodied his views in the evangelical fact-studded essay of exposure. Veblen chose the form of the academic monograph to express himself, but the same ulterior objectives lay behind them all.

Now there are certain advantages, especially if one has sensational things to say, in selecting an unsensational medium for saying them. The scholarly treatise suggests objectivity and authority; its audience is limited, its tone disinterested, and it enables the writer to hide behind a camouflage of erudition. The monographer need not be hortatory, as George was, or Lloyd; he need not declare himself openly.

Veblen happened to be a scholar, furthermore, and a very learned one; the academic essay was a natural and congenial literary form for a person of his training. The orthodox economists and all of the tradition-bound theorists he slyly controverted also resorted to the scholarly tract and textbook, introducing myths even more at variance with the facts than those Veblen introduced. Books like *Progress and Poverty* and *Looking Backward* never bulked very large with the academicians, who regarded George and Bellamy as misty-minded prophets. But Veblen was a Ph.D. and a professor, as another professor, Brander Matthews, was shocked to discover after he had reviewed *The Higher Learning in America*. He knew his Spencer and Mill and Darwin as well or better than his colleagues, and in addition he threw at them references and facts garnered from his extensive readings in anthropology, biology, psychology, and archaeology. He had a command of the classical languages and of German, French, Spanish, Italian, Dutch, and the Scandinavian languages as well. In other words, he could not be dismissed as an amateur.

All of this impressive learning Veblen forged into weapons with which to assault the brazen fortress of capitalist institutions. Instead of attempting to storm such an impregnable barrier directly, Veblen chose to rely upon the long-term siege. He had plenty of time and he was naturally painstaking and thorough. But even when he wrote about subjects apparently remote from the question of the standing social order, he always had an eye cocked in the direction of the enemy and phrased his remarks in such a way that his readers were more or less obliged to make the parallels between the present and the past, between the barbarian and the plutocrat. His omissions were therefore almost as eloquent as his pronouncements.

In spite of the variety and the apparently random scheme of subject-selection in Veblen's writings, it is not very difficult to see the *Gestalt* that breaks out after his books and essays have been inventoried. Basic to his social philosophy are his ideas on human motivation or human nature already partly touched upon. In his raw state, man is essentially peaceful and industrious, Veblen surmised, although capable of fantastic irrationality. He is distinctly not a Benthamite automaton reacting predictably to pleasure/pain sensations and oscillating 'like a homogeneous globule of desire of happiness under the impulse of stimuli that shift him about the area, but leave him intact,' but an active agent who is potentially capable of changing the conditions under which he lives. Or again, according to the behaviorists from whom Veblen freely borrowed, man 'is not simply a bundle of desires that are to be saturated by being placed in the path of the forces of the environment, but rather a coherent structure of propensities and habits which seeks realisation and expression in an unfolding activity.'

The 'instincts' are the motivating forces in human behavior (he uses the term 'instinct' descriptively to 'signify,' as he says, 'a concurrence of several instinctive aptitudes' that seem to combine in human behavior), and the three all-subsuming ones are the Instinct of Workmanship, the Parental Bent, and the Instinct of Idle Curiosity. The first of these unprecise and deliberately metaphorical characteristics, defined as the 'proclivity for taking pains,' is distinguished by a workmanlike approach to anything, an innate appreciation of utility, system, and arrangement. The second might be called a more psychological version of the sympathetic instinct; it implies not only a love of one's kin but of the neighborhood, the nation, and the world, or, as Veblen phrases it, 'the current solicitude for the welfare of the race.' The third, idle curiosity, is reflected in the impersonal urge to know apart from any material benefit to be gained by it.

These instincts, however, are subject to contamination by surrounding influences and need almost laboratory conditions to flourish unchecked. When habit patterns harden into institutions, the instincts may be insulated or misdirected: In a pecuniary culture, for instance, the instinct of workmanship may reveal itself in 'make-believe' occupations, 'in "social duties," and in quasi-artistic or quasi-scholarly accomplishments, in the care or decoration of the house, in sewing circle activity or dress reform, or proficiency at dress, cards, yachting, golf, and various sports.' Again, other less peaceable and useful traits may choke them out for the time being. Institutions and obsolete habit patterns will then dominate in a society for long periods before the resilient instincts can reassert themselves. Thus in the Veblenian scheme a constant war is going on between the elemental nature of man and his cultural fabrications. Man's history is a recurrent cycle of the birth, death, and rebirth of his beneficient proclivities.

During the Savage era of human development, according to Veblen's hypothetical timetable of historical periods, peaceful conditions permitted the indulgence of the workmanlike propensities. Men lived, according to this interesting but conjectural account, in small communities, holding their land and tools in common and advancing rapidly in the peaceful arts. The parental bent in the prehistoric man was very strong, as was the instinct of idle curiosity. Although he was occasionally bellicose, he bore little resemblance to the Social Darwinist's primitive man, blood-thirsty, abject, and credulous. Veblen quite deliberately undercut the prevailing views on primitive society, because he wanted to show that capitalist ethics were not necessarily natural and instinctive, as even some humanitarian apologists implied, and that the traits of the primitive men were precisely those most unsuitable for modern pecuniary culture. For these traits combined, he wrote, 'a certain amiable inefficiency when confronted with force or fraud' together with 'truthfulness, peaceableness, good-will, and non-emulative, non-invidious interest in men and things.'

Veblen did not explain why this savage era, lasting until the early neolithic period, should suddenly pass into the Barbarian era, predaceous and warlike, but he offered some suggestions. The almost ideal conditions of the savage state, it seems, accelerated technological advance and led to an accumulation of wealth in the form of tools and animals. Certain individuals and communities tended to gain more than others and this surplus of things owned (property is the root of all evil) excited cupidity and aggression. War and all forms of predatory exploit gradually became the rule, with the military chieftains and the priests assuming positions of influence. The rapidly increasing disparity in property distribution stimulated distinctions of status and strengthened 'the institution of ownership.' But the most striking and important modifications that came with the barbarian age had to do with the change in human character as men were forced 'to adapt themselves,' in Veblen's words, 'to new exigencies under a new scheme of human relations.' The parental bent diminished, and the aggressively individualistic drives asserted themselves against group solidarity.

The earlier situation [Veblen wrote] was characterised by a relative absence of antagonism or differentiation of interests, the later situation by an emulation constantly increasing in intensity and narrowing in scope. The traits which characterise the predatory and subsequent stages of culture, and which indicate the types of man best fitted to survive under the régime of status, are (in their primary expression) ferocity, self-seeking, clannishness and disingenuousness—a free resort to force and fraud.

Barbarian traits, which took hold during the age of predacity, continued through the middle ages to the third or Handicraft era (lasting until the beginning or middle of the eighteenth century) and the contemporary era of the machine process. Barbarian 'exploit' was refined to pecuniary chicanery during the interval, as property relations became more complex and ownership and industry more sharply differentiated. 'The chivalric canons of destructive exploit and status,' Veblen wrote, also gave place 'to the more solid canons of workmanlike efficiency and pecuniary strength' as the age of handicraft got under way, but 'the egotistic principles of natural rights and natural liberty,' which this age ushered in, ultimately strengthened the pecuniary drift. Natural rights made for equality at a time when a man could justifiably claim as his own what he made through his skill and industry. A 'natural right' in this instance could be distinguished from a 'vested right,' a feudalistic concept based upon 'a prescriptive right to get something for nothing.' But the machine process soon divorced the worker from his tools, and the amassing of property no longer depended upon 'the workmanlike serviceability of the man who acquired it.' Natural rights then became another name for vested interest. By the time that industrial techniques had become firmly established in modern society, ownership and management had been pre-empted by people imbued with the barbarian-pecuniary values and marvelously adapted to a society designed for their perpetuation. Beneath this barbarian-minded elite lay the 'underlying population,' sharing many of the upper-class biases, warped by the same out-of-date institutions, and yet somehow more closely attuned to the codes of their savage forebears, the live-and-let-live and workmanlike tendencies repressed but not extinguished by the institution of property.

Veblen's analysis of social origins, in effect, turned Social Darwinism upside down, as he intended it should, for the abilities and qualities celebrated by the business apologists were transformed by Veblenian logic into predatory holdovers. The 'failures,' on the other hand, the victimized underlying population, were betrayed, according to his account, by a latent amiability and innocence which made them unfit to compete in the battle of the market place. The 'fittest' in the Social Darwinian sense he regarded as historical anachronisms temporarily nourished by decaying institutions but doomed in the long run by a machine culture already undermining their authority. Science relentlessly advanced, inculcating new disciplines, new attitudes, and gradually expunging the metaphysics of the earlier economy. Technology became his *Deus ex machina,* literally as well as figuratively, which would destroy private ownership and all the ritualistic paraphernalia of capitalistic institutions.

The victory of the machine, however, was far away. Veblen respected the strength of the obsolescent clutch and the multiple pressures for coercion that lay at the disposal of the pecuniary elite. The propertyless industrial man, moreover, had not yet emancipated himself from superstition and still responded to upper-class ceremonials. In a rigged economy where a relatively small group could practice all of the 'peaceable or surreptitious manoeuvres of delay, obstruction, ,and friction,' the industrial traits of good will, tolerance, incredulity, and common sense had small chance of expression. Captains of Industry, who managed the industrial plant, operated under the predatory canons of chicane. Like their ancient equivalents, they too went on forages against the supine community and systematically sabotaged and perverted a technology designed for public service and capable of an immense efficiency.

Opposed to the Business-Salesman (the quintessence of all the acquisitive qualities and so constructed that he was unable to understand the casual sequences of science) was the engineer, the masterpiece of the machine discipline, unstained by reactionary culture-traits, matter-of-fact, and practical, under whose disinterested authority the industrial plant could function as it was intended to. Veblen never conceived of the Business Man or the Engineer as literal personages or even as recognizable types; they were the metaphorical archetypes of two warring disciplines in the modern capitalist society.

Here again Veblen departed from the established attitudes, pro and con, toward the business leader, as well as idealizing his efficient antitype. Before the publication of *The Theory of the Leisure Class* and *The Theory of Business Enterprise,* the 'ruthless business man' had been castigated for his greed, dishonesty, and aggressiveness. Veblen differed from most of the outraged moralists in attacking the entrepreneur at his supposedly least vulnerable point. That is to say, he flatly denied businessmen those particular qualities with which they had been popularly endowed for a century: courage, vision, and technical skill. He argued, on the contrary, that as a class businessmen were simply supersalesmen, adepts at getting something for nothing, absentee owners living off the labor of others, 'sabotagers' of industrial productiveness. Incapable of anticipating future problems, timid and cautious in all his undertakings, the American businessman, said Veblen, had utterly failed to live up to his pretensions.

At the same time that Veblen viewed the depredations of business with undisguised distaste, he seemed to regard the paradox of American society's reverence for the class that exploited it with bleak amusement. Much of the satire in Veblen's discussion of business derives from the ridiculous situation of an overfed and excessively sheltered parasitical group exploiting mass credulity and perpetuating obsolescent institutions at community expense.

Veblen did not hold the individual businessman morally responsible for his unabashed acquisitiveness. The fault, if you could call it such, lay in the price system itself and in the conventional values of pecuniary culture. The entrepreneur either observed the rules or got left. 'Should the business men in charge,' Veblen observed, 'by any chance aberration, stray from the straight and narrow path of business integrity, and allow the community's needs unduly to influence their management of the community's industry, they would presently find themselves discredited and would probably face insolvency. Their only salvation is a conscientious withdrawal of efficiency.' Only a type especially adapted to the discipline of the price system and sufficiently devout to believe in capitalistic folklore could maintain itself:

> The successful man under this state of things succeeds because he is by native gift or by training suited to this situation of petty intrigue and nugatory subtleties. To survive, in the business sense of the word, he must prove himself a serviceable member of this gild of municipal diplomats who patiently wait on the chance of getting something for nothing; and he can enter this gild of waiters on the still-born pecuniary gain, only through such apprenticeship as will prove his fitness. To be acceptable he must be reliable, conciliatory, conservative, secretive, patient, and prehensile. The capacities that make the outcome and that characterise this gild of self-made businessmen are cupidity, prudence, and chicane,—the greatest of these, and the one that chiefly gives its tone to this business life, is prudence. And indispensable among the qualities that command that confidence of his associates without which no man can make himself as a business man, is a conservative temper.

The continued supremacy of business, however, was menaced by the fabulous potential of the machine temporarily held in check by the absentee owners. As long as expanding markets absorbed the ever-increasing flow of goods, curtailment or sabotage of the industrial plant was not so imperative. But with the absorption of the available markets and the 'fuller development of mechanistic technology . . . beyond the current needs of business,' self-regulation became a necessity and free competition, in the old-fashioned sense, an impossibility. Ownership and the profits of ownership gravitated toward a small minority, and a substantial number of people belonging to a class that had been most devout in its reverence for the capitalistic animus were now in danger of being disenthralled by the machine discipline and of becoming skeptical and iconoclastic, and intolerant of inefficiency. Capitalism was expropriating its staunchest allies; its institutions could not last unless there were people to believe in them and protect them from the irreligious assaults of men like Thorstein Veblen.

ɪᴠ] Veblen took great pains to break down the elaborate superstructure of capitalist institutions, because in them were embalmed all the legal, political, and moral traditions of defunct cultures, and through them the shamans of the standing order hoodwinked the underlying population. His contemporaries customarily regarded institutions as the inherited wisdom of the race, a wisdom originally implanted 'by a shrewd and benevolent Creator.' For Veblen institutions symbolized 'the bias of settled habit.' Thus, from an evolutionary point of view, Veblen said, the expression 'Whatever is, is right,' ought to be changed to 'Whatever is, is wrong,' because institutions took root in early times and 'are therefore wrong by something more than the interval which separates the present situation from the past.' After their initial usefulness, they quickly degenerated into mere barriers to change and perpetuated the obsolescent. Since most of the prevailing institutions dated back to the pre-industrial eras, the taboos, magic, and fantasies they incorporated were particularly ill-suited to modern conditions, and yet for this very reason they proved invaluable to business and the business hierophants (statesmen, lawyers, scholars, priests) who presided over the pecuniary mysteries.

Like Parker, Bellamy, and Lloyd, Veblen observed with interest how the business ideal penetrated all forms of social and political life. 'There is no branch or department of the humanities,' he wrote, in *Absentee Ownership,* 'in which the substantial absentee owner is not competent to act as guide, philosopher, and friend, whether in his own conceit or in the estimation of his underlying population,—in art and literature, in church and state, in science and education, in law and morals,—and the underlying population is well content.' There was nothing new in his conclusions that business ideas and values motivated politicians, clergymen, and school boards, but Veblen's comments were often as illuminating as they were funny and helped to sustain his gigantic indictment of the competitive order. His unsparing description of a society organized and run by the forgotten dead had its grotesque aspects, which he did not minimize. He never quoted Jefferson's remark about the present belonging in usufruct to the living, as George did, but he described a modern industrial society 'created by the technicians of the twentieth century' run according to the precepts 'framed by the

elder statesmen of the eighteenth century,' who in turn were pre-
serving 'habits of thought' already ancient.

Thus the difficulties of building a rational up-to-date society
were enhanced a thousandfold by this kind of ancestor worship,
and government became a many-sided instrument for the vested
interests. Veblen did not fall into the absurdity of attributing the
business control of government to a small and willful faction; both
government and business antedated the machine industry and both
had long operated on the principle of force and fraud. 'The democratic nations,' Veblen wrote, 'have taken over in bulk the whole
job-lot of vested interests and divine rights that once made the
monarch of the old order an unfailing source of outrage and deso-
lation.' The aggression of a national state was simply an extension
of private corporate enterprise; the state also injured the community and resisted any limitation of its sovereignty as vehemently
as the private corporation opposed threats to property rights.
Stripped of its trappings, the state was a collectivity of special interests dominated by the all-powerful absentee owners. It performed
the work of business in the name of the nation and diffused the
shibboleths of national vainglory and pretension throughout the
lower classes in order to bind them together 'in the service of their
predacious masters by an inveterate and unreflecting solidarity of
national conceit, fear, hate, contempt, and an enthusiastically slav-
ish obedience to the constituted authorities.'

The cult of the state and the patriotic rigmarole had more than
an incidental importance. 'Indeed,' said Veblen, 'they constitute
the chief incentive which holds the common man to an unrepin-
ing constancy in the service of the "national interests." So that,
while the tangible shell of material gain appears to have fallen to
the democratic community's kept classes, yet the "psychic income"
that springs from national enterprise, the spiritual kernel of national elation they share with the common man on an equitable
footing of community interest.' A properly enlightened society,
geared to the matter-of-fact workaday routine of the machine,
would not have been beguiled by the 'picturesque hallucinations' of
the patriots:

the democratic commonwealths would in such event be in a fair way to become what they profess to be,—neighborly fellowships of ungraded masterless men given over to 'life, liberty and the pursuit of happiness' under the ancient and altogether human rule of Live and Let Live. In that event loyal subjection to the national establishment of politicians would have no sacramental value, and patriotic fervor would be no more meritorious than any other display of intolerance.

But the predatory rationale of the dynastic state had been 'ground into the texture of civilized life and thought'; the common man continued his fealty to government by vested interest, which swindled him at home and abroad.

At home big business wrecked the domestic economy by curtailing production and raising prices; abroad big business prevented material progress, diffused ill will, and supported a minority of absentee owners at popular expense. The common man did not benefit tangibly from the war of chicane and fraud on either front, and yet he somehow identified himself with the spirit of 'national prestige and collective honor.' Technically he was the sovereign in the democratic state, and the 'gentlemanly stewards of the kept classes' made a pretence of consulting him on concerns that could not be 'wholly carried through in a diplomatic corner and under cover of night and cloud.' That is to say, the common man was 'managed rather than driven,' unless he belonged to the very lowest level and except during 'the recurrent periods of legislative hysteria and judiciary blind-staggers,' but whether force or cunning were used to keep him in line, all of the national institutions hung over him like so many jealous gods and shrouded his world.

Wherever he turned, the state, the church, the school, and popular arts re-enforced leisure-class assumptions—what Veblen called 'the conservation of archaic traits' or anthropomorphic survivals. Pecuniary canons of waste and conspicuousness everywhere displayed themselves: in the grotesque and neobarbaric architecture, aesthetically and functionally objectionable, in the leisure-class vocations, sports, clothes, and furnishings, in the very papers and magazines turned out for popular consumption under business supervision.

Others before Veblen had recognized the covert affiliation between business and the periodical press—the terms 'venal,' 'corrupt,' 'kept' were commonly applied by reformers from Parker to Lloyd to characterize this tie—but Veblen was among the first to see the phenomenon purely as a business matter rather than a wicked conspiracy. In commercial periodicals, the readers read what they wanted to believe. By editorial design no idea that might be offensive to the advertisers or detrimental to their interests found its way into the columns, for the magazine or newspaper was primarily a business venture—not a vehicle for disinterested communication. Veblen pointed out how the 'literary output' of a magazine served as a filler between the pages of advertising and how it was gauged to blend with the tastes and biases of carefully defined social strata. Ideally the suitable story, Veblen declared, 'should conduce to a quickened interest in the various lines of servîces and commodities offered in the advertising pages, and should direct the attention of readers along such lines of investment and expenditure as may benefit the large advertisers particularly.'

The successful writer of the 'slicks' carefully adapted his wares to the fancies and ideals—'artistic, moral, religious, or social'—of the particular class he selected to entertain, but the richest and most respectable audience was the substantial leisure class, composed largely, according to Veblen, of business-class dependents 'of various shades of conservatism, affectation, and snobbery' whose social reputability 'was less high or less authentic than their aspirations' and who found the 'conservative and conciliatory' tone of the magazines reassuring. Periodical literature adroitly suggested to the reader that he was correct in his values and prejudices and needed only to be reinforced at certain points. In short, as Veblen saw it:

> The literary output issued under the surveillance of the advertising office is excellent in workmanship and deficient in intelligence and substantial originality. What is encouraged and cultivated is adroitness of style and a piquant presentation of commonplaces. Harmlessness, not to say pointlessness, and an edifying, gossipy optimism are the substantial characteristics, which persist through all ephemeral mutations of style, manner, and subject-matter.

> Business enterprise, therefore, it is believed, gives a salutary bent to periodical literature. It conduces mildly to the maintenance of

archaic ideals and philistine affectations, and inculcates the crasser forms of patriotic, sportsmanlike, and spendthrift aspirations.

But it was in education, and especially higher education—supposedly dedicated to the disinterested pursuit of knowledge—that the values and assumptions of the business world were most reverently enshrined.

Veblen conceived of the university as simply another form of business institution organized like a corporation and run, in part, by absentee directors along similar lines. The 'captain of erudition' (the college president) and his staff of 'yes-men' (the deans) were engaged in turning out salesmen according to strict business specifications. Scholarship received little encouragement, since the university administrators seemed largely preoccupied with getting favorable publicity by a conspicuous display of ceremony. Universities paid more attention to the private affairs of their professorial 'help' than they did to their publications (here Veblen wrote from personal experience) and tolerated no radical departures from the 'current conservatism' of the well-to-do. They served as temples of business animism—especially the schools of commerce and law —insuring the 'intellectual quietism' most conducive to the presentation of the culturally obsolete and muffling the free play of idle curiosity and the instinct of workmanship.

The college president 'dear to the commercialized popular imagination,' fitting 'convincingly into the business man's preconceived scheme of things,' and supreme in 'skilled malpractice and malversation' supervised the thought-control and betrayed the educational experiment. His chief function was to dazzle the laity through

quasi-scholarly homiletical discourse, frequent, voluminous, edifying, and optimistic; ritualistic solemnities, diverting and vacant; spectacular affectations of (counterfeit) scholastic usage in the way of droll vestments, bizarre and archaic; parade of (make-believe) gentility . . . promulgation of (presumably ingenuous) statistics touching the volume and character of the work done.

It was quite appropriate that his university, an institutionalized lie which in large measure defeated the very ends for which it was ostensibly created, should be housed in buildings that were both meretricious and studiedly impracticable. And it was inevitable, too, that he should lose his intellectual birthright and even undergo a physical change by virtue of his office. All of Veblen's austerity, his loathing of leisure-class excess, comes out in the following description of the university president, which has the quality of one of George Grosz's early portraits:

A flabby habit of body, hypertrophy of the abdomen, varicose veins, particularly of the facial tissues, a blear eye and a colouration suggestive of bile and apoplexy,—when this unwholesome bulk is duly wrapped in a conventionally decorous costume it is accepted rather as a mark of weight and responsibility, and so serves to distinguish the pillars of urbane society. Nor should it be imagined that these grave men of affairs and discretion are in any peculiar degree prone to excesses of the table or to nerve-shattering bouts of dissipation. The exigencies of publicity, however, are, by current use and want, such as to enjoin not indulgence in such excursions of sensual perversity, so much as a gentlemanly conformity to a large routine of conspicuous convivialities. 'Indulgence' in ostensibly gluttonous bouts of this kind —banquets, dinners, etc.—is not so much a matter of taste as of astute publicity, designed to keep the celebrants in repute among a laity whose simplest and most assured award of esteem proceeds on evidence of wasteful ability to pay. But the pathological consequences, physical and otherwise, are of much the same nature in either case.

The Higher Learning in America, Veblen's baleful survey of the university as a business institution, was probably the most unreservedly personal book he ever wrote. He had languished for many years in the academic factories, where he so obviously did not belong and where his superiors either ignored him or snooped into his private affairs. But this book, like his others, described one more link in the chain of archaic holdovers that helped to keep the common man in subjection.

          v] Unlike the less sophisticated progressives whose oversimplified theories of human nature permitted them to base their hopes of the common man's salvation on a sudden change in head or heart or in a quick revolution through the ballot, Veblen expected no easy or miraculous victory. He distrusted the fervor of the middle-class humanitarians with their schemes of 'equitable' readjustments and redistribution of property. The legality and morality of private ownership were embedded in the common law, ground into 'the moral sense of civilized men.' The underlying population behaved as they did out of long habituation to doctrines preached and exemplified by the 'kept classes.' Only the slow tortuous process of machine discipline might ultimately destroy their fantasies, but that possibility was neither imminent nor foreseeable.

The out-and-out socialists who wanted to abolish ownership completely appealed to him more than what he called the 'contingent of well-to-do irregulars' or polite reformers, but even the socialists, Veblen thought, were moved by 'a faith prompted by their own hopes rather than by observed facts or by the logic of events.' If the humanitarian well-to-do wasted their efforts on futile remedial programs, which Veblen likened to the labors of Sisyphus, so the socialists erred in supposing that the unpropertied classes would rationally and automatically gravitate toward socialism.

The unpropertied classes employed in business do not take to socialistic vagaries with such alacrity as should inspire a confident hope in the advocates of socialism or a serious apprehension in those who stand for law and order. The pecuniarily disfranchised business population, in its revulsion against unassimilated facts, turns rather to some excursion into pragmatic romance, such as Social Settlements, Prohibition, Clean Politics, Single Tax, Arts and Crafts, Neighborhood Guilds, Institutional Church, Christian Science, New Thought, or some such cultural thimblerig.

The shift from an independent to a dependent status did not automatically change a person's outlook, make him less property-conscious or more iconoclastic, unless he was at the same time converted by the discipline of the machine. Veblen's hatred of his pecuniary society did not lead him to underestimate its vitality; business discipline continued to operate simultaneously and always at cross-purposes with the machine.

The socialists, 'those shudderingly sanguine persons' who counted on 'salesmanlike waste and business sabotage to bring on the collapse,' misjudged both the shrewdness of the business leaders and their skill (despite 'their trained ignorance on matters of technology') in bringing about 'what amounts to effectual team-work for the defeat of the country's industrial system as a going concern.' The masses, imbued with business metaphysics, had no desire to prevent 'this miscarriage of civilization,' and even the technicians (the only group who could run the industrial plant for the community) were for the most part the well-fed lieutenants of the vested interests. They co-operated complacently with business, conducted themselves with a reassuring degree of 'filial piety,' and were 'pretty well commercialized.' The working class, characteristically enough, regarded their potential saviors as a 'fantastic brotherhood of over-specialized cranks, not to be trusted out of sight except under the constraining hand of safe and sane business men.' All in all, Veblen concluded, such was the profound deference shown to business sagacity that only a 'harsh and protracted experience' could possibly undermine business reputability.

Yet despite his reservations about the progressive or socialist miscalculations, Veblen's expectation of the eventual success of the leveling and vulgarizing machine is an unacknowledged expression of his utopian bent. Once that connection with the reformers is established, it can be seen that he was interested in socialism and reform not merely as 'an animus of dissent from received traditions' but as current protests against the unfitness of contemporary institutions. He made a more technical analysis than Bellamy or Lloyd; he relied less upon traditional political concepts, such as Natural Rights, but his conclusions were essentially the same, and he started with many of their presuppositions.

All of the progressive reformers previously discussed were 'institutionalists' in the sense that Veblen was. That is to say, they went beyond the limited boundaries that the formal economists had set for themselves—the artificial and mechanical analysis of things as they are—to questions of a social, ethical, psychological, and biological nature. In turning to what they considered the decisive forces shaping social behavior, in dealing with facts ordinarily excluded from the purview of the classical school, they became convinced that the conclusions of the orthodox economists were incomplete and inaccurate, mere apologies, in effect, for things as they are or were supposed to be. It was not enough to understand the theoretical mechanism of society. One had to ask what the good society was, how it could be achieved, and why men were so dissatisfied and frustrated with their lives. Veblen intimated that he was not concerned with these whys and wherefores, but his speculations followed the path already stamped out by the earlier progressives.

Consider his answer to the question, why are men dissatisfied with present society? It was not, as some socialists argued, because capitalism was destructive and wasteful or because some men abused their positions of authority or because the masses were sunk in poverty. Veblen, like the other progressives, attributed much of the class bitterness to the underling's sense of 'slighted manhood,' to the petty mortifications that stirred up more rage in the hearts of the snubbed than the rich ever imagined. 'Man as we find him to-day,' Veblen wrote, 'has much regard to his good name—to his standing in the esteem of his fellow men. This characteristic he always has had, and no doubt always will have.' A society that exalted pecuniary emulation above any other and did not value highly 'efficiency in any direction . . . which does not redound to a person's economic benefit' very definitely limited the possibilities of individual self-fulfillment. It made very little difference that the comforts of the working population had increased during the last one hundred years; statistics proving this were irrelevant. Under capitalism the lot of the average had not declined in terms of subsistence or comfort, but competitive enterprise tended to make the poor 'relatively poorer, in their own eyes, as measured in terms of comparative economic importance.' Current protest ordinarily did not come from the poverty-stricken (their spokesmen usually belonged to another class) but from those whose privation was not strictly necessary, who diverted 'what might be the means of comfort . . . to the purpose of maintaining a decent appearance, or even a show of luxury.' As Veblen observed, it is 'notoriously just as difficult to recede from a "high" standard of living as it is to lower a standard which is already low,' a fact which the great depression bore out. Then, it will be remembered, the middle classes (filled with the Protestant horror of poverty as something shameful) suffered greater spiritual wear and tear from reduced circumstances than the lower-income groups accustomed to precarious living.

Veblen therefore surmised that in a socialist society, with the bane of private ownership removed, the invidious pecuniary appeals would have no force and the principal reason for social discontent would disappear. 'With the abolition of private property,' he concluded, 'the characteristic of human nature which now finds its exercise in this form of emulation, should logically find exercise in other, perhaps nobler and socially more serviceable, activities.' That other incentives existed besides the money urge Veblen simply assumed. To the capitalist mentality, work was irksome and workmen ignoble, but Veblen even allowed himself to conjecture about the time when 'labor might practically come to assume that character of nobility in the eyes of society at large, which it now sometimes assumes in the speculations of the well-to-do, in their complacent moods.' Although he did not entirely discount the familiar Spencerian arguments that the socialist state must necessarily become a tyranny, a 'system of status,' and that its establishment involved certain risks, he saw no reason to suppose, in modern industrial society, that such a likelihood was certain. Constitutional democracy had been a daring innovation and still worked imperfectly; industrial democracy, given the vagaries of human nature, could not operate without knocks and jolts, but Veblen implied that modern society had reached the point where even an imperfect socialism was possible and desirable.

With all of his cautious hypotheses, then, and the invariably tentative quality of his generalizations (he had almost a genius for avoiding the positive, transparent declaration), Veblen propagandized for a liberal industrial democracy. And from there we can go even further and say that Veblen, with a more scientific vocabulary and with more involved arguments, continued the campaign against the competitive order in America that the Fourierists had helped to start and the post-bellum reformers had sustained.

Only in one important respect did he depart from the spirit of his predecessors, and that was on the meaning and value of machine technology. Even here, however, the differences may have been more apparent than real.

The reformers, as we have seen, did not want to dispense with the machine; only to subordinate it to its tenders, the workmen who operated it. Veblen, who regarded the revulsion from machine discipline as a kind of sentimental reaction characteristic 'among the moderately well-to-do, the half-idle classes,' looked upon the *long-term* effect of the machine discipline as beneficent and therapeutic, for by its agency ossified institutions dissolved away. Nowhere in Veblen's writings is there a really satisfactory discussion of this process; one is forced to conclude that on this subject he gave his wishes free rein, and that his arguments did not rest upon observation. Evidently he never scrutinized very closely the day-to-day life of the factory worker (his one important labor contribution dealt with the Industrial Workers of the World, whose members, according to one authority, worked at occupations 'not highly mechanized when Veblen wrote'), and the steps by which the worker could be 'de-institutionalized' Veblen left to the reader's imagination.

On the other hand, Veblen admitted that 'the logic of the machine process' did not 'best comport with the native strain of human nature in those people that are subject to its discipline,' and that in spite of the nonsense about the 'unending "grind" of living' under the machine method, the industrial tempo often broke down the worker prematurely. There is some indication that Veblen attributed the malevolent effects of the machine to the business owners who drove the factory hands to exhaustion and prevented them from 'indulging any possible curiosity' in the facts of technology, but he also acknowledged that machine occupations may be unnatural 'to the common run of civilized mankind.'

Veblen's speculations on the role of technology in modern culture are tinged with utopian-progressive sentiments and Marxian assumptions as well, with the latter certainly less central to his thinking than has sometimes been supposed. No one can say with any assurance just what Veblen took from Marx, since there were so many other sources from which he could have derived his socialism, but the following similarities are at least worth noticing.

Both Marx and Veblen were historical materialists whose views on the character of early primitive society and the origins of class bore many resemblances. Both emphasized the distinction between the economic foundations of society and the intellectual superstructure. Both criticized the fetishes and naïve preconceptions of orthodox economists. Both agreed that workingmen were exploited and both placed great importance on the class structure of society. And yet, while recognizing these points of resemblance, and there were others too, and remembering that Veblen was a careful and appreciative student of Marx for many years, one finds their differences more striking and significant than their correspondences.

Marx's 'metaphysical preconceptions,' his Hegelian overtones, disturbed Veblen, and he rejected the teleology that he found implicit in the Marxian view of the social process. According to the 'neo-Hegelian, Marxian' view, all nations advanced 'unremittingly toward a socialistic consummation.' This indicated a personal, intellectual, and non-evolutionary attitude, whereas the Darwinian scheme saw continuity as a result 'of blindly cumulative causation, in which there is no trend, no final term, no consummation.' Marx was not enough of a Darwinian to suit him, and he appears to have had greater sympathy with the revisionists who were trying to re-equate Marxism in terms of modern science. Veblen flatly repudiated the hedonistic psychology of rational calculus whether he found it in Adam Smith or in Karl Marx:

> Under the Darwinian norm it must be held that men's reasoning is largely controlled by other than logical, intellectual forces; that the conclusion reached by public or class opinion is as much, or more, a matter of sentiment than of logical inference; and that the sentiment which animates men, singly or collectively, is as much, or more, an outcome of habit and native propensity as of calculated material interest.

A 'selfish, calculating class interest' explained neither why economic forces modified institutions nor the pattern of class alignments. Veblen recognized the conflict of interests between the working and owning classes, but the differences went deeper than mere disparity of income. The question of equality, of social status, as I have indicated, was an important psychological consideration, but Veblen saw the real divisions between the two classes as growing inevitably out of the habituation to different disciplines. Until the machine discipline had done its work, no grounds existed for supposing that the worker would automatically side with his self-declared rescuers against the propertied 'tyrants.' It depended entirely upon the influences to which he had been exposed and upon his response to these varied stimuli.

Even more revealing than his disagreement with the Marxian ideas on psychological motivation was Veblen's criticism of the labor theory of value. With his discussion of this point, we are back again with Edward Bellamy and the progressives.

Just as the class struggle with its premise of the dictatorship of the proletariat seemed to Veblen romantic and teleological, so the Marxian doctrine of exploitation was un-Darwinian and irrelevant except as a slogan to excite the working class. For Veblen, the alleged 'natural right' of the workman to the product of his own labor belonged to those crude generalizations that had no basis in fact. That workers were exploited he did not deny, but he did not think of the distribution of rewards in terms of individual or class contributions. Labor power created value, to be sure, but the effectiveness of this labor power, in turn, depended upon the technological information available at the time and other such vital considerations as the size and needs of the population, or, taken collectively, what Veblen called the 'state of the industrial arts.' It seems perfectly evident that Veblen wanted the legacy of man's past achievements to be vested in the community itself ('the only heir,' as Bellamy had said, 'to the social inheritance of intellect and discovery') and not restricted to the business elite who preempted the fruits of this collective wisdom or to the workingmen whose skill and knowledge derived from the corporate body. 'The state of the industrial arts,' Veblen declared 'is a fact of group life, not of individual or private initiative or innovation. It is an affair of the collectivity, not a creative achievement of individuals working self-sufficiently in severalty or in isolation.'

Veblen exalted the community above the predatory schemes of individuals or groups—plutocratic or proletarian—who snatched at the common fund. His conception of the good society (hinted at through implication but never sketched) substituted for the Marxian fancies of a proletarian dictatorship, followed by a withering away of the state, his own benign vision of 'masterless men' living together in comity, working to the rhythms of a beneficent machine, and freed from the depredations of business saboteurs. Under the prevailing economic system, wasteful and conspiratorial, business and organized labor vied with one another in retarding industrial efficiency and in constantly menacing the community. In Veblen's society, directed by passionless engineers, the predacious anachronisms became as extinct as the flesh-eating dinosaur; the technician (another version of Bellamy's Industrial General), who equitably supervised the distribution of the community birthright, usurped the place of the captain of industry.

vi] I have said these things about Veblen with no intention of minimizing his importance as an economist or a sociologist but rather to explain his deep and abiding moral animus. Veblen, I have tried to show, was not only an astute diagnostician of economic institutions; he was also a kind of splenetic prophet. Like Marx, he attracted disciples by his startling insights and remorseless logic, but his appeal was not limited to the reason. He quite consciously overemphasized and oversimplified. He was fond of dramatic dichotomies, or what the semanticists call the two-valued orientation. He juxtaposed 'business' and 'industry,' the entrepreneur and the engineer, the instinct of predation and the instinct of workmanship, the absentee owner and the 'underlying population.' These distinctions, more ethical perhaps than scientific, carry an emotive appeal and imply unstated preconceptions. They offer further proof that Veblen was quite capable of deliberate distortion and bias despite his pose of Olympian detachment.

What Veblen did was to destroy holy shibboleths by means of a language ordinarily identified with ritualistic or pedantic expression; he was, in other words, reverently irreverent. His technique, useful as a kind of protective coloration to misdirect potential enemies, suggested the outrageous solemnity of Swift's *A Modest Proposal* and the weightiness and aloofness of Gibbon's chronicle of Rome.

In his best writing he demonstrated both his bias and his artistry and turned ideas made blunt by excessive handling into sharp-cutting instruments. For style is more than embellishment and contributes immeasurably to the total impression; shreds of additional meaning cling to the apt metaphor, and the bald informative statement is not necessarily the most accurate. Veblen announced his message (men are potentially decent damned fools who honor their oppressors and habitually act against their own best interests) in a series of amusing paradoxes. His strong personal feelings he conveyed through the use of a loaded diction.

Most critics when they praise Veblen's style are thinking primarily of his talent as a phrasemaker. Such unusual but now familiar collocations as 'conspicuous consumption,' 'trained incapacity,' 'business sabotage,' 'sagacious restriction of output,' 'collusive sobriety,' and 'blameless cupidity,' have become the well-known hallmarks of Veblenese. This device of balancing opposites, the arbitrary linking of words with respectable and dishonorable connotations, is a literary expedient not usually employed by scientific writers. It resembles the oxymoron, or the conceit used by the metaphysical poets in the seventeenth century to achieve a new and shocking perspective. Veblen's readers, trained to the automatic response, were sometimes puzzled by the seeming incongruity of his phrases. Does not 'business' suggest efficiency, honesty, respectability, practical results? Is not 'sabotage' associated with anarchy, waste, treachery? In joining the meritorious with the blameworthy, Veblen was of course making a value judgment and imprisoning a whole philosophy in a single phrase.

By using language in this way, he reduced the prestige of business, contemplating it, as it were, through the wrong end of a telescope. The words *petty, nugatory, conciliatory, reliable, cupidity,* when applied to businessmen, are less pejorative and picturesque than *pirate* or *robber baron* or *Titan* or *tycoon,* but they strip away the romance and glamour that so frequently has mitigated dishonesty on a grand scale. The businessman, Veblen is saying, is not an audacious and genial freebooter, a gambler, an unscrupulous but God-struck empire builder. He has none of the larger wisdom. He is small, mean, circumspect, and useless—a creature formed by the price system and victimized by the values of his own pecuniary culture.

As a more specific illustration of Veblen's artifice, consider the sentence with which Veblen winds up his discussion of the similarity between religious and business institutions. The very fact that he identifies the Church with Big Business is significant, if not original, but the sentence itself deserves closer analysis:

All told—if it were possible—it will be evident that the aggregate of human talent currently consumed in this fabrication of vendible imponderables in the nth dimension, will foot up to a truly massive total, even after making a reasonable allowance, of, say, some thirty-three and one-third per cent., for average mental deficiency in the personnel which devotes itself to this manner of livelihood.

Here the language of economics, morally toneless, is applied to a subject that is not ordinarily associated with the market places. The conceit ('fabrication of vendible imponderables') not only puns on the word 'fabrication' but relates in a particularly insulting manner the tricks of salesmanship with spiritual salvation. Veblen, in an earlier passage, had been admiring the 'perseverance, tact, and effrontery' of the propaganda of the faith, that 'magnificent' institution whose 'enterprise in sales publicity' makes 'the many secular adventures in salesmanship' seem raw and crude by comparison. Now, in the sentence quoted above, he joins the most material and the most spiritual of institutions, identifying them both with mumbo jumbo and deceit. Business and the Church, exploiting the credulity of the 'underlying population,' take on the 'same air of stately benevolence and menacing solemnity.' Disarming, insolent, or official—always ostensibly neutral—Veblen can slant his judgments without explicitly committing himself.

Much may be said in jest that would be intolerable if uttered with perfect seriousness, and Veblen is apt to adopt the character of the playful satirist when he is being the most subversive. His humor is very largely the humor of incongruity, the grotesque or willful rearrangement of conventional word patterns into droll and unusual combinations: business schools specialize in 'widening the candidates' field of ignorance'; academic opportunists succeed by virtue of a 'ready versatility of convictions and a staunch loyalty to their bread.' But Veblen also likes to embellish his writing with witty epigrammatic touches. Illegitimate births 'may be rated as an undesigned triumph of the hormones over the proprieties.' The 'watchful waiting' policy of the cautious entrepreneur is likened to 'a toad who has reached years of discretion and has found his appointed place along some frequented run where many flies and spiders pass and repass on their way to complete that destiny which it has pleased an all-seeing and merciful Providence to call them.' The captain of industry, he continues, is motivated by the same 'safe and sane strategy' of 'sound business principles' that governs the toad. 'There is a certain bland sufficiency spread across the face of such a toad so circumstanced, while his comely bulk gives assurance of pyramidal stability of principles.'

Veblen's dead-pan manner, according to some critics, places him in the same tradition as the frozen-faced humorists of the frontier and the 'cracker barrel' school, but this resemblance is only superficial. As a general rule American humorous writers (the more consciously 'literary' and popular ones, at any rate) have ridiculed the aberrations from the norm and indirectly supported national prejudices. Primarily they are the amiable guardians of the middle classes. Veblen made use of the stock American trick of being seriously unserious, but instead of jesting at the deviations from conventional behavior, he flouted the unquestioned beliefs of bourgeois folkways.

He is, in fact, much closer to Thoreau than, let us say, to Artemus Ward. Both Thoreau and Veblen, diametrically opposed in so many ways, announced ideas outrageous to their contemporaries; both, to borrow Emerson's description of Thoreau, resembled 'some philosophical woodchuck or magnanimous fox'; both, if we are to believe the accounts of their friends, were reserved and antisocial; both, in their principal works, revealed the craziness of everyday life and exposed the conspiracy of institutions; and both—the one directly and the other by implication— advocated the drastic simplification of living and the stripping away of unessentials. All of these attitudes and characteristics were incorporated in the sardonic jokes they made at the expense of

moldy cultural hangovers and established patterns of conduct. Unlike the majority of American humorists, folksy and homely,
Thoreau and Veblen were the queer ones who stood beyond the
pale and made fun of the solid citizens.

vII] When a man feels strongly about the bad state
of the world and wants to put his feelings into words, he can convey his disapproval and his suggestions for amendment in an infinite number of ways. He can spoof and debunk. He can expatiate
warmly and tolerantly. He can fume, tabulate, preach, lament. The
vehicle he chooses for self-expression will depend partly upon his
personal make-up and partly, perhaps, on the degree of concern
he feels for the situation he wants to remedy.

Thoreau, hostile to the values of his generation and holding
fast to what his contemporaries (had they read him) would have
regarded as an incomprehensible position, spoke with measured
force and insolent assurance. Obligated to no one and unintimi-
dated by a public opinion he habitually disregarded, he affronted
his world with impunity; requiring no elaborate subterfuges, he
subverted society in broad daylight.

Veblen could not afford to make the frontal assault. As the
angry recluse and mocking Prometheus, he required a style and
vocabulary that would muffle his rage and allow him to stalk his
victims without their being conscious of his intentions. His milieu
was the university, ostensibly dedicated to the quest for truth but
guided in actuality by a 'meretricious subservience' to the Philistines. Veblen may be said to have betrayed the betrayers by
thinking unholy thoughts on holy ground and by using the ritualistic paraphernalia of scholarship—ordinarily employed in but-
tressing the social order and impressing the gullible—for profoundly subversive purposes. Had he been a cynic or debunker,
content to shock and to smash images, he could have been dismissed as a troublesome smart-aleck. But Veblen was too much
of a moralist and a conspirator. He diverted his readers while he
systematically undermined their social order. He attacked the institutions and culture of capitalism while at the same time laying
the foundations for a more humane and natural way of life.

PART THREE

. . . .

Latter-day Progressives

. . . .

CHAPTER 8

Theodore Roosevelt and Brooks Adams: Pseudo-Progressives

1] What has been called the 'Progressive Movement' officially began with Theodore Roosevelt's incumbency in 1901. During the next ten years, the 'muckrakers' he was finally to denounce continued to expose the tools and tactics of the plutocracy even more sensationally than the earlier reformers, piling up columns of damaging evidence and showing in a hundred different ways how business adventurers pillaged America. The latter-day progressive philosophers, men nourished on George and Bellamy and Lloyd, began to rewrite American history; practical politicians like Robert M. La Follette translated progressive ideals into political action. Whereas a Veblen smuggled progressive-utopian theories into the university campuses of America (and started his unobtrusive but fatal influence among a younger generation of intellectuals), a number of journalists and lawyers of a non-utopian cast—Louis D. Brandeis, Clarence Darrow, Lincoln Steffens, Brand Whitlock, Frederic C. Howe, Walter Weyl, and Herbert Croly among others—preferred to work for immediate and tangible reforms. Ideals, as Theodore Roosevelt told a Harvard audience in 1910, had to be realizable, or at least partially so; good intentions without efficiency produced nothing. The latter-day liberals were, for the most part, pragmatists.

Possibly this new emphasis upon concrete legislation, upon getting things done, was a salutary change from the days when emotional men confidently awaited the impossible. In any case, it was almost inevitable that the ambitious public figures who now began to speak in the accents of George and Bellamy should hedge and qualify where the older radicals bluntly denounced. It paid to be cautious when the stakes were high.

The two-men destined to provide the national leadership for the Progressive Movement were both marvelously adept at thrilling the populace with the old progressive rhetoric and at the same time soothing the suspicious men of property. Sandwiched in between the Square Deals and the New Freedoms, the ringing periods of Roosevelt's 'A Confession of Faith' and Wilson's first inaugural address, were the reiterated affirmations that radical economics must be sanely radical. Roosevelt carefully and frequently disassociated himself from 'the wild preachers of unrest and discontent,' and Wilson repeatedly offered similar reassurances. He was no radical who 'pulls up roots to see if the thing is growing,' Wilson told a Nashville group in 1912. 'The true radical,' he went on, 'goes down to the roots to see that the soil is wholesome and that the tap-root is getting the pure nutriment that ought to come from the soil. That is the kind of radicalism I believe in; recultivation, thence reformation of the whole process.'

Neither Roosevelt nor Wilson deserved the title of 'progressive' as much as Robert La Follette, who early in his career had preferred to act rather than to talk progressively and who never truckled to the interests. La Follette read Henry George at a time when the two future presidents had scarcely heard of the Single Tax; Republican though he was, he co-operated with Bryan when Roosevelt was denouncing the populist orator as 'the cheapest fakir we have ever had proposed for President,' and Wilson was condemning his 'foolish and dangerous theories.' It is ironic that the two standard bearers of progressivism in 1912 should both have experienced the shining vision of the people's commonwealth comparatively late in life and that their progressive fervor (particularly Roosevelt's) was always tempered by an adroitness and prudence that the less successful La Follette, the lineal heir of the nineteenth-century progressives, never acquired.

Theodore Roosevelt, the Bull Moose candidate of the Progressive party in 1912, may have been 'the best publicity man progressivism ever had,' as one of his recent biographers has claimed, but his progressivism was of the most dubious sort, despite his often repeated remarks about his instinctive democracy. Adored by his followers (he had a genius for inspiring loyalty and love) and radiating an astonishing ebullience, vitality, and charm, he could identify himself with a new cause so quickly and completely that it appeared to his admiring public as if conservation or trust-busting or progressivism had originated in his fecund mind.

Those who had known him during his Harvard days or who were in positions to watch his shifts and stratagems before and during his presidency did not succumb so readily to the Roose-veltian glitter. Shrewd leaders of the Old Guard, such as Mark Hanna, distrusted him, but so did intimates like Henry Adams and John Jay Chapman. Chapman's judgments are perhaps the most revealing, since he had gone through the stages of near rap-ture and disillusionment experienced by many of Roosevelt's other acquaintances. What most disturbed him about T.R. (and he had many brilliant and devastating things to say) was Roosevelt's chronic dislike for the kind of man he sometimes paid lip-service to—the idealist.

This testy condemnation of the idealist as an enemy to society was never far from Roosevelt's thought [Chapman wrote] and cropped out in his conversation. A philosopher might wonder why the man whose whole life was one long fight for righteousness should feel harshly towards men of any sort for being inexpediently, rashly, and ignorantly righteous—fools of idealism and mere prophetic agitators. One would think that such persons might be commiserated but must certainly be approved by the standard bearer of righteousness.

Other reformers—Charles Edward Russell, Henry Demarest Lloyd, Mark Twain, to mention only a few—concurred with Chapman's estimate. They sized Roosevelt up as a bogus liberal and concluded with William Howard Taft that he was an 'emotionalist,' a 'neu-rotic,' and a 'megalomaniac.'

Nothing in Roosevelt's background except a family tradition of stewardship gave promise of the ardent Square Deal candidate and the self-styled leader of the common man. From his first gin-gerly dip into the political waters, when he was elected as a 'silk-stocking' assemblyman in 1882 (John Swinton labeled him soon

after 'the Crested snob, Roosevelt,' who 'tried to terrify mankind
by shouting "Socialism! Communism!" and other blood curdling
words'), until his death in 1919 he conceived of himself as a
natural leader, if not an aristocrat, who knew what was best for
the people and expected them to appreciate his disinterested devotion to their welfare. He overcame his early hostility to labor unions
and played less self-consciously the role of the blue blood mingling
incognito with the *hoi polloi,* but his conviction of his superiority
is evident in almost everything he did or wrote. The ideal citizen,
he apparently believed, was the sturdy yeoman, neither money-
grubber nor mobocrat, who would drop whatever he was doing
when the country was being threatened by a Spanish or Mexican
invasion and enlist in one of Colonel Roosevelt's cavalry brigades.
This 'virtuous demagogue,' as Chapman called him, would have
been content to rule over a kingdom of cowboys. His political allegiances may have fluctuated according to the national temper,
but whether he voted for Blaine or blasted Taft, he always har-
bored a passion for order and a disgust for what he referred to as
'mushy sentimentalists.'

The young Roosevelt possessed to a high degree three traits,
which carried him from a minor New York office to the presidency:
ambition, energy, and adaptability. Very early he worked out a convenient rationale of compromise, which permitted him to support
James G. Blaine in 1884, when all of his tender-spirited Mugwump
friends bolted the party ticket, and then later to temporize with
his political and financial overlords while he worked out his apprenticeship in New York politics and as McKinley's vice-presi-
dent. During the two terms of his presidency, he did nothing to
offend the House of Morgan, and inadvertently helped to consolidate the United States Steel Company by permitting Frick and
Gary to buy the stock of the Tennessee Coal and Iron Company.
And then, paradoxically enough—or rather naturally enough—
after the four years had elapsed between the end of his second
term and Taft's single administration, Roosevelt, having recognized the political significance of the progressive tide, snatched
the leadership of the movement from the man who was chiefly responsible for building it up—Robert La Follette. After usurping

the position that belonged rightly to another, Roosevelt, with the help of other 'progressives,' proceeded to wreck the Progressive party.

Roosevelt himself did not break faith with La Follette in a literal sense; he never acted meanly or treacherously, and he had made no bargains. But his willingness to accept the support of La Follette's untrustworthy and disingenuous allies and to save the country from a standpatter and a 'rural tory' illustrates again his cosmic vanity and his inveterate opportunism. As Mark Twain said:

Mr. Roosevelt is always talking about his policies but he is discreetly silent about his principles. If he has any principles they look so like policies that they cannot be told from that commodity, and they have that commodity's chiefest earmark—the quality of impermanency, a disposition to fade and disappear at convenience.

These less attractive features of Roosevelt's personality, which bulk so large especially in the early and final stages of his life, should not blind us to the fact that he was a person of culture and great charm and that with all of his muddle-headedness and truculent boyishness he was a high-minded and a completely honest public servant. Conscious of his own superiority and the superiority of his class, he nevertheless felt a solemn obligation to the lesser orders and worked as conscientiously as he could to make every citizen equal before the law and to restrain the 'predatory monopolists' from gobbling up the 'people's heritage.' His most distinguished achievement was his work in conservation reform, his securing for the public hundreds of thousands of acres of valuable forest and grazing land, much to the rage of the spoilsmen. It is a tribute to his abilities and to his personal magnetism that he won the reelection in 1904 with the greatest plurality enjoyed by any president since Grant; and it is quite characteristic of him, too, that he should have been so worried about the outcome that he is reported to have beseeched the railroad tycoon, E. H. Harriman, to contribute more money to his campaign chest.

In spite of his protestations to the contrary, Roosevelt never trusted the instincts of the voting masses enough to put himself completely in their hands, and he was quite capable of making embarrassing commitments to the very millionaire-malefactors he ripped up and down before delighted audiences. He disliked the bloated moneybag as any gentleman would, but the Hamilton in him and the Gouverneur Morris (his beau ideals of American statesmanship) made him distrust even more the extreme democrats of the Jefferson-Jacksonian stamp. He despised Jefferson with all of the vigor of his Federalist forbears. Jefferson was the 'timid, shifty, doctrinaire,' the most incompetent chief executive in American history, 'not even excepting Buchanan.' Roosevelt admired Jackson as a soldier and a nationalist, but Jackson also did his country more harm than good and aggravated 'caste antagonism.' If Roosevelt loved the people and proclaimed his faith in the superiority of human rights over property rights, he loved stability still more. He had resolutely condemned populism and Governor Altgeld as the philosophy and agent of anarchy, and in his liberal phase, when he spoke out honestly against 'the dull purblind folly of the very rich men,' in the back of his mind was the old and ever-present fear of socialism and revolution. Taft correctly interpreted Roosevelt's criticisms of the unthinking rich as an effort to withhold the socialist momentum, which the flagrant and ostentatious expenditures of the plutocracy encouraged. When Roosevelt became a 'radical' in 1912, his old friends, the ones who really knew him, were not taken in. 'He has merely picked up certain popular ideas which were at hand,' Elihu Root observed, 'as one might pick up a poker or a chair with which to strike.'

Roosevelt used as one of his slogans for the third-term fight 'The New Nationalism,' a term he borrowed from Herbert Croly's *The Promise of American Life*. This book, which Roosevelt read with avidity in 1909, provided the kind of ideology he had been looking for. Croly glorified the theory of the Hamiltonian elite and the positive national state, but he argued that such a conception should be given 'a democratic meaning and purpose.' Roosevelt had always slightly tempered his enthusiasm for the Federalists by criticizing their excessive distrust of the masses. What pleased him about Croly's disquisition was the latter's insistence that the new national government should not be used as a bulwark against the people but as an engine for harmonizing all the national energies for the public welfare. Monopolies could not be penalized or broken up (Croly and Roosevelt agreed that the trusts were inevitable) but harnessed and regulated; then the advantages that came with centralization could be put to democratic ends.

The Croly-Roosevelt program, with its plan for 'co-operating' with and 'regulating' big business and its unmitigated anti-Jeffersonian cast, broke with the earlier progressive tradition and substituted in its place a kind of pseudo-progressive makeshift which bore only a superficial resemblance to the original philosophy. It turned out to be a compromise with monopoly capitalism, and it was engendered more from a fear of social revolution than a dream of democratic fulfillment. The New Nationalism ill accorded with the aspirations of many of the progressive crusaders who sang 'Onward Christian Soldiers' at the Progressive party convention in Chicago. Liberals like Brandeis, more attuned to the values and views of Henry Demarest Lloyd and Henry George, saw the unprogressive implications of the New Nationalism and turned to Wilson. Others did not understand them until it was too late. Charmed by the candidate's rhetoric, they identified the Rooseveltian brand of liberalism with their own.

Lloyd, who had different ideas about the alleged efficiency of the trusts and their so-called natural evolution, never made that mistake. As early as 1901 he had expressed his doubts about the reliability of T.R.

> As to Roosevelt [he wrote to W. T. Stead], I do not know. He is a man of infinite energy, but when I read his speeches, there seems to be more emotion than matter in his mind. I am afraid he is in large part an illustration of atavism, as Bonaparte was, with much the same appetite for the spread of ideas by explosion which Napoleon had. I do not think he has any ear at all for the new music of humanity that you and I would like to hear from the orchestra of history of our times, but he is probably an admirable instrument for the 'Americanization of the World,' commercial and military.

Lloyd correctly sized up the President as an ambitious man (he predicted in 1901 that Roosevelt would try to break the two-term tradition), a timorous reformer, and a fire-eating militarist;

several years of the Roosevelt administration did not change his views. In 1903, he exploded: 'His spitting way of talking is no accident. He is a mad dog. I don't detect a single trait or purpose in R. sympathetic to anything truly sane and good. I wish he had himself and his Lodge in some vast wilderness.'

The last outburst was unfair if not absolutely unwarranted, but the jingoistic side of Theodore Roosevelt, Lloyd realized, indicated more than a youthful aberration. The militarist and the disciplinarian was the real Roosevelt, not the belated reformer, and his contempt for what he called the 'flabby, timid type of character, which eats away the great fighting features of our race,' revealed more about the Roosevelt character than his admirers have cared to admit. Much of Roosevelt's distaste for the vulgar plutocracy was not inspired by his humanitarianism so much as it was by his feeling that too much luxury debilitated the Anglo-Saxon race and the American fighting spirit. Hence his palaver about race suicide which so disgusted Howells.

But to see what the Rooseveltian system really amounted to and where it might have actually taken the country had Roosevelt been more resolute and intelligent and (most important) more successful in 1912, we must turn not to Roosevelt's public declarations, not even to his franker and more revelatory private correspondence, but to the writings of a far more brilliant and incisive thinker, who probably had a deeper influence upon Roosevelt than the Colonel realized himself—Brooks Adams. Adams is the real philosopher of the pseudo-progressives, a man whose theories ran parallel to the progressive tradition in a few important respects but whose basic assumptions, like Roosevelt's, were deeply conservative. But Adams was consistent where Roosevelt was not. Had Roosevelt followed his counsels (as he sometimes did, for Roosevelt instinctively agreed with Adams on some issues even though he prudently rejected Adam's suggestions when the times called for compromise), he might have become an even greater and perhaps a more sinister figure.

II] Brooks Adams has been dead for more than twenty years now, but there are still many people in Boston and

Cambridge who remember this eccentric and arrogant man, the last-surviving of the children of Charles Francis Adams. His nephews and nieces recall his gruff manner and his penchant for saying shocking things at dinner parties, his love of argument, his endless jaunts to watering spas, his fondness for the Scottish lays he compelled his niece Abigail Adams to memorize. To some people, it seems, he was known as a crank, 'that damned fool, Brooks,' and Boston never quite accepted the man whom, during the fiery days of '96, it had ostracized as a dangerous incendiary. Even his brother Henry, certainly closer to Brooks than to any other member of his family, saw a mulish streak in the youngest Adams, and continually cautioned him not to kick so violently against the obnoxious aspects of American life they both loathed but to which Henry had become resigned.

Brooks never became resigned to anything, no matter how vehemently he boasted to Henry that he had. He remained the rebel, the unreconstructed individualist, knowing all the time that he was an anachronism, an 'unusable man,' as his niece put it, preaching to uncomprehending ears. The few times in his life when he did manage to interest a small audience always astonished him, and he would sometimes announce with a curious air of triumph to Cabot Lodge or to Henry that he was not a maniac. 'I feel I am not mad,' he wrote to Lodge in 1894, as if to reassure himself. 'I am after all like other men. I am not the victim of an illusion. I am not a man with a maggot in my brain—and all the years when I have been wandering from New York to Jerusalem speculating on the causes which seemed to be crushing the world, I have not been morbid, crazy or ill.' This is the cry of the 'unusable man,' the prophet in the wilderness, and it is only after we have discovered more about this misplaced American that we can understand his despair. It is agonizing to believe that one has a revelation that one's contemporaries are incapable of responding to, and Brooks Adams's eccentricity and neuroticism were aggravated if not actually produced by what he chose to regard as the blockheadedness of his fellow citizens.

Adams took some consolation in the thought that posterity might find some merit in his views and even wrote to Henry in a moment of pride, 'I shouldn't wonder if I had quite a reputation after I'm dead,' but his recognition has come slowly. It is ironic that Vernon Louis Parrington, whose political philosophy he would have found completely repugnant, should be one of the first to write favorably about him. Parrington's essay was genial but thoroughly misleading, and most of his successors have erred in taking literally Henry's joking reference to his brother as a 'Jeffersonian, Jacksonian, Bryanian democrat,' a judgment that clashes with almost everything Brooks Adams ever wrote. While an immense literature has grown up about Henry, Brooks (if we except the valuable introduction by Charles Beard to *The Law of Civilization and Decay* and R. P. Blackmur's perceptive essay that appeared some years ago in *The Southern Review*) has received only the most cursory treatment and that of a very inferior sort.

That Adams might be a more considerable person than the historians had supposed has been made clear in Mr. Blackmur's essay and also in the few pages that Matthew Josephson devoted to Adams in his book, *The President Makers* (1940), where he appears for the first time as a flamboyant and somewhat sinister figure. The quotations Mr. Josephson cites from Adams's letters to Theodore Roosevelt reveal the imperialist and the Darwinian, the snob and the frustrated aristocrat. According to Mr. Josephson, Brooks Adams had become, after a brief flirtation with political reform, the historical theoretician and international strategist for the younger group of statesmen who came into power during McKinley's administration. Adams's speculations on trade routes, international exchanges, and the historical responsibilities of peoples were extremely congenial to men like Roosevelt, Lodge, and Beveridge, and although Mr. Josephson makes far too much of Adams's influence, he is correct in pointing out the similarity between the ideas of Adams and the neo-Hamiltonian expansionists who were cheered by America's reviving nationalism and who sought to substitute the martial values for the spirit-destroying materialism of plutocrat and socialist. Roosevelt and Lodge shared Adams's distaste for what T.R. called 'the lawless capitalist' and 'the Debsite type of anticapitalist.' They too believed in the 'stewardship' principle, in the desirability of a public-spirited but aristocratic elite of skilled administrators representing the nation as a whole and jealous of its honor.

It is rather surprising that Adams's geopolitical speculations have not attracted more attention during the last decade, for Adams was one of the first American strategists of *Realpolitik* to be taken seriously by the Germans, and his remarks upon America's place in the world and her future course with Russia make less eccentric reading to us than they did to his provincial contemporaries. It seems likely, however, that as his papers become available, he will become less important as an authority on the dynamics of international change and more interesting as a kind of American phenomenon, a complement to his brother Henry whose ideas he helped to shape and who furnished him, in turn, with his only sympathetic audience.

III] From his birth in 1848 until his death nearly eighty years later, Adams lived a life that was not, on the surface, very different from the lives of his older brothers; that is, he was graduated from Harvard College, married well, traveled extensively, and wrote from time to time on public issues. But he seems to have been a chronically dissatisfied man, conducting a one-man mutiny against the world as he found it. He never attained the popular success of his brothers Charles and John Quincy, to whom apparently he never felt particularly drawn, nor could he acquire the disciplined resignation of Henry, who taught himself to stare into the horrid abyss of the future without quivering.

As a young man Brooks hoped for political preferment or at least for some post of power and authority, and persisted in his ambitions for a much longer time than Henry. With the retirement of his father from politics, he lost for a time his last intimate connection with the men guiding American affairs, and it was not until Lodge and Roosevelt came into the ascendant during the 'nineties and Henry began to move in the Washington orbit that he once again found access to the inner circle. Out of office himself, he still had the pleasure of knowing and advising men who were in. He enjoyed playing the role of the amateur statesman and offered his ideas and services to properly oriented people in Washington who had the wit to appreciate his expert counsel. It is not too much to say that Adams's pessimism about the future of the country fluctuated with his friends' political successes and failures.

During his early years, after his father had returned from his post as Minister to England, Adams practised law, served as private secretary to his father when the latter represented the United States on the Alabama Claims Commission, and married the sister of Mrs. Henry Cabot Lodge. For a short time he flirted with the Mugwump reformers, but he quickly repudiated their ideals as sentimental and unrealistic, and from the 'nineties on he developed his particular brand of romantic conservatism, which distinguished his writings from this time until his death.

We cannot be sure what influences or forces changed Adams from a genteel reformer to a hard-headed geopolitician, but this much seems clear. After his marriage he retired from the active practice of law and began to write history. Fortunately for him, he was not obliged to earn his living, for, as he remarked to Henry, he was too original a person to survive in a world that protected a man only if he joined a guild and listened to him only if his ideas were stolen. The reception of his first book, *The Emancipation of Massachusetts* (1887), convinced him that the public was far stupider than he had dreamed possible, and from this time on he played the misunderstood prophet with gusto. Ostensibly the book was a ferocious attack on the Puritan founders of Massachusetts Bay, whom Adams excoriated as monsters, sadists, and hypocrites. So, at least, Boston interpreted the book. But Adams, in letters to Cabot Lodge, Henry Adams, and William James, protested that such was not his intention at all. 'What I feel the lack of,' he wrote to Lodge, 'is appreciation of the unity of cause and effect in the notices I see of my book. It is really not a history of Mass. but a meta-physical and philosophical inquiry as to the actions of the human mind in the progress of civilization; illustrated by the history of a small community isolated and allowed to work itself free.' He insisted that he could have done the same for any other similar community: 'This is not an attempt to break down the Puritans or to abuse the clergy, but to follow out the action of the human mind as we do of the human body. I believe they and we are subject to the same laws.'

Whether or not Adams was justified in censuring his audience or in confiding to Henry that no one seemed bright enough to review him, his explanations to his friends clearly show that already he was thinking along the lines he was to develop most completely in *The Law of Civilization and Decay* (1895). He was attempting to show, as he told William James, 'that mind and matter obey the same laws and are therefore probably the same thing.' In this same letter he outlined one of his cardinal theories and defended his historical approach:

My dear sir, the deepest passion of the human mind is fear. Fear of the unseen, the spiritual world, represented by the priest; fear of the tangible world, represented by the soldier. It is the conflict between these forces which has made civilization. And it is the way in which the problem has worked itself out which interests me. . . If you mean I have given a side, it is very true; I can't conceive what is meant by impartial history, any more than impartial science. There are a set of facts; your business is to state them accurately and then criticise the evidence, and draw a conclusion; and at the same time, if you can, throw in enough interest to sugar-coat the pill. I have tried to show what I believe to be the crucial point of a certain phase of development, and then to show that what is true of this is universally true. . . I have perhaps erred in making the story too personal, but the temptation to try to interest your audience, I admit, is too strong for me; and I can't resist the desire to make all the men and women as real to other people as they are to me.

The explanation to James is most revealing, for it helps to show what prompted Brooks Adams to apply his theory on a larger scale as well as offering a hint of what he took to be the function of the historian.

The initial result of his first political fiasco was to send him to Europe and to a set of experiences that he later cherished as the most rewarding of his life. Europe, the Near East, and afterward India not only confirmed and expanded the ideas he first propounded in America but opened up the endless vistas of a past, which even his mercenary and vulgar contemporaries, he told Henry, could not desecrate. In 1888 he began his introduction to the Middle Ages, his discovery of the meaning of the Gothic, and what he described to Henry as 'the heart of the great imaginative past.' At a cathedral in Le Mans, the meaning of the mass and the medieval spirit struck him with a strange intensity, and it was here that he received the impetus to go on to Jerusalem, to Syria, and to see 'what it was that made the crusades' and 'the remains of the age of faith.' In Jerusalem, at Beaufort, at the Krals, and 'most of all it may be,' he reminisced to his brother, 'in that tenderest of human buildings, the cathedral of the Templars at Tortosa, I suppose I had an intenser emotion that I could ever have again.'

Out of these experiences came *The Law of Civilization and Decay,* perhaps his greatest book and as much a glorification of of the pre-industrial age of fear and of the imagination as it was a demonstration of the inexorable movements of the trade routes and money centers. Simultaneously with this sudden and ravishing illumination came the numbing realization of what it all portended. In the past he read the degeneration of the present and glimpsed the chaos toward which he saw his own world rapidly heading. The revelation heightened his nostalgia for an age forever closed, and increased his disgust for the age in which he found himself entrapped. His subsequent writing can be understood only in the light of this dilemma.

Long before his European adventure, Adams indicated that his sympathies lay with the obsolescent standards of a defunct past rather than with the capitalistic ethic of his own America. As early as 1874, he confessed a strong distaste for Benjamin Franklin's doctrines of self-interest. 'No man who has elevated ideas of morality,' he wrote to Lodge, 'is willing to put the duty he is under to keep his word of honour to the account of profit and loss.' Franklin's morality was perfectly suited to

counter jumpers but well I know that George Washington would never have indulged in any such calculation nor yet would have been proud to become the preacher of such small ware if he had. I never said Franklin wasn't useful—so is the constable and so are your account books—but you don't set the constable by the side of your God nor make a bible of your ledger—though many folks have no other.

These assumptions Adams developed more fully some years later in a remarkable essay on Scott and Dickens, in which he made out his case for the pre-industrial man.

According to Adams, Scott expressed the ideals of the non-economic man, while Dickens spoke for the economic man. Scott's heroes, and we may assume they were Adams's too, were extremely brave, held honor more precious than life, displayed the utmost naïveté about money matters, and clung fervently to an ethic that, on the eve of the industrial period, was becoming obsolescent. The soldier-hero, the religious enthusiast, the loyal retainer (creatures of the age of fear) are ennobled by Scott, and the attributes that characterize them, Adams believed, derived from a decentralized, rural, policeless society. Only the courageous and the physically strong could flourish in that kind of world. But when these conditions disappeared, Adams continued, with the rise of the industrial community in the eighteenth century, a new and timid social stratum came to power (creatures of the age of greed), differing from the preceding one as the organism of the ox from the wolf. Charles Dickens was its chronicler. Where the antique world of Scott had singled out courage as the 'essential quality of the ruling class,' in Dickens's novels the prevailing trait is a kind of scaredness, the fear of a timid class that has applied craft and guile rather than valor to the struggle for survival. 'Accordingly,' Adams concludes, 'when Dickens wished to personify force, he never did so through the soldier, or the swordsman but through the attorney, the detective, or the usurer.'

Beginning with *The Law of Civilization and Decay* and continuing in books, articles, and letters, Adams ranged the idealized types from the age of faith against the mercenary and unheroic figures of his own day. He deplored this world of Dickens, a world devoid of statesmanship, of art, of manners, of adventure, even while he traced its inevitability. Hence his attacks against plutocrats, bankers, Jews—collectively subsumed in the word 'gold-bug,' the quintessence of everything vile and rotten in his generation.

The term 'gold-bug' for both Brooks and Henry was an epithet and conveyed no exact designation. The gold-bug or Jew or banker (Brooks used the words interchangeably) embodied the spirit of

the modern, the genie of money. Essentially they were poetic conceptions personifying the forces of commerce. In his more rational
moments, he recognized that 'to hate the gold-bug is not the attitude of the historian. The gold-bug sucks because he is a gold-bug,
and nature causes him to suck.' He also knew perfectly well, as
Henry did, that the family income depended on the sovereignty
and well-being of the money-changers. But history had also persuaded him that the money power had poisoned his world. 'I never
should have hated Wall Street as I do,' he wrote to Henry in 1896,
'if I had not just dug the facts out of history, and convinced myself
that it is the final result of the corruptest society which ever trod
the earth. I tell you Rome was a blessed garden of paradise beside
the rotten, unsexed, swindling, lying Jews, represented by J. P.
Morgan and the gang who have been manipulating our country
for the last four years.' This is a romantic statement and typical
of the naïve over-simplifications to which so-called 'realists' are
often susceptible. That a money power existed, that it exerted an
influence dangerous to a democratic people was certainly true, and
many thousands of Adams's contemporaries agreed with this view,
but Brooks, and Henry too, attributed to international finance an
almost occult energy and pervasiveness that hardly differed from
the fantasies of the primitive Populists they ridiculed.

Brooks Adams's mightiest effort to overcome the legions of gold
came in 1896, when he lent some tangible and much moral support
to the Democrats. He had spent the last year in India studying
reverently, almost ecstatically, the vestiges of a warlike, poetic,
and imaginative culture. Modern India, with its crumbling shrines,
its commercialized temples, its vulgar, arrogant officialdom
epitomized for him the deteriorating effects of the money economy
on human institutions, and he returned to Quincy full of resolve to
strike at gold if the opportunity arose.

The campaign of 1896 seemed to offer that opportunity. In a
long and interesting series of letters, Brooks recounted to Henry
what he later referred to as the last great servile insurrection. It
was characteristic of Adams that he should quixotically associate
himself with the Nebraska farmers (a group as obsolete, he be-

lieved, as the Templars and the English monks) while at the same
time having no respect for the Populists or their candidate Bryan,
'one of the very most empty, foolish, and vain youths, ever put in
a great crisis by an unkind nature.' He informed his brother that
the election of Bryan would mean revolution, for the bankers
would never let him assume office, even granting the remote possibility that he could win the election. Bryan was only a clever agitator, he reported to Henry, with no understanding of economics,
and he early came to the conclusion 'that the Republicans had better win' over the 'honest incompetents' of the silver movement.
Adams had everything to lose by a Bryan victory. The Adams's
estate had gone on the rocks in '93, and a Democratic administration, as he told Henry, 'would disarrange many things which have
taken me three long, harassing years to get in order.' Adams had
backed the conservative movement within the Democratic camp,
but he was not prepared to support actively 'a raving Populist
stump speaker' and his bob-tail following.

Believing as he did that the country and the family fortunes
would remain safer with McKinley as president, Adams could still
enjoy the spectacle of the struggle ('it is like a cold bath, it is like
looking into a heavy surf where you know you must plunge') and
take the most exquisite pleasure in the consternation of the gold-
bugs. The Republicans, moving 'in their course like a squad of
police against a mob' had everything on their side. Mark Hanna,
Adams mentioned to his brother, took two millions out of one
Boston office building alone during the first week of August 1896.
And yet the Democrats, lacking 'ability, or judgment, or capacity
of any kind' and led by an 'empty vessel,' still managed to keep the
election in doubt and terrify business. The violence of the agrarian
storm astonished him:

I have never seen so impressive a sight as the election. A rising of
miserable bankrupt farmers, and day labourers led by a newspaper reporter, have made the greatest fight against the organised capital of
the world that has ever been made this century—or perhaps ever. . .
No money, no press, no leaders, no organisation. Amidst abuse, ridicule, intimidation, bribery—against forces so powerful and so subtle
that they reach the bravest and most honest men in the country.

Brooks, as a gesture, sent money to Chicago and induced Henry to do the same, but he reluctantly reached the conclusion that the gold-bug must retain control until the inevitable rot should set in. 'Henceforth,' he wrote to Henry, 'the old travesty of popular government must be abandoned and the plutocracy must govern under its true colors.' Nature had so constituted the gold-bug mentality that it alone could survive; the rest were mere anachronisms, the rejected, animals 'who might have done well in the glacial or the torrid or some other age, but who can't live now.' And the worst of the defeat, Adams lamented, was the absolute impossibility of a renaissance:

Out of it all observe, that for the first time in human history there is not one ennobling instinct. There is not a barbarian anywhere sighing a chant of war and faith, there is not a soldier to sacrifice himself for an ideal. How can we hope to see a new world, a new civilization, or a new life? To my mind we are at the end; and the one thing I thank God for is that we have no children.

IV] During the exciting days of '96, Adams had been reflecting on other subjects besides silver and gold, and in the closing years of the century he continued his European travels, watched carefully what he believed to be the signs of decay in the British Empire, studied the campaigns of Napoleon, for whom he developed an intense admiration, and scrutinized the great Russian state sprawling to the eastward. It was at this time that he thought through the ideas embodied in his next books, *America's Economic Supremacy* (1900) and *The New Empire* (1902). These ideas can be reduced to the following axioms: (1) that 'man is an automatic animal moving along the paths of least resistance' without will and dominated by forces over which he has no control, and that what is true of men is true of nations; (2) that 'by nature, man is lazy, working only under compulsion,' and that 'when he is strong he will always live, as far as he can, upon the labour or the property of the weak'; (3) that the history of nations is simply the success or failure of adaptation (the flexible live; the rigid die) and that 'intellectual variations are the effect of an attempt at adaptation to changing external conditions of life'; (4) that since the life of nations centers around the fiercest competition (with war as the extreme form) and since nations 'must float with the tide,' it is foolish for men to talk of 'keeping free from entanglements. Nature is omnipotent.' Nations either respond to challenges or decline. There is no standing still.

The corollary economic laws worked out by Adams made national survival depend upon energy and mass, or, to put it in another way, upon concentration and the cheap and efficient administration of large units. 'From the retail store to the empire,' he wrote, 'success in modern life lies in concentration. The active and economical organisms survive: the slow and costly perish.' Throughout the history of man, Adams decided, civilizations have expanded or receded according to their control of trade routes and their access to mineral deposits; but military and commercial successes frequently destroyed national traits responsible for engendering these successes, and newer and more virile nations rose upon the ruins of the old. As society comes to be organized into 'denser masses,' he reasoned, the 'more vigorous and economical' unit 'destroys the less active and more wasteful.' Hence the modern state, if it is to survive, must move in the direction of collectivism, whether private or state. For the realist political principles become less important than success in underselling one's rival. Victory in the war of trade depends, in turn, upon ready access to raw materials and a cheap, efficient administration.

Political principles are but a conventional dial on whose face the hands revolve which mark the movement of the mechanism within. Most governments and many codes have been adored as emanating from the deity. All were ephemeral, and all which survived their purpose became a jest or a curse to the children of the worshippers; things to be cast aside like worn-out garments.

Adams's attitude toward governments rested finally upon the degree to which they could exploit material and human resources and survive in the continuous struggle between nations. To see him solely as an anti-plutocrat and a radical, as some have done, is to oversimplify as well as to misconstrue his true position. The clue to his character and the explanation for his various stands are suggested by his dual role of romantic and conservative. In the first, he glorified the pre-industrial man, lashed out against the money-power, and identified himself with the obsolete organisms who retained the vestigial attributes of the age of faith. In the second, he played the ambitious opportunist, the lover of power, the geopolitical schemer mapping the course of his country's destiny and bolstering the *status quo*. These two seemingly antithetic guises were actually complementary.

As a historian and a realist, Adams knew that to protest against the change in the character of society was foolish, and that the sensible man adjusted himself even in a world for which he felt himself unsuited. He saw no reason why he should make himself a martyr to gold. 'Only those who have a faith to die for want to suffer,' he wrote to Henry, who needed no convincing. 'I see no future to this thing but a long, sordid, slow, grind lasting, may be, indefinitely, with no hope of anything better, and no prospect of what you call anarchy, even supposing anarchy an agreeable condition.' The wise strategy for the philosopher in a dying world was to survive as comfortably as he could. 'If I believed in a god, or a future, in a cause, in human virtue right or wrong, it would be another thing; but I have not enough lust for martyrdom to want to devote myself to misery simply for the sake of suffering.' One did not have to make one's peace with the gold-bug to endure in his society.

Given the stupidity of the average man, certainly one of Adams's primary postulates, and the iron laws of history, the sheer task of staying alive was difficult enough to preoccupy any man. He knew for certain that the world was disintegrating, and he had no faith, as we have seen, in man's ability even to comprehend the complexities of modern living. Man moved instinctively toward self-gratification by the shortest possible route, the 'human mind so constituted that whatever benefits an individual seems to that individual to benefit the race.' What his grandfather had discovered about the people who spurned his services, Adams professed to have discovered about his own generation: that the American people rejected the great dream of his idol, George Washington, of a 'constructive civilization,' that science and education only aggravated the problem, since man was not, as John Quincy Adams at first hopefully surmised, an intelligent, rational animal. Science only permitted man to 'control without understanding.' It hastened the process of disintegration, since 'an education of conservation was contrary to the instinct of greed which dominated the democratic mind, and compelled it to insist on the pillage of the public by the private man.' With such human stuff to work with, no government could evolve 'capable of conducting a complex organism on scientific principles.' Democracy was by its very nature disintegrative, 'an infinite mass of conflicting minds and of conflicting interests, which, by the persistent action of such a solvent as the modern or competitive industrial system, becomes resolved into what is, in substance, a vapor which loses its collective intellectual energy in proportion to the perfection of its expansion.'

These conclusions (which illustrate again the Adams brothers' fondness for applying the second law of thermodynamics to human institutions) spelled ultimate disaster for the race; but Brooks nevertheless felt that a strategy might be worked out whereby America's prosperity and potential supremacy could be at least temporarily sustained and which could once more revive the old heroic virtues. As a property holder and a gentleman, he opposed the thrusts of populism, socialism, and trades-unionism. As a statesman and an economist, on the other hand, he saw the policies of the plutocracy, with their unintelligent domination of the banks and the courts, as suicidally stupid and leading straight to revolution. His criticism of the rich, therefore, must in no sense be interpreted as adventures in muckraking, but as warnings to a a class in danger of being overthrown by forces within and without. Most of his writings after 1896 should be seen as lectures to the members of his own class on the tactics of survival. Governments, he says, are not accidents but growths 'which may be consciously fostered and stimulated, or smothered, according as more or less intelligence is generated in the collective brain.' In modern society their duration depends upon the successful application of Adams's talismans: consolidation, conservation, administration.

Adams's domestic ideas were radical enough to anger most of the conservatives, but as he turned more and more to the international scene around the close of the century, an apparent inconsistency began to appear in his writings, which disturbed even Henry, always in close rapport with his brother. Adams had started as a young man in the Mugwump camp and had worked with the New England reformers of the 'Goo-Goo' variety. He had refused to support James G. Blaine, 'the continental liar from the state of Maine,' and for some time had plumped for Cleveland, a conservative Democrat who wanted, as Adams saw it, to scale down a revolution-provoking tariff and maintain sound money. He came out flatly at this time against the McKinley tariff as a device of capitalists to destroy capitalism; for it was the oppressive protective duties, he felt, that indirectly lured the ignorant into supporting confiscatory and socialistic financial schemes like the unlimited coinage of silver. Harrison in 1892 he labeled a gold-bug. Cleveland steered a path between socialism and plutocracy, and Adams supported him for that reason. And then, rather dramatically, Brooks Adams, the anti-gold-bug, the secret sympathizer of the populists, the man who wanted to see McKinley hanged in front of the White House, became one of the Republican administration's strong supporters.

Actually the shift was not so bewildering as an innocent populist who had read *The Law of Civilization and Decay* as an antigold-bug tract might have supposed, and Henry, out of sympathy with Brooks's new jingoistic phase, need not have been surprised. This book, as Adams pointed out to Lodge in 1894, did trace 'the origin, rise, and despotism of the gold-bug,' but he advocated no heretical monetary theories and had seen silver as a feasible solution only in so far as it might be controlled by conservative businessmen in the Democratic party. Adams feared revolution in 1896 and thought that an intelligently controlled silver policy might reduce its threat by relieving the impoverished farmers. His pamphlet on the gold standard published in that year (described by Samuel Bowles of the influential *Springfield Republican* as 'perhaps the most insidious and powerful argument ever made in demonstration of the ruinous consequences of silver demonitization') provided useful ammunition for the anti-gold-bugs. But he found no difficulty in coming to terms with the other side a few years later, because his own friends, the imperialists, were moving into positions of power. The war with Spain had alleviated the pressure at home by opening up new markets. Surplus production could now be handled without tampering with the monetary system. Adams announced his change of views at a press interview in 1898:

The party [he was quoted as saying] which takes advantage of the opportunity afforded now for the nation to advance and takes its place as a power in the world, is bound to be victorious, no matter what its name, and the men and parties who are content to stand still, and who cannot see that the country has outgrown the system of government which did very well a century ago, will be swept aside. I believe in the war . . . and in the policy of expansion which it forced the nation. I am an expansionist, an 'imperialist,' if you please, and I presume I may be willing to go farther in this line than anybody else in Massachusetts, with, perhaps, a few exceptions.

Certain world patterns were beginning to take shape that called for a different strategy. From 1898 to 1912 Adams was eager to provide it.

v] From his studies and travels, Adams became convinced by the early 'nineties that the old European balance of power was beginning to shift. Watching the money centers moving further westward from Lombard Street to Wall Street, always a sign of impending convulsion and revolution in Adams's prognosis, he calculated that the United States stood at last upon the threshold of a new era. By 1897 (a crucial date in the Adams's chronology, when Pittsburgh steel began to undersell European steel) America was on its way to becoming the greatest creditor nation in the world. The rapid liquidation of British assets abroad—the dissolution of the British Empire was a favorite theme of both Brooks and Henry—had placed tremendous demands upon the supply of American specie. But owing to the superb and remarkably efficient reorganization of American industry through the great trusts, we met our obligations and then proceeded to undersell Europe. In addition to our clearly superior manufacturing facilities and our rich endowments of natural resources, especially the all-important minerals, our prohibitive tariff, formerly assailed by Adams, permitted us to pay for the losses suffered temporarily in the trade invasion abroad. We were carrying on the war of commerce with commendable energy, impoverishing European farmers, reducing the profits of Europe's industry, excluding large, potentially productive areas from European penetration, and, in general, making our position economically unassailable.

For the moment Adams could support the party of the plutocrats and the trusts. 'The trust must be accepted,' he said in 1901, as the corner stone of modern civilization, and the movement toward the trust must gather momentum until the limit of possible economies has been reached.' Not only did he feel that the trust produced more cheaply and efficiently than small concerns, reducing waste and providing low prices for the consumer, but he saw the trust also as a form of Western collectivism which would meet the challenge of the collectivist peoples of the East. He summarized his ideas when he wrote to Lodge:

I must honestly and seriously believe that we are now on the great struggle for our national supremacy, which means our existence. I believe, from years I have given to the study of these matters in many countries, that we must be masters or we must break down. We must become so organized that we can handle great concerns and vast forces cheaper and better than others. It is fate. It is destiny. I believe that, unsatisfactory in many ways as our present system is, the overthrow of McKinley, or even the failure to strengthen his administration, would be a blow to our national life.

After his conversion to McKinleyism in 1900, he saw no reason why McKinley's administration should not go down 'as the turning point in our history. As the moment when we won the great prize. I do believe,' he assured his friend Lodge, 'that we may dominate the world, as no nation has dominated it in recent time.' In this happy and aggressive frame of mind, the country's prospects looked particularly good. To Henry he wrote:

I look forward to the next ten years as probably the culminating period of America. The period which will hereafter be looked back upon as the grand time. We shall, likely enough, be greater later, but it is the dawn which is always golden. The first taste of power is always the sweetest.

His temporary good spirits did not delude him into the belief that America's ultimate future was any brighter, 'but the bloom,' he concluded, 'will last our time. We have vitality enough for one generation at least—perhaps more. And we shant last that long.' A trip to Spokane in the spring of 1901 provided more evidence of America's incredible energy:

> The journey was tiresome [he wrote to Henry] but very interesting. I came home straight, and sat most of the time in an observation car. It is no use for the world to kick, the stream is too strong, nothing can resist it. Beginning on the crest of the rockies the tide flows down into the Mississippi valley, and then across to the eastern mountains in an ever increasing flood, with an ever heightening velocity. At last you come to the lakes and Buffalo. There, I take it, modern civilization reaches its focus. No movement can keep pace with the demand; no power can be found vast enough. . . No one who has watched that torrent from its source on the Divide to its discharge in New York Bay can, I think, help feeling the hour of the old world has struck.

Confident in America's destiny, close to his friends Lodge and Roosevelt, and eager to receive information or offer what he considered to be sound advice, his utterances took on a magniloquence, a bellicosity, and a fervor that he showed neither before nor after.

Both Roosevelt and Lodge understood geographical necessities; they shared Adams's distaste for plutocrats and socialists and appreciated the soldierly virtues. But it was Roosevelt who seemed particularly attuned to Adams's aggressive message and who most clearly reflected the influence of his scholarly friend. From the time of Roosevelt's sympathetic review of *The Law of Civilization and Decay* until the days of the Bull Moose party, Adams closely followed T.R.'s career. He had sympathized with Roosevelt's ambitions in 1896, for Roosevelt too felt the pain and frustration in a gold-bug age, and he had advised his friend to sell himself. 'It is of course a poetical conception to fight and die for what is right, what is pure and true and noble, but after all is it not the dream of a poet, or at least a poetic age? Is not to live the first, the most pressing demand of nature; and to live must we not bend to nature? Can anything be wrong for us to do which is imperiously demanded by the instinct of self-preservation?' After Roosevelt had tempor-

ized with Wall Street and found himself by accident in the White
House, Adams congratulated his protégé as the new Caesar:

'Thou hast it now: king, Cawdor, Glamis, all—' The world can give
no more. You hold a place greater than Trajan's, for you are the embodiment of a power not only vaster than the power of the Empire,
but vaster than men have ever known.
You have too the last and rarest prize, for you have an opportunity.
You will always stand as the President who began the contest for
supremacy of America against the eastern continent.

Roosevelt, in short, was to carry out the policies of McKinley,
whose death Adams deeply regretted and whom he now described
as the best President since Lincoln. McKinley had kept pace with
the times, changing his cabinet after the war, reorganizing the
army, checking Russia and Germany in the east without causing a
panic, and revising America's trade policy. Roosevelt must continue and implement these achievements or we were doomed. This
was to be the theme on which he continually harped to the new
President and which lay behind all of his subsequent counsel, both
on foreign and domestic relations.

Dreams of peace, Adams had long argued, were the will-o'-the-
wisps luring nations to destruction. Human destiny called for war.
Nations destroyed or were in turn destroyed. Our trade methods
actually despoiled the world, whether or not they were intentionally
devised to do so, and if we meant to retain our commercial hege-
mony, we had to face the facts. If we played the braggart, 'rich, aggressive, and unarmed,' we should most certainly be stripped by our
adversaries; nor could we cautiously withdraw. 'If we retreat from
our positions,' he wrote Henry in 1901, 'we might keep the peace,
but I fancy our retreat would mark our culmination. It would mark
the point you were always speculating about when America would
be overweighted by the combination of all Asia from the Atlantic
to the Pacific. It would be all Asia then, Europe would be absorbed.'
For the certain success of the new American push, Adams added
one more proviso. Our political administration would have to be
as flexible, up-to-date, and energetic as our economic; our political
machinery would have to be recast into a cheaper, more elastic,

and simpler form. Finally, we should have to develop a new kind of administrator, well-trained, audacious, and disinterested.

Now by their very natures, the rulers of American society were specialists, whose skill in aggrandizing themselves and whose heroic devotion to their own interests incapacitated them for public service. The ideal administrator represented no special interest but all the interests, and his mind was not bounded by the narrow concerns that made the capitalist unfit to rule a vast, complex, and centralized economy. Unfortunately, America, said Adams, had no administrators, and in 1903 his letters to Henry are filled with apprehensive references to this dearth of trained personnel:

We need a new deal of men and we need it very bad, and everyone agrees with it. Only we can't raise the men. . . As I see it, everything is ripening for a plunge. We must have a new deal, we must have new methods, we must suppress the states, and have a centralized administration, or we shall wobble over. The most conservative as well as the most radical seem to agree to this.

Adams used the analogy of the 'new high steel building' to suggest the powerful, compact, administrative system he had in mind. 'Our whole civilization,' he warned, 'must consolidate to match the high building.'

In daily life we have outgrown the specialist, and for that reason the specialist fails and is a positive danger. We are now attempting to produce the generalizing mind. We are attacking administration scientifically. If we succeed in training the next generation right, and their nervous systems do not give way under the strain, we shall, likely enough, pull through and land a big fish . . . the change is represented by the steel cage of thirty or forty stories. Everything has to pass onto the basis of steel from a basis of brick and stone. It means a social revolution going down to the family and up to the government.

An intelligent administration subordinated the indispensable monopolies to the service of the state, obviating the necessity of a biased judiciary (which hastened the movement toward revolution), and taught the people how to obey and take responsibility. Adams's dream envisioned a kind of modified state socialism, run along the lines of a big modern corporation, with a trained and conservative elite solidly in control, a powerful but amenable industrial aristocracy, and an orderly, responsible electorate. 'The older I grow,' he wrote to Henry, 'the more I am convinced that the administrative mind is the highest vehicle of energy, and that is what makes the power of the soldier, for the soldier must also be an administrator.' The time was rapidly approaching, he hazarded with more prophetic insight than he usually showed, 'when we shall be reorganized by soldiers.' From 1900 his cry was for discipline—a disciplined Business, a disciplined Nation, a disciplined Home, 'Life is tolerable,' he concluded, 'under any form of orderly government.'

Adams placed his hope in Roosevelt as the man who might bring about the necessary administrative reforms. He welcomed his incumbency and remained in close touch with him until T.R.'s death. Roosevelt, he thought, at least approximated the ideal type of administrator, despite his occasional aberrations, his volatility, and his penchant for addressing hard-bitten party men as if they were Groton boys. He too shared Adams's disgust for 'moral platitudinizing' about war ('hogwash without admixture,' Adams called it) and feared the loss of national virility if the feminists had their way. Adams backed Roosevelt, admitting all of the latter's limitations, not only because of his sincerity and honesty, but because Roosevelt represented the kind of intelligent conservatism that, through limited concessions to reform, would preserve their class and protect the country. Writing to the President in 1903 about the railroad problem, he remarked:

I think all conservative men owe you and the Attorney-General a great debt—for it is your policy or State ownership. There is no middle course. In a word, to live, this country must keep open the big highways leading west, at equitable rates, and must command the terminus in Asia—if we fail in this we shall break down.

Throughout Roosevelt's administration, Adams constantly advised him on the railroad issue. His own affairs happened to be involved here, but he saw the arrogant and irresponsible practices of the roads, supported by what he regarded as a stupid and reactionary judiciary, as an invitation to social convulsion as well as an injurious blow to our foreign interests. 'I apprehend that we are entering on a social revolution,' he wrote Roosevelt in 1906, 'which must either wreck or reorganize our society. The community, or the monopoly must control prices, and therefore all wealth.' Under Taft, Adams was now certain, the gold-bugs had regained lost ground; it was for this reason that, in 1912, he urged his friend to seek a third term and save the country. 'This two term business,' he agreed with his grandfather, was 'vicious and preposterous Jeffersonian rot,' and as Roosevelt seemed to respond to Adams's ideas, he grew more excited about his campaign for re-election. He warned Roosevelt that he was attempting to defeat the strongest and best-defended entrenchment in the world and that the gold-bugs would treat him no better than an anarchist. But then, he concluded, 'it has always been so':

I think I know this thing to the bottom. What I want, and have always wanted, is order and authority, and we can have neither unless the law is equally enforced. Capitalism, as always, seeks unequal enforcement of the law—or privilege. Just now, to get privilege, they use the courts, as they are using the Commerce Court to upset the Interstate Commerce Commission. To attain this immediate end they expose the courts to popular attack, as the vested slave interest did the Dred Scott Case. Capital always will. But in so doing it undermines the foundation of order. It works chaos. And chaos is straight before us.

These ideas he presented in greater detail in his *Theory of Social Revolutions* (1913), which reflected the 1912 campaign as *The Law of Civilization and Decay* embodied the issues of '96. As Adams saw it, Roosevelt's job, if elected, was to rebuild a broken-down administrative system, unable to cope with modern complexities, in a scientific way. He could not succeed by making emotional speeches against the bosses. Bryan and his followers had failed in a similar contest because they relied too much on emotion, and Roosevelt's task was immeasurably more difficult than Bryan's.

The question [he told Roosevelt] is whether we can construct a central administration strong enough to coerce those special interests, or whether they can prevent such a consolidation. Call it what you will: empire, dictatorship, republic, or anything else, we have the same problem which Caesar had in Rome when he suppressed the plundering gang of senators led by Brutus, who murdered him for it. We must have a power strong enough to make all the interests equal before the law, or we must dissolve into chaos. All of these special interests are now banded against you in Chicago and they are capable of anything, including murder.

After Roosevelt failed to win the Republican nomination at Chicago, Adams advised him not to run independently and to bide his time, but to Henry he confided his disappointment. Roosevelt had tried hard, but his mind was not elastic and he never fully understood the issues; with a tenth of Caesar's ability he faced problems ten times as difficult. Adams found the emotion of the Bull Moose crusade extremely distasteful, and the antics of Roosevelt and his followers reminded him of 'these volatilized women who run about in motors and can't keep still.' Henry was sure by this time that Roosevelt's mind had 'disintegrated like the mind of the country,' but Brooks still believed that some use remained in his erratic friend, even though Teddy made 'plenty of mistakes' and was 'as headstrong as a mule.'

Adams had never really approved Roosevelt's brief alliance with the progressives ('They do not know what they want and, if they were told what must be done, they would run like rabbits'), but as Roosevelt moved back again to reality and began his crusade against Wilson and unpreparedness, Adams warmed up considerably. The war he had predicted in 1903 had already embroiled Europe and threatened to drag in the United States. American participation at this time would be disastrous, he told Roosevelt in 1914, because only by remaining neutral could we reconstruct our obsolete political system and defend ourselves. A German victory he thought preferable to an English, 'for Germany will not dare attack us with the English fleet on her flank, whereas England, I suspect, if she has the better, must control our competition on the sea if she is to carry her debt and feed her people.' The Germans, at least, might teach our plutocrats and our mercenary proletariat that 'we men owe a paramount duty to our country.' Our salvation lay in substituting for the money standard of Wall Street the military standards of West Point.

By 1916 Roosevelt's chances for the presidency were slim, but Adams thought his friend might carry enough influence to have himself appointed Secretary of War or see to it that a man like Leonard Wood got the job. Adams wanted to see a series of military schools on the order of West Point set up all over the country, in which 'obedience, duty, and self-sacrifice' would be taught 'on a great scale.' If Roosevelt succeeded in his all-important assignment, which was nothing less than changing the moral values of people raised for two generations on the gospel that money is the chief end in life, he would have made his greatest contribution to the nation. 'Our troubles,' according to Adams, 'now arise from the false standards of our people. Is it not logical for men to reason that if money is the only end in life, then peace at any price is a sound policy?'

Roosevelt, however, could not prevent the re-election of Wilson, the President who had become for Adams a 'flagrant ass' and the symbol of our national disunity. He detected the hand of his old enemies, the bankers, behind the League of Nations and suspected that Mr. Schiff was 'somewhere near the focus of the hell-broth.' Adams should have realized by this time that his recommendations had little chance of being taken seriously, but he could not resist the temptation to preach in spite of Henry's pointed remarks that he avoid didacticism; he still felt obliged to warn his uncomprehending and bemused contemporaries. In the debates of the Massachusetts Constitutional Convention in 1917 and 1918, he unfolded all of his favorite arguments and admonitions: the necessity of national supremacy and the subordination of all special interests to the collective will; the dangers that would follow from our failure to collectivize in the face of European tendencies; the tyranny of the courts as brakes on progress; the importance of a flexible bureaucracy that could administer without obstruction ('All modern government means administration, and that is all it does mean'); the certainty that 'everything is to be cured by the concentration of power in some one who really will protect the whole community, the interest of all of us'; the natural inequality of men and the inevitable concommitant, competition; the necessity of recasting our society and girding ourselves for the future struggle that is most certain to occur.

These ideas, amusingly and sometimes brilliantly elaborated in the Massachusetts debates, drew polite applause but no one pretended to know what he was talking about. Only one person really understood Adams's remarks, the person who had provided his first and most sympathetic audience—his brother Henry.

vi] Henry had been following Brooks's strenuous theorizings from the beginning and had found little to disagree with. Always more reserved and skeptical, if no less pessimistic than Brooks, he still found his brother's economic analyses stimulating and instructive; indeed, his own thinking was frequently so similar that it is sometimes hard to discover which brother anticipated the other. Although Henry refused to take credit for the ideas in *The Law of Civilization and Decay,* he exhibits many of Brooks's pet preconceptions—not only his loathing for the gold-bugs, Jews, and socialists, but his views on the inevitability of some kind of state socialism. Both brothers predicted the bankruptcy of England, Henry with more regret, for he did not share Brooks's inveterate hatred of England or accept his vision of an American empire. America, he felt, could not manage its own concerns, much less the world's (a view Brooks returned to), and Henry preferred to see Germany and Russia direct the machine after Britain went under. But Henry's geopolitical speculations resemble Brooks's in large part (he too believed 'that superiority depends . . . on geography, geology and race energy'), and he accepted unchanged Brooks's hypothesis of civilization:

All Civilisation is Centralisation.
All Centralisation is Economy.
Therefore all Civilisation is the survival of the most economical (cheapest).

Henry's heavy correspondence with Brooks, earnest for the most part and without the veneer of flippancy that characterized most of his other correspondence, is merely one indication of their close intellectual relationship. 'We are too much alike, and agree too well in our ideas,' Henry remarked to a friend. 'We have nothing to give each other.' Both used different methods to approach identical ends and acted upon each other as counterirritants or whetstones. Each submitted favorite hypotheses to the other and criticized each other's ideas with brotherly candor.

Brooks had a younger brother's respect for Henry's genius and the highest admiration for his literary talents. *Mont St. Michel and Chartres* he called 'the best literary production of America, if not Europe, at least upwards for two generations,' and he took a family pride in this 'gem of thought, of taste, of execution' that redeemed his generation. 'I perhaps alone of living men can appreciate fully all that you have there,' he wrote to Henry, 'for I have lived with the crusaders and the schoolmen.' Of the *Education* he was less certain, although he allowed that it was perhaps 'the broadest and, in many ways, the best thing you have ever done.' His criticisms or recommendations seem a little cryptic to the outsider, but apparently he felt that Henry had not written the last half on the scale of the first and had 'tried to relieve the shadow.' Brooks may have meant by this last remark that the 'failure' of Henry's life was not seen clearly enough as an individual reflection of a general predicament: man's tragic inability to adapt himself to a changing universe. Such a meaning is certainly suggested in Brooks's reply to Henry after receiving his essay on 'Phase.' Here he recommended that the *Education* be rewritten on the basis of this radical theorem:

> You have at last overcome your obstacle. Here is unity whereby to measure your diversity. The theorem which should precede the experiment. Your education has been the search for the 'new mind.' The contrast you wish to draw is the absolute gap between the thing nature demands and the human effort. If you can strip from your book all semblance of personal irritation against individuals, eliminate the apparent effort to write fragments of biography, and raise the story of your life to the level in dignity of the vast conception against which you are to measure the result, you will have created one of the masterpieces of literature, psychology and history. But I can only say again to you what I have said before . . . that this is a huge and awful tragedy.

Henry had begun to complain to Brooks in 1908 about failing powers of mind, and his brother's praise and encouragement must have been especially welcome. Brooks assured him that his work had steadily improved and that his best work, like his grandfather's, had been done after sixty. 'The only trouble with you,' he wrote, 'is the trouble he felt and we all feel, that is an increase of mental power as the bodily power declines. I suffer from that myself.' As for himself, Adams noted that he was losing his 'faculty of expression' and that he could not rid himself 'of that rigid, didactic and school-mam manner, which drives me to frenzy but which holds me like a vice.' Certainly Henry wrote far better than Brooks. He was more successful in presenting systematically and meticulously his well-considered ideas, sustained, as R. P. Blackmur says, by an all-pervasive imagination. But it should be added that Brooks knew perfectly well the strength and limitation of his method. Always deferring to Henry and regarding him as one of the greatest minds of his age, he nevertheless stoutly defended his own kind of writing against his brother's criticisms. He never thought of his books as being history or literature in the strict sense. They were written for an 'occasion,' for crises, and the times were too crucial to allow him the luxury of being a mere chronicler. History for him had no particular interest unless a practical lesson could be extracted from it:

I try to present a method, not an historical study. I use history as little as possible, and only as illustration. Anyone can gather facts if they only have a plan upon which to arrange them. Hence I have a perfectly plain task, very narrowly limited. I have to state a theory or a method. I have to illustrate it enough to be understood. . . I have to take a definite starting point, and I have to deduce a practical conclusion bearing on our daily life. I have last of all to be ready at the precise moment when the catastrophe is impending evidently—or I shant be read.

Henry and Brooks clearly differed in method—Brooks choosing to be didactic and active, Henry non-committal and passive—but they saw eye to eye on laws of social change and the probable future of the world.

After Henry's stroke and gradual debilitation, Brooks foresaw his brother's death and recoiled from the prospect of being left alone, the last of his generation. Writing to Henry in the spring of 1915, he reminisced:

And as I look back through the long series of years to the days when I was a schoolboy and you used to take me to walk in England, more than fifty years ago, I wonder more day by day what it has all been about and why I am here at all. You have been closer to me than any other man, I suppose, and I cannot with equanimity contemplate parting with you. At this moment my whole life rises before me. I am a coward. I do not want to stay till the last. You must wait and keep me company.

A few months later he wrote almost shyly:

You have helped both of us over many a wet place in our path. . . It is my birthday—so I may be forgiven an emotion. You always were the best of us four brothers—you are so still now that we are reduced to two. I wish I could have done more to justify my life—but I think I have done nearly my best—good or bad, the best part has been yours ever since I was a boy. And now, as an old man, I look at your worth and thank God that you have redeemed our generation.

Brooks's last tribute to Henry was his long introduction to the latter's *Degradation of the Democratic Dogma,* in which he re-iterated his and Henry's theory of exhaustion of resources by waste and its human equivalent. The introduction was mainly an ac-count of John Quincy Adams and, by indirection, of Brooks him-self, for he had come gradually to identify his own career with that of his grandfather. In 1909, while he was preparing a biog-raphy of John Quincy Adams that he never published, he wrote to Henry that Washington and their grandfather were

the only two men who ever conceived of America as a unity and tried practically to realise their idea. They failed and with them our civiliza-tion has failed. Adams stood alone because no one else saw the se-quence of relations. He felt this and the sense of failure made him bitter and morbid.

Brooks and Henry, facing the same problem, had failed too. No one ever understood their grandfather, Brooks concluded, and 'no one will ever understand us—but he was right: and we are right.'

Brooks Adams died in 1927, the same arrogant, blunt, audacious man that he always was, with a few years to spare before the crackup he anticipated and had hoped to escape. With him died his prejudices, which were later to crop up in uglier forms, and his yet unfulfilled predictions. He had wanted to serve his countrymen, for he never seemed quite able to resign himself to the pessimistic implications of his own message, but they responded neither to his promise of national glory nor to his threats of disaster. He had much to suggest which was pertinent and valuable, but he always stood aloof from the democracy he wanted to save and believed that men were 'doomed eternally and hopelessly to contend' against a blind and purposeless universe. And yet he did not gloat over the world's destruction as Henry Adams liked to do. He made a great show of being fatalistic and of enjoying the *Götterdämmerung,* but behind the façade of scientific detachment can be discerned a prevailing sympathy for man in his uneven contest with nature.

CHAPTER 9

. . . .

In Retrospect:

1912-1950

1] Brooks Adams voted the straight Progressive ticket in 1912, but the Democrats won with a candidate whom Roosevelt in his 'elegant billingsgate' later described as a 'conscienceless rhetorician,' a 'logothete,' a 'very adroit and able (but not forceful) hypocrite,' a 'silly doctrinaire,' and 'an utterly selfish and cold-blooded politician.' Wilson's hesitancy to involve the United States in a war with Germany (thereby dulling 'the national conscience,' T.R. complained, and 'teaching our people to accept high-sounding words as the offset and atonement for shabby deeds') particularly angered Roosevelt, but the whole tone and direction of Wilson's administration enraged him. However similar the New Nationalism and the New Freedom appeared on the surface, the more genuinely progressive philosophy of the ex-college president differed fundamentally from the political theory of the big-game hunter.

Like his opponent in the 1912 campaign, Wilson had also started as a conservative. He had come a long way since the days when he spoke about knocking Bryan into a cocked hat, but he retained his conservative bent and, like Roosevelt again, quite consciously worked to save society from revolution and socialism. Wilson had his counselor, too, in 1912—Louis D. Brandeis, the 'people's attorney' and one-time co-worker with Henry Demarest Lloyd. It was Brandeis who convinced Wilson that the New Nationalist-Roosevelt-Adams plan of trust domestication was unworkable. Roosevelt's policies, according to Brandeis, simply legitimized

281

monopolistic practices by making large economic blocks official parts of the government. Under the policy of regulation, the President became, in effect, the chairman of a board of business trustees, a director of a kind of corporate oligarchy. The government that started out to 'regulate' would soon be regulated by the forces it ostensibly intended to manage. Only by making certain 'that the methods by which monopolies have been built up are legally made impossible,' Wilson declared in the spirit of Lloyd and Brandeis, could the American people control their own affairs.

The alternative to a people's government, Wilson argued, was government by a corporation elite. He rejected the system of trustee control, whether the trustees were self-regarding plutocrats or Adams's disinterested administrators, and spoke out eloquently for representation by all the people as against rule by a class 'which imagined itself the guardians of the country's welfare.' After 1910, Wilson never introduced the naïve and irrelevant categories of 'good' or 'bad' wealth and never, in discussing corporate malpractice, spoke intemperately. Where Roosevelt called names and kept his connections with the objects of his tirades, Wilson saw his opponents as stupid or misguided. He preferred the role of schoolmaster to that of the angry prophet.

And yet, although we admit Wilson's closer kinship to the spirit of progressivism and acknowledge his courageous and persistent attempts to legislate democratic ideas into the law of the land during the early years of his presidency, it must be confessed that he remained a progressive very largely in the latter-day or party sense of the term. The liberal influence of men like Brandeis and George L. Record, the exigencies of the times, and political expediency modified his earlier conservatism and account for his progressive tendencies after 1910. But he held to his conviction that change must proceed in a regular and orderly fashion and that reform should not go too far. After the dramatic success of his New Freedom program, designed to aid the small entrepreneurs in their one-sided struggle against big business, Wilson felt he could relax. The American economy, he thought, had been set back on the highway of free enterprise; the business brigands had reformed and no longer molested the little fellows racing toward El Dorado.

So Wilson believed, at any rate, and so he told Congress in his second annual message:

> Our program of legislation with regard to the regulation of business is now virtually complete. It has been put forth, as we intended, as a whole, and leaves no conjecture as to what is to follow. The road at last lies clear and firm before business. It is a road which it can travel without fear or embarrassment. It is the road to ungrudged, unclouded success. In it every honest man, every man who believes that the public interest is part of his own interest, may walk with perfect confidence.

Wilson's remarkable ignorance of the real nature and direction of business enterprise and his never-relinquished faith in the workings of 'free competition' as contrasted with 'illicit competition' induced this complacent note of satisfaction. After America entered the war, it became clear that business had not made the honorable capitulation to popular government Wilson had supposed. His second administration helped to undo the reforms of the first, and in 1918 Veblen's absentee owners, who had made enormous profits during the war, were more solidly in control than ever.

To reformers like Frederic C. Howe, who had believed in the New Freedom and hoped for its perpetuation, the President's alliance with men he had formerly denounced seemed particularly shameful. How could a man who had spoken so eloquently in behalf of progressive ideals act so implacably toward those who continued to affirm them? Howe, commenting more regretfully than bitterly, realized that Wilson's commitments abroad distracted him from his domestic responsibilities, but nevertheless he came reluctantly to the following conclusions about his former hero:

> Conflict disclosed his loneliness, his fearfulness, his hatred of men who challenged his power. Conflict disclosed the Wilson who had bewildered liberals while he was President; who turned on old friends, who hated Cabot Lodge, who excoriated imperialism, and seized Haiti and San Domingo and sent battleships to Vera Cruz. It disclosed the Wilson who imprisoned men who quoted him against himself. When he himself was subjected to a personal test, he abandoned the ideals he had held before America.

Inadvertently, Wilson betrayed the progressive ideal by covering the mercenary policies of finance capitalism with a fog of perfervid rhetoric; he was either unable or unwilling to see the connection between international peace and the economic and social structures of the powers involved. In the last years of his administration he tried to blend national unity and private profits, service and salesmanship, manifest destiny and dollar diplomacy without any awareness, apparently, that such ingredients would not mix. He saw no paradox, once he had embarked upon his course of war leadership, in conducting the fight against autocracy and militarism abroad and giving the superpatriots a free hand at home. For Wilson, democracy had simply become a battle cry.

It was not that Wilson and the anti-German elements in the United States blundered in breaking our traditional neutrality and siding with the Allies. Veblen, perfectly familiar with the dynamics of imperialism and untouched by the war hysteria, wanted to see Germany defeated for reasons incomprehensible to Colonel Roosevelt and President Wilson. Other progressive-minded men saw in German militarism some of the ruthlessness and terror that another war did not disprove. But Wilson lost his perspective with the rest of the country and failed to offer a postwar program that any genuine progressive could support. The blunt suggestion of his friend George L. Record that Wilson call for the public ownership of the railroads, the utilities, and the trust-controlled natural resources, and the restriction of large fortunes through high inheritance and income taxes, made no impression upon the star-struck President.

The letter recommending these measures which Record sent to Wilson in March of 1919 makes clear just how far the President had drifted from the progressive sentiments of the New Freedom. Record, one of the most remarkable and far-sighted of the later progressives, derived straight from Henry George, whose land theories impressed him deeply, and from Henry Demarest Lloyd. He had been largely instrumental in drafting the progressive program carried through by Wilson during his New Jersey governorship, and he had continued to advise him from time to time in the period following Wilson's election to the presidency. Now in 1919, surveying the wreck of the Democratic party, Record frankly blamed his none-too-appreciative friend for ignoring the 'great issue which is slowly coming to the front, the question of economic democracy, the abolition of privilege, and the securing to men the full fruits of their labor or service.' It required no special courage, he told the President, to fight for political democracy; that battle had been largely won. Industrial democracy, however, still remained a dream. In proof he cited the recent five to four decision of the Supreme Court (Hammer *v.* Dagenhart), which declared unconstitutional an act of Congress 'forbidding the relic of barbarism, the employment of little children in mills.' Impossible conditions still obtained in the 'industrial slave pens' where poorly paid men worked long hours at monotonous jobs. Record, like his mentor George, repudiated socialism, but he wanted Wilson to fight for a democratic equivalent and to turn his wrath against the powerfully entrenched law-breakers, the profiteers, and the monopolists, and not against the 'poor, weak socialists,' imprisoned for protesting against what Record termed 'the monstrous injustice involved in the immunity of these wealthy criminals, and other similar inequalities of our industrial system.' Although he enthusiastically approved of Wilson's championing the League, he challenged his friend to assume an even greater and more imperative task: to 'become the real leader of the radical forces in America, and to present to the country a constructive program of fundamental reform.'

What Record proposed in 1919, Randolph Bourne, hounded by government agents and driven into silence, had demanded two years before. For Bourne, Deweyan pragmatism led directly into the cul-de-sac of Wilsonian compromise and the suffocation of the progressive ideal. He had been an ardent instrumentalist while keeping a faith in his private utopia. But Bourne suddenly realized that instrumentalism was bankrupt without a vivid poetic vision. The philosophy of 'adaptation' or 'adjustment,' he found out before Woodrow Wilson did, ends in a 'radiant cooperation with reality,' but it stops there.

An impossibilist élan that appeals to desire will often carry further. A philosophy of adjustment will not make for adjustment. If you merely try to 'meet' situations as they come, you will not even meet them. Instead you will only pile up behind you deficits and arrears that will some day bankrupt you.

Bourne asked the ex-radicals, bogged down in compromise, to construct a valid democratic program if they wished to allay the suspicions of the impossibilist.

But when [he wrote] the emphasis is on technical organization, rather than organization of ideas, on strategy rather than desires, one begins to suspect that no programme is presented because they have none to present. This burrowing into war-technique hides the void where a democratic philosophy should be. Our intellectuals consort with war-boards in order to keep their minds off the question what the slow masses of the people are really desiring, or toward what the best hope of the country really drives. Similarly the blaze of patriotism on the radicals serves the purpose of concealing the feebleness of their intellectual light.

Bourne argued that 'vision must constantly outshoot technique.' The progressive in 1919 had neither vision nor technique, and Brooks Adams's 'money power' (as blind and stupid and reckless, in all but its own peculiar line, as ever was a drunken soldier, or a crazy Nero') took over in due course as George Record had predicted.

The defeat of Wilson cannot be attributed solely to Wilson himself. His liberal supporters, even men like Record or Brandeis, who criticized his failure to prepare an adequate postwar reconstruction program, had no program or organization of their own to sustain him. Isolated more and more from the progressive-minded rank and file, both by circumstances and by choice, and entirely preoccupied with the Peace Conference and the League, he found it easier to compromise with his conservative critics than to fight them and to sanction legislation (as Howe observed) that he never would have tolerated during the opening years of his administration. He seemed to have no qualms about sacrificing one set of ideals in the hope of approximating another. In the end, not even his courage, sincerity, and audacity were enough to salvage his wrecked administration.

During the next decade, the battered idols of *laisser-faire* were once more enshrined in the American temples and the business oracles resumed their glorious prophecies.

II] By 1920 the progressives found themselves without a party, a leader, or a philosophy. The old Progressive party had fallen to pieces since the days when Theodore Roosevelt provided a dubious leadership, and now the insurgents from the two major parties had no place to go. In the election following the war a bobtailed Farmer-Labor party managed to poll a quarter of a million votes, and the Socialist candidate, Eugene Debs, picked up a million more, but the magnitude of the Republican victory left no doubt that whatever progressivism was or could be, the bulk of the American voters wanted no truck with it.

During the next few years the progressives took stock. Why did they fail and what now remained for them to do? Did they share a common set of beliefs? Was it possible to build up a national party that would come to something more than a loose confederation of malcontent groups, each harboring a different grievance? From the discussion of these questions in the liberal press, one can see that the answers were not reassuring to the progressive cause.

The various definitions of the 'progressive' which cropped up from time to time did suggest a kind of agreement on the meaning of the term, although most of them merely expressed a vague liberal creed. The composite progressive turned out to be a person who worked for the wider diffusion of economic, political, and social equality, who sought to approximate the moral code in politics, who combined a zeal for service with a curiosity for facts, who worked for the gradual displacement of the obsolete by the new, who understood the relation between human conduct and unjust economic conditions, who believed in 'purposeful change.' One contributor to the *Nation* brought these ideas together in the following credo:

A progressive is one who recognizes the fact that the past does not fit into the present and that the present will not fit the future. He is one who advocates such changes in our social and economic structure as will best serve the interests of a majority of the people now and present the least resistance to ready adjustments to meet coming needs in the future. He is one who is always ready to take one constructive step forward, even if he cannot go the whole distance. He is one who stands on the past that he may reach farther into the future, but does not try to take the past with him.

Unfortunately, it required more than an enunciation of progressive criteria to launch an effective political party. Progressives could agree on how a progressive ought to feel and what he ought to think, but the more perceptive among them also recognized the ideological conflicts within the movement itself, which had not yet been resolved. Progressivism, as one of them noted, shook and wobbled because it represented little business, which 'shades off into big business on the one hand and into labor on the other in such a vague and indefinite fashion that it is inevitable that progressives are divided in their counsels.' Both conservative and radical progressives believed in advancing, but they did not agree on how wide the steps should be or how frequently taken.

Even more serious in the eyes of some critics, notably the editors of the *New Republic,* progressivism still smacked of the unreflective insurgency of the Bull Moosers and expended more effort on denunciation than on constructive planning. The progressives emphasized evils rather than remedies; they lacked a 'moral and intellectual binder,' an 'ardent belief in some fundamental principle or purpose which will establish and sharpen the fighting issue between them and their opponents.' According to Herbert Croly and his associates, no progressive movement could succeed until large numbers of voters still loyal to the old parties and to the old economic system could be persuaded to abandon their allegiance. A campaign of education was needed to provoke this mass apostasy, which in turn required the formulation of a realistic program. Ideas by themselves were not enough, nor were good intentions. If the farmers and the wage earners were to be won over, they must be made to see that progressivism was a method, not a principle, and that they had something to get by supporting it.

This strong pragmatic approach to politics, which gained currency with some of the progressive theorists in the early 'twenties, had been developing since the outbreak of the First World War. Disgust for Theodore Roosevelt's camp-meeting tactics and Wilsonian rhetoric and a profound respect for power prompted such a man as Herbert Croly to re-examine progressive policies. The defects of progressivism or liberalism, as Walter Lippmann (speaking for his master) wrote in 1919, lay in 'its apathy about administration, its boredom at the problem of organization, its failure to make its own what may be called roughly the constructive tradition of Alexander Hamilton.' These were Croly sentiments, for Croly combined an admiration for Hamiltonian techniques with an at least ostensible preference for democratic ends. Progressivism, as he understood it, was 'fundamentally the attempt to mold social life in the light of the best available knowledge and in the interests of a humane ideal.' It lived 'by the definite formulation of convictions.'

Croly saw the task of the progressives as chiefly one of class reconciliation. In order to achieve this end the progressives had to take the leadership in restoring a larger measure of economic power and social privileges to the masses of farmers and wage earners. Such a restoration of power would do much to relieve class tensions increasingly exacerbated by business rule and to prevent the domination by a single class either from above or from below. Progressives in the past had weakened their position by remaining aloof from the very classes whose support was indispensable, and they could not 'repair this mistake,' he wrote in 1921, "without reviving the primitive association between liberalism and radicalism and a conscious and militant humanism.'

In taking this stand, Croly, for the moment at least, allied himself with the early progressives, but during the next few years he seemed to play down the ideological imperative and concentrate upon naked appeals to economic interests. As the 1924 election approached, the *New Republic* kept hammering at the La Follette supporters not to crusade for social justice, not to talk about helping the oppressed or ameliorating conditions, but to promise a fairer distribution of economic power.

It is an illusion [declared an editorial] to suppose that a society like our own which is made up so largely of competing as well as cooperating classes can generate automatically out of this class competition an amount of public spirit and enlightenment which will enable the existing state, which necessarily reflects these prevailing standards, to become the trustworthy agent of a program of social reform.

Croly's objectives were progressive, but here spoke the Hamiltonian. He stated frankly that any successful party had to be not only numerous but also conscious of its objectives and resolute enough to fight for them. It was up to the progressives to make this issue clear to an electorate who still did not 'understand the function of conflict in the social economy of a democratic people,' who were satisfied always with 'immediate agreements,' and who failed to realize 'that conscious conflict is often the only means by which the obstacles to co-operation are removable.'

The failure of La Follette to win more than a small percentage of the votes in 1924 further testified to the 'massive inertia' of the American public and confirmed Croly's conviction that the progressives would never come to power until they had a workable program and an educated following to back it up. The conservatives, he pointed out in December 1924, possessed the program and the personnel to administer it. Until the progressives built up an organization powerful and capable enough to assume power, he advised them to transform themselves into an opposition party whose function it would be to force a clarification of political issues. Two parties, he maintained, now dominated national politics, 'neither of which has allowed questions of ultimate political and economic power to become the subject of partizan controversy.' Conservatives therefore had no obligation to take a definite stand and administer seriously for the country's welfare. Given a unified radical party instead of the 'liberal' Democratic party (which proposed to do 'nothing much' instead of 'nothing at all'), it might be possible to convert the present negative conservatism of the Republican party into something more nearly resembling the more enlightened Conservative party of England. Certainly 'radical progressives' had much more to gain by allowing the businessmen to administer the as yet workable machine of capitalism and forcing upon them the desperate problems they would undoubtedly be obliged to cope with during the next thirty years, than by struggling to gain control over an economy the progressives had not the capacities to manage. An intelligent conservatism, he believed, would respond to the popular demands, preferring to make concessions than to risk the loss of power. Progressives, in turn, might continue their political agitation while preparing themselves to overcome their handicaps. Croly told his fellow progressives they had nothing to fear from the conservatives. Their real enemies were 'the stubborn limitations of the existing economic and social system which are created by and confirm the existing disabilities of human nature' and 'the lack of a sufficiently alert, conscious and educated body of workers.'

Croly's astute diagnosis of progressivism may have stimulated his *New Republic* readers, but it did not halt the dissolution of the progressive movement. The disappointment of the 1924 defeat increased, as the *Nation* had predicted, the 'abstention from political life' and the 'contaminating cynicism' that had begun to infect many intellectuals since the end of the war. The impregnability of the business system, the huge Republican pluralities, and episodes such as the Sacco-Vanzetti case all seemed to prove the impossibility of compromising with the American rulers. However dull and vulgar their culture, they had apparently devised a system that provided for the physical needs of the citizens if not their spiritual wants. To Herbert Croly, the businessmen were 'operating a more efficient and flexible economic and political machine than did the kings and aristocrats of the eighteenth century . . . operating it more efficiently than their opponents would or could.'

Four years after Croly's tribute to American business efficiency came the economic collapse that the progressives had neither expected nor prepared for.

III] With the victory of the Democrats in 1932, an administration came into power which at least attempted to continue the progressive struggle for industrial democracy. Franklin Roosevelt was a spiritual descendant of Jefferson and Jackson if not Ralph Waldo Emerson, and his belief in the positive role of government, of government as a popular instrument, resembled closely the attitudes of the men discussed in the preceding chapters.

In many ways, however, Roosevelt stood poles apart from these reformers, even though the liberals at first had him pegged as a lesser Wilson. The ethical tones of nineteenth-century liberalism sounded in his own pronouncements, but he showed hardly a trace of the ideologue. He had little of the evangelist and not a great deal of the practical social architect; in certain respects his notions of government resembled those of Brooks Adams (during Adams's progressive moments) more than those of George or Bellamy. Several years before his election he had observed that 'that nation or state which is unwilling by government action to tackle new problems caused by the immense increase of population and the astonishing strides of modern science is headed for a decline and ultimate death from inaction.' Roosevelt attempted nothing less, to borrow Henry Adams's metaphor, than to convert 'our old Mississippi raft of a confederate state into a brand-new ten-thousand ton, triple screw, armored, line-of-battle ship,' a job that Adams predicted would take a thousand years. It required vision to carry out such a scheme, but it also required the combination of firmness and cunning, which many of our successful Presidents, most notably Jefferson and Lincoln, never hesitated to employ.

When Hawthorne called on Lincoln in 1862, he detected in this kindly and sagacious man a touch of slyness, a kind 'of tact and wisdom,' Hawthorne wrote, 'that are akin to craft, and would impel him . . . to take an antagonist in flank, rather than make a bull-run at him right in front.' Roosevelt had something of that quality variously interpreted by his contemporaries as shrewdness or trickiness, depending on their political orientation. He listened to the theorists and liked them, but the technical aspects of his job appealed to him the most. He saw quite correctly that it was the task of government not only to formulate the national policy but to use 'the political technique to obtain so much of that policy as will receive general support; persuading, leading, sacrificing, teaching always—because the greatest duty of statesmen is to educate.' Roosevelt served as a salesman for the new progressivism, breaking down the resistance of a people long inured to political and economic superstitions.

The new President showed no more inclination than Theodore Roosevelt or Woodrow Wilson to embark on socialist schemes. He informed his constituents that capitalism, in its unadulterated state, worked well enough, but unfortunately it had been perverted by a group of insiders ('grafters' and 'chiselers' in the F.D.R. parlance) who fouled up the engine of private enterprise. Roosevelt compared these business parasites to the carbon in the engine of the car: the engine would not knock quite so loudly, he declared, when the carbon was removed. In other words, the President and his aides looked upon reform as a technical rather than a moral question, even though Roosevelt deeply felt his responsibility to the people and was a sincere humanitarian. As Edmund Wilson remarked in 1933, Roosevelt was at his worst when he imitated the 'pastoral unctiousness' of his great Democratic predecessor. 'He is himself most impressive,' Wilson continued, 'not in the role of political prophet, but as a sensible public servant trying to straighten out a bad mess in the interests of what he conceives to be the American democratic tradition.' Roosevelt was more interested in increasing the buying power of each citizen than in discussing man's spiritual potentialities, less concerned with plans for developing unplumbed genius than in overcoming the heavy inertia of ignorance and prejudice.

The Rooseveltian strategy of compromise and restraint, of working for realizable goals, of never getting too far ahead of public opinion, of speeding up and slowing down, depending upon national and international exigencies, was understandable and probably necessary. Certainly, a moon-crazed Quixote could never have gone as far toward the liberal goal as the canny Roosevelt, and we can be thankful that a person of his temperament and abilities succeeded to the presidency in 1932.

It does not minimize Roosevelt's achievements to say that New Dealism was a crisis philosophy, reconstructive rather than radical, inconclusive, temporary, makeshift. After acknowledging the valuable legacy of New Deal reforms in the fields of banking, agriculture, labor, and social security (the policy of the do-nothing state was finally and permanently discredited), we can see from the vantage of today that the basic power structure of the country was substantially untouched, even admitting the large and probably lasting gains of organized labor. The tendencies in our society which shocked and frightened the nineteenth-century progressives still exist; unwholesome accumulations of private wealth, inequalities of real opportunity, the monopolization and despoiling of natural resources, the power of special interests to block the majority will. Under the New Deal (once defined by Max Lerner as a 'fighting coalition of the productive groups in America headed toward a socialized community, using the technique of democratic planning') it seemed for a time as if ideals and technique really were working in conjunction and that the co-operative common-wealth, so long in the blueprint stage, was at last under construction. By the middle of Roosevelt's second term, however, the movement had already flagged. The inevitable 'breathing spell' that follows periods of intense reformist activity set in; the bold experiment had ended.

Historians are still speculating about the reasons for the New Deal relapse, which occurred even before World War II indefinitely postponed its continuation. But looking back to the Rooseveltian era and judging it by progressive standards, one might say that the New Deal was not radical and far-reaching enough, that it came to terms too readily with the opposition, that the necessity of halting the panic and reviving a sick economy absorbed its early impetus and drained its energies before the real job of reconstruction began. This is the dilemma facing every liberal regime coming to power under similar circumstances; it must undo the work of accumulated stupidity and mismanagement and at the same time surpass the peak performance of the old order whose blundering brought about the collapse. The British Labour Government faces that job today.

The New Deal did not depart very radically from the earlier anti-big-business protests. Like Greenbackism or Populism, New Dealism had utopian overtones, but by and large, it was merely another popular effort to get a larger slice of the American pie. Both Bellamy and Lloyd finally saw the People's party for what it was, and there is little doubt that Veblen, had he lived, would have quickly seen that the New Deal program introduced few if any radical transformations in American life. It was Veblen's utopian bias that enabled him to see the *ideological* nature of the American labor movement and the ineffectuality of liberals dallying along the fringes of reform.

The New Deal succeeded in giving the people a feeling of purpose for a short time, but it based its appeal almost exclusively upon the same desiderata that had motivated the previous Republican administration. In dropping the ethico-religious baggage of the old progressives and in focusing their attentions almost entirely upon raising economic levels and increasing social benefits, the New Deal leaders missed the opportunity of driving home the social and economic lessons of the great depression: that every citizen has obligations as well as rights, that the responsibility for the 1929 debacle could not be foisted upon a small group of corrupt insiders, that the stability and health of a community is not measured by the number of automobiles and washing machines in operation, that reform must be a continuous process and not a short interlude of delirious agitation sandwiched in between decades of reaction and social irresponsibility.

IV] Progressivism, during the 'thirties, had to buck up not only against conservative opposition that bitterly contested almost every New Deal measure (an opposition that arose soon after the panicky days of 1932), but also against a communist opposition unknown in the days of Bellamy and George and hardly formidable until the depression.

The story of communism's rise in the United States is a separate one in itself, but what concerns us here is the defection from the progressive ranks of many intellectuals who, in the space of a few years, became Marxists and party sympathizers. The reasons for this break, already discernible in the middle 'twenties and dramatically evident by 1932, are numerous and varied, but this much can be said by way of explanation.

A number of writers and intellectuals had come to distrust the democratic idealism of the older progressives and the middle-class values they upheld. They saw no hope in either the leadership or the program of progressivism, committed, in their opinion, to the preservation of the *status quo* and to the continued domination of the ruling class. Croly's recommendation that the progressives cooperate with the established powers seemed both cowardly and unworkable. Such a policy brought no immediate relief to the workers and offered further proof that the progressives preferred to sacrifice the rights of the submerged proletariat rather than to cut themselves off from the middle class. What had the progressives done to prevent the 'legalized murder' of Sacco and Vanzetti? How could one speak of co-operation with 'reactionaries' and 'bloodsuckers' who had no compunctions about putting to death anyone who seriously challenged their tyranny? The execution of these two anarchists was more than a miscarriage of justice to many embittered progressives; they saw it as a symbolic capitalist rite that divided America into the 'two nations' of John Dos Passos and conclusively exposed the fraudulence of the middle-class ideal.

The depression dispelled what for many radicals was the last myth of capitalism—the myth of prosperity. In place of the vacillation, confusion, and timidity of progressivism, the renegades now turned to a movement that had a creed, a bible, and a cause. The mere example of the Soviet Union, according to one of them, 'made all progressive movements and liberal programs seem superficial, long and rather hopeless.' Waldo Frank, writing in the *New Masses*' symposium, 'How I Came to Communism,' in the fall of 1932, expressed the feelings of many former progressives when he remarked: 'I have lost my last faith in the middle-classes, in all middle class action, and in the efficacy of middle class groups who are identified, either openly or indirectly, with middle class values.' He was ready to agree with Marx that only 'the communist society can go forward to the creating of a real *human* culture.'

Any such expression of faith in the communist cause would be regarded today as merely another example of leftist rascality or naïveté, but the fact that many honest and idealistic people agreed with Frank in 1932 is highly significant. We cannot minimize its influence by impugning the intelligence or the motives of its supporters. The Communist party challenged a progressivism that hesitated too much and neglected too much. During the early 'thirties, it exhibited a resolution and audacity that made most progressive agitation seem tepid by contrast, and it publicized national evils—race discrimination and the treatment of minorities, for example—with a flair that was new in radical movements. The propagation of Marxist ideas invigorated our universities, stimulated scholarship and teaching. If the results were not always good, a large number, if not all, of the novelists, poets, historians, and critics who passed through and out of the communist phase were none the worse for their experiment; indeed they were better qualified to expose the totalitarian state than the professional 'red-baiters,' who never took the trouble to understand what they feared and hated. Finally, it must not be forgotten that the fervent sincerity of many communists impressed young men and women who, in an earlier generation, would have turned to the Christian Socialists or to the Fabians. To them, progressivism in the 1930's was 'corpse cold,' communism a warming fire, a hope, a faith.

All of this is quite understandable in retrospect. What seems harder to comprehend today is why an allegedly cynical and creedless generation could accept so uncritically the communist vision after emphatically rejecting its native middle-class equivalent. The communists distorted reality far more than did the progressives. Bellamy and George had the good sense to project their utopias into the future; the Communist party succeeded in convincing a good many intelligent people that the utopia existed already in the workers' republic across the ocean. The communists and their friends had a touching faith in Soviet statistics and a highly unrealistic notion about the recuperative powers of American capitalism. They sentimentalized the working man as no progressive ever did and placed their faith, as one of them said, in 'the proletarians and farmers who *alone* as a class have not been hopelessly corrupted by the sources and methods of the capitalistic order.'

The glorification of the proletariat went on simultaneously with the debasement of the bourgeois decadent. During the early 'thirties the strange spectacle could be observed of middle-class writers apologizing for their middle-class origins and acknowledging 'that the workers alone can give militant and effective leadership to the fight against reaction.' Even the word 'people,' with its bourgeois overtones, was declared to be a reactionary slogan, whereas the words, 'proletariat' and 'worker' were considered appropriate symbols for the communist propagandist. The Marxists, in abandoning the middle-class values, also spurned the tactical insights of the progressive agitators, men and women far more familiar with national prejudices and assumptions than their communist successors. The communists were correct enough in seeing progressivism as an embodiment of middle-class values; they simply miscalculated when they concluded that these values were obsolete and irrelevant. At best the ideas of the nineteenth-century reformers had a kind of historical interest for the radical critics in search of the 'usable past' (such men as Lloyd or George or Bellamy were interesting as precursors of scientific socialism and helped to confirm the line that communism was twentieth-century Americanism), but according to the Marxists, the progressive-liberals had nothing to offer the post-Leninist world. Historical liberalism, V. F. Calverton wrote in 1933, was retrogressive and harmful. It found its expression in Wilsonian platitudes and in the 'infantile proposals' of La Follette. The outmoded democracy still professed by John Dewey, Charles Beard, Jane Addams, James Harvey Robinson, and others

was not the industrial or proletarian democracy of the modern radical but the democracy of the small farmer and the small business man and entrepreneur in the cities. In a word, they were not interested in proletarians as proletarians, but in proletarians as potential bourgeois. They were determined to think of American society as a classless phenomenon, uncognizant that what they were doing was supporting the middle class, first as agrarianites and later as urbanites as well, with its futile stress upon an individualistic economic outlook which has been rendered anachronistic by the technical processes of production and social organization.

Calverton's understanding of the progressive view was correct enough, but we may now wonder why he placed so little stock in the judgment of a John Dewey or a Morris Cohen, why he assumed that they were unaware of the implications of their position, and why he was so certain that nineteenth-century American liberalism was dead.

To Calverton and the other Marxists, the 'day of the individual' had passed and the 'day of the classes' had arrived. America was at last 'Europeanized.' The middle class, the source of enlightened leadership for the reformers, would now have to choose, in their disintegrated state, between a rising proletariat and a doomed upper-*bourgeoisie*. A suggestion like Howells's, that the working class vote itself into power, was patently ridiculous, because anyone who had read Marx (or better, his popularizers) knew that no ruling class relinquished power in the manner hoped for by the reformers. Utopianism or gradualism, in fact any theory that seriously broached the possibility of peaceful change, was contemptuously rejected by orthodox communists in the 'thirties. As one of them wrote, 'only a liberal could entertain the fantastic notion that the few who run civilization for their profit can be induced to change their purpose by any other method than by shooting them.' No plan short of taking over the means of production by the proletariat seemed worth discussing.

The revolutionary radical's impatience with the wishy-washy progressive mentality can be illustrated rather dramatically by Lincoln Steffens's review of Charles Edward Russell's recollections, *Bare Hands and Stone Walls,* which appeared in the *Nation,* December 20, 1933. Russell, a reformist-muck-raking-progressive-socialist, had participated in or observed practically every liberal movement of any significance for the past sixty years and had emerged from the battle with his ideals still whole and his optimism undimmed. His professional duties had taken him all over the world, to New Zealand, Australia, India, Ireland, and Russia. Invariably and characteristically, he sided with the rebels and the underprivileged, but in Russia, to the disgust of Steffens, Russell shied away from Lenin and the Bolsheviks and supported unequivocally the more visionary and soon-to-be liquidated Social Revolutionaries, the men, as he put it, who were 'shot to death by the rifles of men that professed to want the same things but insisted upon getting them in a different way.'

Steffens's observations on this episode are most revealing. Russell, said Steffens, represented the predicament of the liberal theoretician who goes through life with an open mind and open mouth and cannot grasp the necessity for action. 'There is a time for thinking and planning,' he admitted, but after that 'there comes a time to close our open minds, shut up talking, and go to it. Lest Hitler do things his way. That time is when we don't need good fellows and liberal compromisers who want to get together. The goal is in sight and we must be Bolsheviks and—do it.'

As an old friend and co-worker of Russell, Steffens should have

known that what disturbed him was not that the Bolsheviks acted
(the Social Revolutionaries also had plans as well as visions); he
appreciated as well as Steffens the immediate practical tasks that
had to be accomplished, and knew that revolutions so long de-
layed and of such magnitude could not occur without bloodshed.
Russell, nevertheless, was shocked by the Bolsheviks' treatment of
dissenters, even those who had languished for years in Czarist
prisons, and what seemed to him the betrayal of the ideals of the
revolution. Steffens accused him, in effect, of sitting back and de-
ploring, of being a 'nice socialist' instead of a 'socialist.' Russell,
however, could not reconcile Leninism with socialism or a the-
ocracy (with Lenin as the 'titular deity') with democracy. 'If so
far the story of mankind has taught anything,' he remarked, 'It is
that a people's progress must be self-achieved. You cannot take
them by the throat and jab progress into them as a cook stuffs a
turkey. The doctrine of doing good to the people because they are
too incapable to do anything for themselves is bearded with age.
It has been the excuse of every tyrant and bloody minded murderer
that ever sat on any throne.' The myth of the Soviet paradise
flourished in a capitalist wasteland where generous-spirited men
and women, disgusted with the callousness and ineptitude of a fal-
tering business civilization, saw their hopes embodied in what they
believed to be a vigorous and democratic socialist state; it faded
when the nature and tendencies of Soviet Communism became
better known. Then Russell's strictures against Leninist tactics
could no longer be dismissed as the old-fogyism of a sentimental
muckraker.

Morris Cohen, giving his reasons, a year after Steffens's review,
why he was not and could not become a member of the Communist party, restated the liberal-progressive creed quietly and eloquently and explained why the liberal must always oppose the communist 'fallacy of simplism.' Like Russell, he rejected the communist plea 'that the denial of freedom is a temporary necessity'
as an argument 'advanced by all militarists. It ignores the fact,' he
observed, 'that, when suppression becomes a habit, it is not readily
abandoned.' He could not agree with the Calvertons that liberalism was dead, but even if it were, he said, 'I should still maintain

that it deserved to live, that it had not been condemned in the court of human reason, but lynched outside of it by the passionate and uncompromisingly ruthless war spirit, common to Communists and Fascists.'

The liberalism of Morris Cohen, unfortunately for progressivism, did not have a wide appeal in the 'thirties, nor did it carry much weight in the next decade with the managers of the 'Progressive party' of Henry Wallace, those of them, at any rate, who did not share Morris Cohen's conviction about the incompatibility of democracy and dictatorship. The new 'Progressives' suffered from political astigmatism; their view of democracy was imperfect and indistinct. Whereas the progressives in the 'eighties and 'nineties felt obliged to denounce Czarist tyranny and capitalist oppression as equally reprehensible, the organizers and strategists of the self-styled 'Progressive party' (if not the bulk of the membership) seemed to be more chary with their condemnations, more qualifiedly antitotalitarian, more adept in separating theory from practice. Their failure in the 1948 presidential election to attract more than a scant proportion of the voters can be attributed partly to the fact that they borrowed the rhetoric but rejected the spirit of progressivism, and identified what had once been an authentic radical movement with a reactionary ideology.

v] The current attack on liberal-progressivism by the non-communists is explainable in some measure as a revulsion from the pseudo-progressive mentality so much in evidence during the last decade, but it would be much too simple to see it merely as that. For many radicals who had long regarded Russia as their spiritual home, the Great Betrayal produced a violent reaction, which carried them far to the right, politically, and compelled them to reconsider all of their ideas about the nature of man and the meaning of progress. The Second World War, with its calculated atrocities, also prompted a reassessment of old values. One could find, it seemed, a more valid interpretation of man and human conduct in the writings of Kierkegaard, Dostoevsky, or Kafka than in the optimistic prophets of progress and sanity. Neo-Calvinists and Freudians justified the recognition of the reality of sin; the 'tragic sense' almost became a literary cliché. And thus during the 'forties American intellectuals turned increasingly to those writers and artists who had experienced the vision of evil, and they found in their books, written with 'the fine hammered steel of woe,' the confirmation they expected and wanted.

In contrast, the ebullitions of the liberal and quasi-liberal press seemed to them mawkish, insensitive, and false. Their quarrel was not so much with liberalism as with the corruption of its doctrines, yet in their attacks on the 'middle-brow'-progressive mentality, their contempt for the banalities of the progressives revealed, unconsciously perhaps, a contempt for progressivism itself and an impatience with the program as well as with the tastes and the ideals of the middle-class groups engaged in political action. Lionel Trilling, an intelligent and discriminating antiprogressive, could detect little difference between the cultural level of the Wallace Progressives and the Americans for Democratic Action; both seemed to him vulgar and pedestrian and ripe with the defects liberalism seems perpetually heir to.

The criticisms of Trilling and the people whose views he represents have a real basis. 'There is no odor,' as Thoreau said, 'so bad as that which arises from goodness tainted.' Progressivism, unlike more austere and pessimistic faiths, is peculiarly susceptible to the insipid and the sentimental; neighborliness can easily degenerate into the 'folksy,' confidence into smugness, conscience into self-righteousness. All this can be conceded without becoming disenthralled about progressivism because of its alleged incapacity to comprehend the irrational and the brutish.

What is so often overlooked in the current onslaught against progressivism is that its most significant spokesmen, although never quite appreciating the limitlessness of human depravity, did not slight the potency of evil. Nor did they all take for granted that progress was inevitable and irreversible. They believed in the kind of liberalism defined by Morris Cohen as 'a pride in human achievement, a faith in human effort, a conviction that the proper function of government is to remove the restraints upon human activity,' but they did not minimize the distance between the desirable future and the undesirable present. They assumed that under

favorable circumstances society could 'progress,' and that man was not entirely the helpless creature of chance the nineteenth-century naturalists made him out to be, nor the sin-soaked, neurosis-ridden patient of the twentieth century. For, they reasoned correctly, if one begins axiomatically with the proposition that individual man is hopelessly corrupt, then it is impossible to conclude from this, to quote Professor Toynbee, 'that a fortuitous concourse of worthless souls behaving despicably toward one another can produce an ever more healthy and prosperous society.'

The progressives rejected the determinism of the doctrinaire biologist and priest. If they overemphasized, perhaps, the harmful or beneficent influence of social institutions, their awareness of the effects of anxiety, of spiritual wear and tear on human beings trapped in a dislocated society came close to the conclusions of the post-war social psychology. Eric Fromm, Karen Horney, Clyde Kluckhohn, Henry Stack Sullivan, and many others denied that man is doomed by his biological nature, or that social institutions that prevent the harmonious development of personality and exacerbate aggressions and fear are unchangeable. Like the old progressives, they were 'possibilists.' At least their writings implied that people have it within themselves to improve their mental and material conditions as well as to worsen them.

VI] When it comes to the point of evaluating the effectiveness and measuring the influence of the middle-class, reformist-progressive tradition as defined above, opinions will differ. Liberals who have seen the emergence of a people's democracy solely in terms of a strongly organized and dynamic working-class movement may feel that the reformers lived too much in the clouds. Realists and other down-to-earth men may dismiss them as authors of fanciful panaceas, who finally succumbed to the money and power arrayed against them. Judged from a narrow point of view, the failures of reform seem to justify this skepticism. The Single-Tax movement is moribund if not dead. Bellamy's Nationalists have long been forgotten despite the Bellamy clubs that still carry on. Henry Demarest Lloyd's *Wealth against Commonwealth* is merely a dated tract to the casual student, but the Standard Oil

Company remains. Faced with these bleak realities, we may well wonder if any lasting good resulted from one hundred years of moral crusading.

But a more careful scrutiny of these sporadic episodes of reform will assure us, I think, that the efforts of discontented American 'do-gooders' (as their counterparts today have been derisively labeled) were not so fruitless as they might appear to be. They kept alive the spirit of equality and an interest in community welfare in a class that had long forgotten its earlier revolutionary crusade against feudalistic restraints and subordinated all considerations—political, social, and cultural—to the immediate job of business. This one fact alone is of great importance, because the work of the nineteenth-century reformers immensely facilitated the tasks of the latter-day progressives and prevented the development of an unbridgeable gap between the propertied and the unpropertied groups. The American middle class had been inoculated with a virus it could not throw off; within it there remained a number of benignly subversive individuals who periodically betrayed the immediate interests of their class for more enduring objectives. It is Philistinism, then, to dismiss them as mere talkers and of no account. The reformers, although more than closet philosophers, were preeminently men of words, 'visionaries' if you will (using that word in its customary opprobious sense), but they often showed more real foresight than the men who ridiculed them.

Emerson's disciples preached his inspiriting message to a later generation, and it was then that Transcendentalism rocked State Street and Wall Street. We know now that the Populist movement was inspired and directed by eastern intellectuals as well as by agrarian malcontents, that fighting Bob La Follette drew his support not only from frustrated farmers and aggrieved proletarians but from men nourished by *Progress and Poverty* and *Looking Backward*. The fact that a pseudo-progressive, a press agent for reform, Theodore Roosevelt, rode the popular current for a time should not blind us to the genuine underlying forces that made it possible.

One is struck, in turning back to these forgotten and unread men, by the size and quality and diversity of their audiences in both America and Europe, and by the serious consideration their

ideas received. The books they wrote struck at the very roots of the capitalist system, and yet lawyers, bankers, and businessmen read them with attention and frequently succumbed to the power and logic of their arguments.

The success of a book like *Progress and Poverty* with its, practically speaking, preposterous solution, suggests that late nineteenth-century readers possessed a degree of tolerance and idealism that has long vanished, but the popularity of the reformers cannot be attributed solely to the intelligence and receptiveness of their fellow citizens. They had to contend with the same vilification, the same public inertia, which have been the lot of social critics at all times and in all countries. Nor can the wide hearing they received be explained entirely as a result of the unsettled economic and political situation. It is true that during the years between 1865 and 1896 class antagonisms sharpened considerably and that the Georgian paradox—unemployment, poverty, and labor strife dramatically accompanied by the blossoming of enormous fortunes— jolted hitherto complacent Americans; but the sense of crisis was probably no less profound in subsequent years and certainly no less intense than it is today.

If the superiority or the seriousness of the nineteenth-century reading public or the gravity of the times were not the only reasons for the tremendous vogue of the reformers at home and abroad, how can we account for their popularity? The answer to this question has already been given, but this much can be said by way of summary. All of the men dealt with here were either powerful and eloquent speakers or persuasive writers. In some instances they were both. Not only did they thoroughly understand their audience, but they couched their theories and recommendations so appealingly, so strikingly, that they charmed the reluctant into belief as much by their words and sentence rhythms and metaphors as by their logic. They were generally well-informed men, naturally intelligent, and they had wise things to say. Unlike our timid specialists, made inarticulate through excessive caution and fearful of hazarding a generalization, they assumed the duties of the preacher-prophet now very largely monopolized by cranks and charlatans. Most important of all, they appealed to the practical as well as the

idealistic preconceptions of the American people, always the irresistible combination, and anchored their fundamental principles
in the traditions of a democratic past that had been formed before
the dawn of our industrial age.

What needs to be emphasized now is that these men were radicals, in the sense that we use that term today. Their demands for
a real social equality and a more equitable distribution of the national wealth belong in the category of those simple but overwhelm-
ing requests that require a drastic overhauling of our economic
system and a transformation in our social ethic—one might almost
say a religious revival— if they are to be realized. They hoped and
expected to achieve what we should call their utopian goal by appealing to the good sense and justice of their fellow Americans.
They envisaged a Christian society where all would have a comfortable sufficiency, where the atmosphere would be wholesome and
polite, where perfect equality would exist as a matter of course, and
where the citizen would not be offended, either by the vulgar plutocrat or the rude proletarian.

There is something naïve and strait-laced in many of their proposals, and we in the twentieth century who have become wiser
and more cynical about human perversity may smile at the simplicity of the progressive paradise. And yet it has been demonstrated that the progressives were less timid and cautious, less hypothetical, than their modern counterparts, and less sentimental too.
The open society may be an anachronism, but it is a valid and a
sensible ideal. And for all their lapses, the progressives, although
completely absorbed in the cause of the underprivileged, seldom
romanticized 'Labor' or the 'Little People' or degenerated into the
sloppy and maudlin rhetoric of which so many of our present-day
liberals are guilty.

Today progressivism, properly interpreted, provides a philosophy
for America that is deeply radical in its implications, thoroughly
rooted in the American experience, and irreconcilably antitotalitarian. It is a humanist philosophy, undisguisedly ethical, riveted
to principles. It is not a creed for opportunists, for the politically
ambitious (although it has inadvertently brought fame and popularity to its seers and expounders), but it is a very satisfactory faith,

as Charles Russell said, for a person who wants to stay on good terms with himself.

The progressives may have erred in their views of man's nature —certainly that would be the fashionable criticism to make today; some of them may have assumed too trustingly that history was on their side and progress foreordained. But they did not make a cult of science or exaggerate the importance of techniques. Even Veblen, with his unVeblenian faith in the power of machine discipline, respected it not so much as something intrinsically good but as a means of bringing forth man's potential goodness by destroying the encrustations of superstition and prejudice. The progressives believed a better society could be established, even though they knew as well as the 'tough-minded realists' that no society of free and equal people had yet emerged. What is more, they actually began to plan for such a society with hope and enthusiasm, undeterred by the capriciousness and fallibility of the human material with which they proposed to work, and willing to take the abuse from the down-to-earth men who kept their eyes trained upon 'what is.' If their strategy of reform sometimes seemed naïve and impractical, their goals and values were specific. These could be summarized as follows: that the chief business of government, to use Emerson's phrase again, is the care and culture of men; that just as human weakness explained the injustice and irrationality of the social order, so human genius, released from institutional restraints and given free play, could establish it on a humane and efficient basis of equality.

We think of them now, not unnaturally, as malcontents rather than builders and architects, for these men felt obliged to break down the self-satisfaction and false security of their contemporaries before pointing the way to something better. As publicists of unpleasantness, they were superb, exposing the blighted areas of American life from which the comfortable had learned to avert their eyes, and contradicting the claims of the boosters. But the reformer's complaints and denunciations only served as a prelude to the final vision of his progressive America, the open and untrammeled commonwealth where men co-operated in order to be free.

The progressive tradition thus provides the foundations for an indigenous radicalism peculiarly tuned to the American historical experience. It undercuts the contentions of the super-patriots, with their curious and erroneous notions of 'Americanism' and 'un-Americanism,' by showing that a stand against privilege and monopoly has been characteristically American and that forms of socialism are not incompatible with democracy. Progressivism is preeminently the philosophy of social experimentation, of the mixed economy. It is neither for nor against the government; it is against faction, special interests, monopoly, and privilege. Instead of pretending that class bitterness is some kind of foreign poison and that it is indecent even to suggest the possibility of one class or group exploiting another, progressivism proposes to eliminate the conditions that aggravate this tendency and to re-establish a classless or open society. It attempts to carry out this program not through a temporary dictatorship of the working class, not by autocratic fiat, but by abolishing special privileges and by restoring in greater measure the equality of opportunity.

The middle-class rebels who practiced and preached this philosophy of progressivism have not appealed very much to the myth-makers. America has never deified its iconoclasts. But the disturbers of the peace, although ordinarily unappreciated and ignored by the majority when they are making nuisances of themselves, are a complacent nation's most precious possession. A true evaluation of America's great men would include not only the generals and statesmen and athletes, the builders of mousetraps and pipe lines, but our 'prophetic agitators,' excluded from the American pantheon, who devoted themselves to the unprofitable and thankless task of human betterment.

NOTES ON SOURCES

. . . .

CHAPTER 1

Emerson
and the Progressive Tradition

PRIMARY MATERIAL:

The Complete Works of Ralph Waldo Emerson, ed. by E. W. Emerson, Centenary Edition, Boston, 1903-4, 12 vols.
The Journals of Ralph Waldo Emerson, ed. by E. W. Emerson and W. E. Forbes, Boston, 1909-14, 10 vols.
The Letters of Ralph Waldo Emerson, ed. by Ralph L. Rusk, New York, 1939, 6 vols.

RELATED MATERIAL:

Chapman, John Jay, *Emerson, and Other Essays,* New York, 1898.
Curti, Merle, 'The Flowering of New England,' in *The Cultural Approach to History,* ed. by Caroline F. Ware, New York, 1940.
Schlesinger, Arthur M., Jr., *The Age of Jackson,* Boston, 1945.
Shephard, Odell, *The Journals of Bronson Alcott,* Boston, 1938.
Smith, Henry Nash, 'Emerson and the Problem of Vocation,' *The New England Quarterly,* XII, March 1939, 52-67.
Tocqueville, Alexis de, *Democracy in America,* Cambridge, Mass., 1864, 2 vols.
Ward, Lester, *Pure Sociology,* New York, 1925.

. . . .

CHAPTER 2

Theodore Parker:
'The Battle of the Nineteenth Century'

PRIMARY MATERIAL:

The Parker Letter Books, Massachusetts Historical Society.
Parker Journals, November 1844 to November 1849, Massachusetts Historical Society.

Journals, 1840, 1841-3, 1851-6, 1859-60, American Unitarian Association, Boston.

Newspaper cuttings, Boston Public Library.

The Collected Works of Theodore Parker, ed. by Francis E. Cobbe, London, 1863-74, 14 vols.

The Works of Theodore Parker, Centenary Edition, Boston, 1907-13, 15 vols.

Lessons from the World of Matter and the World of Man, ed. by Rufus Leighton, Boston, 1865.

RELATED MATERIAL:

Alcott, Louisa May, *Work: A Story of Experience,* Boston, 1873.

Chadwick, John W., *Theodore Parker, Preacher and Reformer,* Boston, 1900.

Cheney, Ednah D., *Louisa May Alcott. Her Life, Letters, and Journals,* Boston, 1890.

Commager, Henry Steele, *Theodore Parker, Yankee Reformer,* Boston, 1936.

Dirks, John E., *The Critical Theology of Theodore Parker,* New York, 1948.

Donald, David H., *Lincoln's Herndon,* New York, 1948.

Emerson, R. W., *Works,* Centenary Edition, x, xi.

Frothingham, O. B., *Theodore Parker: A Biography,* Boston, 1874.

Higginson, Thomas W., *Contemporaries,* Boston and New York, 1899.

Ladu, Arthur I., 'The Political Ideas of Theodore Parker,' *Studies in Philology,* xxxiii, 1941, 106-23.

Richards, Laura E., ed., *Letters and Journals of Samuel Gridley Howe,* Boston, 1909, 2 vols.

Rusk, Ralph L., ed., *The Letters of Ralph Waldo Emerson,* New York, 1939, iv.

Weiss, John, *Life and Correspondence of Theodore Parker,* New York, 1864, 2 vols.

Williams, C. R., ed., *Diary and Letters of Rutherford Birchard Hayes,* Columbus, Ohio, 1922, i.

. . . .

CHAPTER 3

Henry George:
The Great Paradox

PRIMARY MATERIAL:

Henry George Papers, Manuscript Division, New York Public Library.

Letters from Henry George to William Lloyd Garrison Jr., Smith College Library.

Henry George Scrap Books, Economic Division of the New York Public Library.

The Standard, January 1887-August 1892.

The Complete Works of Henry George, Library Edition, Garden City, New York, 1906-11, 10 vols.

RELATED MATERIAL:

De Mille, Anna George, *Henry George: Citizen of the World*, Chapel Hill, 1950.

Geiger, George H., *The Philosophy of Henry George*, New York, 1933.

—— 'The Forgotten Man: Henry George,' *Antioch Review*, I, 1941, 291-307.

George, Henry, Jr., *The Life of Henry George*, New York, 1911. (*Works*, IX, X.)

Howe, M. A. De Wolfe, *John Jay Chapman and His Letters*, Boston, 1937.

Keller, A. G., and Davie, M. R., eds., *Essays of William Graham Sumner*, New Haven, 1934, I.

Nock, Albert J., *Henry George: An Essay*, New York, 1939.

Post, Louis F., *The Prophet of San Francisco*, Chicago, 1904.

Williams, C. R., ed., *Diary and Letters of Rutherford Birchard Hayes*, Columbus, Ohio, 1922, IV.

—— *The Life of Rutherford Birchard Hayes*, Boston, 1914, II.

Young, A. N., *The Single Tax Movement in the United States*, Princeton, 1916.

· · · · · · · ·

CHAPTER 4

Edward Bellamy:
Village Utopian

PRIMARY MATERIAL:

Unpublished writings of Edward Bellamy, Harvard University Library. See Arthur E. Morgan, *Edward Bellamy*, New York, 1944, pp. 421-3, for a complete description of the manuscript collection.

Letters of Edward Bellamy to William Dean Howells, Howells Correspondence, Harvard University Library; to Henry Demarest Lloyd, Lloyd Papers, State Historical Society of Wisconsin, Madison.

Six to One: A Nantucket Idyll, New York, 1878.

Dr. Heidenhoff's Process, New York, 1880.

Miss Ludington's Sister: A Romance of Immortality, Boston, 1884.

Looking Backward: 2000-1887, Boston, 1888.

Equality, Boston, 1897.

The Blindman's World and Other Stories, Boston, 1898.

The Duke of Stockbridge, New York, 1900.

The Religion of Solidarity, ed. by A. E. Morgan, Yellow Springs, Ohio, 1940.

Edward Bellamy Speaks Again, Kansas City, Mo., 1937.

Talks on Nationalism, Chicago, 1938.

The Nationalist, 1889-91.

The New Nation, 1891-4.

RELATED MATERIAL:

American Federationist, The, III, July 1897, 5-6.

Brooks, Van Wyck, *New England: Indian Summer,* 1865-1915, New York, 1940.

Gronlund, Laurence, *Socialism vs. Tax Reform. An Answer to Henry George,* New York, 1887.

—— *The Co-operative Commonwealth,* New York, 1884 and 1893.

—— *Our Destiny,* New York, 1891.

Howells, William Dean, 'Two Notable Novels,' *Century,* XXVIII, August 1884, 632-4 (review of *Miss Ludington's Sister*).

—— 'Editor's Study,' *Harper's Monthly,* LXXVII, June 1888, 151-5 (review of *Looking Backward*).

—— 'Edward Bellamy,' *Atlantic Monthly,* LXXXII, June 1898, 253-6.

—— 'Mr. Howells on Mr. Bellamy,' *Critic,* n.s. XXIX, 11 June 1898, 391.

—— Introduction to *The Blindman's World,* Boston, 1898.

Madison, Charles, *Critics & Crusaders,* New York, 1947.

Morgan, Arthur E., *The Philosophy of Edward Bellamy,* New York, 1945.

Morris, William, *Collected Works,* London, 1910-15, XVI (*News from Nowhere*).

Mumford, Lewis, *The Story of Utopias,* New York, 1922.

Nation, The, XLVI, 29 March 1888, 265-6.

Our Day, IV, 1889, 542.

Riesman, David, 'Some Observations on Community Plans and Utopia,' *Yale Law Review,* 57, December 1947, 173-200.

Roberts, J. W., *Looking Within. The Misleading Tendencies of 'Looking Backward' Made Manifest,* New York, 1893.

Sadler, Elizabeth, 'One Book's Influence. Edward Bellamy's "Looking Backward," ' *New England Quarterly,* XVII, December 1944, 530-55.

Smith, Goldwin, 'Prophets of Unrest,' *Forum,* IX, August 1890, 599-614.

Springfield Union, 12 February 1876 and 28 February 1877.
Standard, The, v, 27 April 1889, 4; vi, 31 August 1889, 1-2.
Taylor, Walter F., *The Economic Novel in America,* Chapel Hill, 1942.
Von Helmholtz-Phelan, A. A., *The Social Philosophy of William Morris,* Durham, 1927.

. . . .

CHAPTER 5

Henry Demarest Lloyd:
The Middle-Class Conscience

PRIMARY MATERIAL:

Henry Demarest Lloyd Papers (letters, manuscripts, and notebooks), State Historical Society of Wisconsin, Madison.
A Strike of Millionaires against Miners, or the Story of Spring Valley, Chicago, 1890.
Wealth against Commonwealth, New York, 1894.
Labour Copartnership, New York, 1898.
A Country without Strikes, New York, 1900.
Newest England, New York, 1900.
Man, the Social Creator, New York, 1906. Assembled by Jane Addams and Anne Withington from early manuscripts and notebooks, together with fragments of essays and addresses.
A Sovereign People. A Study of Swiss Democracy, New York, 1907. Assembled by John A. Hobson from Lloyd's notes.
Men, the Workers, New York, 1909. Essays and addresses on labor.
Mazzini and Other Essays, New York, 1910.
Lords of Industry, New York, 1910. Essays on business chicane.

RELATED MATERIAL:

Destler, Chester M., 'A "Plebeian" at Columbia, 1863-1869,' *New York History,* July 1946.
—— *American Radicalism,* 1865-1901, New London, Conn., 1946.
—— 'Entrepreneurial Leadership among "Robber Barons": A Trial Balance,' in *The Tasks of Economic History,* Supplement vi to *The Journal of Economic History,* December 1946.
—— 'A Commentary on the "Communication" from Allan Nevins in the *American Historical Review,* April 1945,' mimeographed pamplet dated Connecticut College, New London, Conn., 15 April 1945.
Latchford, Henry, 'A Social Reformer,' *The Arena,* x, October 1894, 577-89.

Lloyd, Caro, *Henry Demarest Lloyd, 1847-1903*, New York, 1912, 2 vols.

Nevins, Allan, *John D. Rockefeller*, New York, 1940, 2 vols.

—— 'Letter to the Editor of the *American Historical Review*,' *American Historical Review*, 50, April 1945, 676-89.

. . . .

CHAPTER 6

William Dean Howells:
The Gentleman from Altruria

PRIMARY MATERIAL:

William Dean Howells Correspondence, Harvard University Library.

William Cooper Howells Correspondence, Yale University Library.

Life and Letters of William Dean Howells, ed. by Mildred Howells, New York, 1928, 2 vols.

The Minister's Charge, Boston, 1887.

Annie Kilburn, New York, 1888.

A Hazard of New Fortunes, New York, 1890.

The Quality of Mercy, New York, 1892.

The World of Chance, New York, 1893.

A Traveler from Altruria, New York, 1894.

The Landlord at Lion's Head, New York, 1897.

The Son of Royal Langbrith, New York, 1904.

Through the Eye of the Needle, New York, 1907.

A Boy's Town, New York, 1890.

Three Villages, Boston, 1884.

Criticism and Fiction, New York, 1891.

My Year in a Log Cabin, New York, 1893.

Impressions and Experiences, New York, 1896.

Literary Friends and Acquaintances, New York, 1900.

Years of My Youth, New York, 1916.

Atlantic Monthly articles:

　　Review of Henry James Sr., *The Secret of Swedenborg*, XXIV, December, 1869, 762-3.

　　'Politics,' XXX, July 1872, 127-8.

　　Remarks on Theodore Parker, XXXIV, July 1874, 109-10.

　　'Police Report,' XLIX, January 1882, 1-16.

Harper's Monthly articles:

　　'Editor's Study,' LXXVI, January 1888, 316-21 (remarks on equality, democracy, and realism.

　　'Editor's Study,' LXXVI, February 1888, 476-82 (remarks on Emerson).

'Editor's Study,' LXXVI, April 1888, 801-6 (reviews of Laurence Gronlund's *Ca Ira* and *The Co-operative Commonwealth*).

'The Modern American Mood,' XCV, July 1897, 199-204.

'Editor's Easy Chair,' CIII, July 1901, 311-14 (thoughts on classes).

'Editor's Easy Chair,' CVIII, March 1904, 640-44 (review of A. R. Wallace's *Man's Place in the Universe*).

'Editor's Easy Chair,' CXVII, June 1908, 147-50 (on lockouts and unemployment).

'Editor's Easy Chair,' CXVIII, May 1909, 965-8 (reflections on reform).

'Editor's Easy Chair,' CXIX, November 1909, 957-60 (collective effort in society).

Harper's Weekly articles:

'Was There Nothing to Arbitrate?' XXXII, 21 April 1888, 286.

'Life and Letters,' XXXIX, 31 August 1895, 820 (review of J. T. Codman's *Brook Farm*).

'Life and Letters,' XL, 4 January 1896, 6-7 (remarks on patriotism).

'The Worst of Being Poor,' XLVI, 1 March 1902, 261.

'Diversions of the Higher Journalist, A Scientific City,' XLVII, 25 July 1903, 1220.

North American Review articles:

'Are We a Plutocracy?' CLVIII, February 1894, 185-96.

'Some Unpalatable Suggestions,' CLXXXVIII, August 1908, 254-61.

'John Brown after Fifty Years,' CXCII, January 1911, 26-34.

Century articles:

'Recent American Novels, "The Breadwinners,"' XXVIII, May 1884, 153-4.

'Equality as the Basis of Good Society,' LI, November 1895, 63-7.

'Who Are Our Brethren?' LI, April 1896, 932-6.

Literature articles:

'American Letter, American Civic Life,' III, 19 November 1898, 474-5.

'American Letter, A Human Document,' III, 3 December 1898, 528-9.

'Rosenfeld's Songs from the Ghetto,' n.s. I, 17 January 1899, 97-8.

Forum articles:

'The Nature of Liberty,' XX, December 1895, 401-9.

RELATED MATERIAL:

American Fabian, The, IV, February 1898, 1-2 (on Howell's socialism).

Arms, G. W., 'Further Inquiry into Howells's Socialism,' *Science and Society*, III, 1939, 245-8.

Arms, G. W., 'The Literary Background of Howells's Social Criticism,'
    American Literature, XIV, 1942, 260-76.

Arvin, Newton, 'The Usableness of Howells,' *The New Republic*, XCI,
    30 June 1937, 227-8.

Belcher, H. G., 'Howells's Opinions on the Religious Conflicts of His
    Age as Exhibited in Magazine Articles,' *American Literature*, XV,
    November 1943, 262-78.

Cady, Edwin H., 'The Neuroticism of William Dean Howells,' *Publications of the Modern Language Association*, LXI, 1946, 229-38.

De Voto, Bernard, *Mark Twain in Eruption*, New York, 1940.

Getzels, J. W., 'William Dean Howells and Socialism,' *Science and
    Society*, II, 1938, 376-86.

Gibson, William M., 'Mark Twain and Howells, Anti-Imperialists,'
    New England Quarterly, XX, December 1947, 435-70.

—— and Arms, George, *A Bibliography of William Dean Howells*,
    New York, 1948.

Howells, William Cooper, *Recollections of Life in Ohio from 1813 to
    1840*, Cincinnati, 1895.

James, Henry, *The Letters of Henry James*, New York, 1920, 2 vols.

—— *The Notebooks of Henry James*, ed. by F. O. Matthiessen and
    K. B. Murdock, New York, 1947.

—— 'William Dean Howells,' *Harper's Weekly*, XXX, 19 June 1886,
    394-5.

Matthiessen, F. O., *The James Family*, New York, 1947.

Paine, Albert B., *Mark Twain: A Biography*, New York, 1912, 3 vols.

Whitman, Walt, *Complete Prose Works*, Boston, 1901.

Williams, C. R., ed., *Diary and Letters of Rutherford Birchard Hayes*,
    Columbus, Ohio, 1922, IV.

Wright, Conrad, 'The Sources of Mr. Howells's Socialism,' *Science and
    Society*, II, 1938, 514-17.

'William Dean Howells,' *Twentieth Century*, XV, 3 October 1895, 6-7.

Yarros, Victor, *Liberty*, 2 May 1896 (article on Howells).

. . . .

CHAPTER 7

Thorstein Veblen:
Moralist and Rhetorician

PRIMARY MATERIAL:

The Theory of the Leisure Class: An Economic Study of Institutions,
New York, 1899.

The Theory of Business Enterprise, New York, 1904.

The Instinct of Workmanship and the State of the Industrial Arts, New York, 1914.

Imperial Germany and the Industrial Revolution, New York, 1915.

An Inquiry into the Nature of Peace and the Terms of Its Perpetuation, New York, 1917.

The Higher Learning in America: A Memorandum on the Conduct of Universities by Business Men, New York, 1918.

The Vested Interests and the Common Man, New York, 1919.

The Place of Science in Modern Civilization, and Other Essays, New York, 1919.

The Engineers and the Price System, New York, 1921.

Absentee Ownership and Business Enterprise in Recent Times: The Case of America, New York, 1923.

Essays in Our Changing Order, ed. by Leon Ardzrooni, New York, 1934.

RELATED MATERIAL:

Anderson, K. L., 'Unity of Veblen's Theoretical System,' *Quarterly Journal of Economics,* XLVII, August 1933, 598-626.

Clark, J. M., 'Thorstein Bunde Veblen,' *American Economic Review,* XIX, 1929, 742-5.

Dorfman, Joseph, *Thorstein Veblen and His America,* New York, 1934.

Duffus, R. L., *The Innocents at Cedro,* New York, 1944.

Gambs, John S., *Beyond Supply and Demand: A Re-appraisal of Institutional Economics,* New York, 1946.

Gruchy, Allan G., 'The Institutional Economics of Thorstein Veblen,' in *Modern Economic Thought: The American Contribution,* New York, 1947.

Harris, Abram L., 'Types of Institutionalism,' *Journal of Political Economy,* 40, 1932, 721-49.

Hobson, John A., *Veblen,* London, 1936.

Howells, William Dean, 'An Opportunity for American Fiction,' *Literature,* n.s. I, 28 April, 5 May 1899, 361-2, 385-6.

Johnson, Edgar, 'Veblen, Man from Mars,' *The New Republic,* 105, 28 July 1941, 121-3.

Lerner, Max, 'Editor's Introduction' to *The Portable Veblen,* New York, 1948.

Queeny, Edgar M., 'The Prophet and His work,' in *The Spirit of Enterprise,* New York, 1943.

Traywick, L. E., *Parallelism in the Economic Ideas of Karl Marx and Thorstein Veblen,* Urbana, Ill., 1942.

Tugwell, 'Veblen and "Business Enterprise," ' *The New Republic*, 98, 29 March 1939, 215-19.

Veblen, Florence, 'Thorstein Veblen: Reminiscences of His Brother Orson,' *Social Forces*, x, 1935, 187-95.

Wallas, Graham, 'Veblen's *Imperial Germany and the Industrial Revolution*,' *Quarterly Journal of Economics*, xxx, 1916, 179-87.

. . . .

CHAPTER 8

Theodore Roosevelt and Brooks Adams:
Pseudo-Progressives

PRIMARY MATERIAL (Roosevelt):

The Works of Theodore Roosevelt, National Edition, New York, 1926, 20 vols.

Theodore Roosevelt Cyclopedia, ed. by A. B. Hart, New York, 1941.

Selections from the Correspondence of Theodore Roosevelt and Henry Cabot Lodge, 1884-1918, ed. by H. C. Lodge, New York, 1925, 2 vols.

RELATED MATERIAL:

Bucklin, Joseph B., *Theodore Roosevelt and His Times Shown in His Own Letters*, New York, 1920.

Croly, Herbert R., *The Promise of American Life*, New York, 1909.

De Voto, Bernard, ed., *Mark Twain in Eruption*, New York, 1940.

Hofstadter, Richard, *The American Political Tradition and the Men Who Made It*, New York, 1948.

Hurwitz, H. L., *Theodore Roosevelt and Labor in New York State, 1880-1900*, New York, 1943.

Howe, M. A. De Wolfe, *John Jay Chapman and His Letters*, Boston, 1937.

Josephson, Matthew, *The President Makers*, New York, 1940.

La Follette, Robert M., *Autobiography*, Madison, Wisc., 1911.

Link, A. S., *Wilson: The Road to the White House*, Princeton, 1947.

Lloyd, Henry D., Letters and Notebooks, State Historical Society of Wisconsin, Madison.

Mowry, G. E., *Theodore Roosevelt and the Progressive Movement*, Madison, 1946.

Padover, Saul K., *Wilson's Ideals*, Washington, D.C., 1942.

Pringle, H. F., *Theodore Roosevelt*, New York, 1931.

Pringle, H. F., *The Life and Times of William Howard Taft,* New York, 1939, 2 vols.

Russell, Charles E., *Bare Hands and Stone Walls,* New York, 1933.

PRIMARY MATERIAL (Adams):

Brooks Adams Correspondence with Henry Adams, Harvard College Library.

Henry Cabot Lodge Papers, Massachusetts Historical Society.

Theodore Roosevelt Collection, Harvard College Library.

The Emancipation of Massachusetts, Boston, 1887; revised and enlarged with new introduction, Boston, 1919.

'*The Plutocratic Revolution,*' an address delivered before the New England Tariff Reform League, 15 June 1892.

The Gold Standard: An Historical Study, Boston, 1894.

The Law of Civilization and Decay, London and New York, 1895; and New York, 1943, with introduction by Charles Beard.

America's Economic Supremacy, New York, 1900.

'Public Art—The Test of Greatness,' *Municipal Affairs,* v, 1901, 810-16.

'The New Industrial Revolution,' *Atlantic Monthly,* LXXXVII, 1901, 157-65.

'Reciprocity or the Alternative,' *Atlantic Monthly,* LXXXVIII, 1901, 145-55.

'Meaning of the Recent Expansion of the Foreign Trade of the United States,' *Publications of the American Economic Association,* III, third series, New York, 1902, 80-96.

'John Hay,' *McClure's Magazine,* XIX, 1902, 173-82.

'War as an Ultimate Form of Economic Competition,' reprinted from *The Proceedings of the United States Naval Institute,* XXIX, no. 4, whole no. 108, Annapolis, Md., 1903.

The New Empire, New York, 1903.

'Economic Conditions for Future Defense,' *Atlantic Monthly,* XCII, 1903, 632-49.

'Legal Supervision of the Transportation Tax,' *North American Review,* 179, 1904, 371-87.

'Nature of Law: Methods and Aim of Legal Education,' and 'Law under Inequality; Monopoly,' in *Centralization and the Law,* ed. by M. M. Bigelow, Boston, 1906.

Railways as Public Agents, Boston, 1910.

'A Problem in Civilization,' *Atlantic Monthly,* CVI, 1910, 26-32.

'The Seizure of the Laird Rams,' *Massachusetts Historical Society Proceedings,* XLV, October 1911- June 1912, 243-333.

'The Collapse of Capitalist Government,' *Atlantic Monthly*, CXI, 1913, 433-43.

The Theory of Social Revolutions, New York, 1913

'The Revolt of Modern Democracy against Standards of Duty,' *Proceedings of the American Academy of Arts and Letters*, IX, 1916.

'The Incoherence of American Democracy,' an address to the Bunker Hill Memorial Association, 17 June 1916.

'Introduction' to Henry Adams, *The Degradation of the Democratic Dogma*, New York, 1919

'Collective Thinking in America,' *Yale Review*, VIII, 1919, 623-40

Debates in the Massachusetts Constitutional Convention, 1917-1918, I, Boston, 1919, chs. I-XV

RELATED MATERIAL:

Adams, J. T., *The Adams Family*, New York, 1935.

Blackmur, R. P., 'Henry Adams and Brooks Adams: Parallels to Two Generations,' *Southern Review*, V, 1939-40, 308-34.

Cater, H. D., *Henry Adams and His Friends*, Boston, 1947.

Ford, W. C., 'Brooks Adams,' *Harvard Graduate Magazine*, XXXV, 1927, 615-27.

——*Letters of Henry Adams*, 1858-1891, Boston, 1930

——*Letters of Henry Adams*, 1892-1918, Boston, 1938.

Madison, Charles, *Critics & Crusaders*, New York, 1947.

Parrington, V. L., *Main Currents in American Thought*, New York, 1930, vol. III.

Roosevelt, Theodore, *Forum*, XII, 1896-7, 575-89 (review of *The Law of Civilization and Decay*).

Springfield Republican, 20 September 1898 (report of an interview with Adams) and 21 September 1898 (editorial by Samuel Bowles on Adams)

. . . .

CHAPTER 9

In Retrospect:
1912-1950

Bourne, Randolph, *Untimely Papers*, New York, 1919.

Cohen, Morris, *The Faith of a Liberal*, New York, 1946.

Cowley, Malcolm, *Exile's Return: A Narrative of Ideas*, New York, 1934.

Diamond, William, *The Economic Ideas of Woodrow Wilson*, Baltimore, 1943.

Hawthorne, Nathaniel, 'Chiefly about War Matters,' *Works*, Boston, 1900, XVII.

Hofstadter, Richard, *The American Political Tradition*, New York, 1948.

Howe, Frederic C., *The Confessions of a Reformer*, New York, 1926

Josephson, Matthew, *The President Makers*, New York, 1940.

Joughin, G. Louis, and Morgan, Edmund M., *The Legacy of Sacco and Vanzetti*, New York, 1948

Kemler, Edgar, *The Deflation of American Ideals*, Washington, D.C., 1941.

Kerney, James, *The Political Education of Woodrow Wilson*, New York, 1926.

Lindley, Ernest K., *Franklin D. Roosevelt: A Career in Progressive Democracy*, Indianapolis, 1931.

Link, Arthur S., *The Road to the White House*, Princeton, 1947.

Mason, Alpheus T., *Brandeis*, New York, 1946.

Modern Monthly, The, 1932-4.

Nation, The, 1918-26.

New Masses, The, 1932-6.

New Republic, The, 1918-26.

Noble, Ransom E., *New Jersey Progressivism before Wilson*, Princeton. 1946.

Partisan Review, The, February to June, 1949, vol. XVI.

The Public Papers of Franklin D. Roosevelt, ed. by Samuel Rosenman, New York, 1938, 1941, 9 vols.

Russell, Charles E., *Bare Hands and Stone Walls*, New York, 1933.

The Public Papers of Woodrow Wilson, ed. by R. S. Baker and W. E. Dodd, New York, 1925-7, 6 vols.

Wilson, Woodrow, *The New Freedom*, New York, 1913

. . . .

New Perspectives on
the Progressive Tradition:

The following books approach some of the same men and issues discussed in *Men of Good Hope* from different and sometimes contradictory points of view. Foremost among them are Morton G. White, *Social Thought in America, The Revolt Against Formalism* (1949), Eric F. Goldman, *Rendezvous with Destiny* (1952), and Richard Hofstadter, *The Age of Reform. From Bryan to F.D.R.* (1955), all three of which are available in paperbound editions. Louis Hartz, *The Liberal Tradition in America* (1955) presents a challenging thesis on American liberalism, and *The California Progressives* (1951) by George E. Mowry contains a suggestive chapter on the progressive mind. Other American reformers are perceptively treated in Arthur Mann's *Yankee Reformers in the Urban Age* (1954) and in David W. Noble's *The Paradox of Progressive Thought* (1958). *American Radicals: Some Problems and Personalities*, edited by Harvey Goldberg (1957) is an uneven but sometimes useful collection of essays on a number of radical intellectuals, labor leaders, journalists, and politicians, including Lloyd, Debs, Veblen, La Follette, and Beard. Henry May, *The End of American Innocence: A Study of the First Years of Our Time, 1912-1917* (1959), R. H. Bremner, *From the Depths: The Discovery of Poverty in the United States* (1956), and Sidney Fine, *Laissez Faire and the General-Welfare State: A Study of Conflict in American Thought, 1865-1901* (1956) are valuable reference works.

A number of volumes have appeared since 1950 on Emerson, George, Bellamy, Howells, Veblen, and Brooks Adams. Stephen Whicher's *Freedom and Fate: An Inner Life of Ralph Waldo Emerson* (1953) is a striking and original analysis. Charles A. Barker's substantial biography, *Henry George* (1956) is an indispensable source. The latest full-scale treatment of Bellamy is Sylvia Bowman's dense and somewhat mechanical biography, *The Year 2000: A Critical Biography of Edward Bellamy* (1958). A selection of Bellamy's social writings, *Edward Bellamy: Selected Writings on Religion and Society* (The American Heritage Series, 1955), has been edited by Joseph Schiffman with a long and informative introduction. Howells has enjoyed a minor revival. E. H. Cady's two volume biography, *The Road to Realism; the Early Years, 1837-1885, of William Dean Howells* (1956) and *The Realist at War; the Mature Years, 1885-1920, of William Dean Howells* (1958), is the most recent and authoritative account. Clues to Howells's social thought may also be found in Everett Carter, *Howells and the Age of Realism* (1954), R. L. Hough, *The Quiet Rebel: William Dean Howells as Social Commentator* (1959), and *Mark Twain—Howells Letters: The Correspondence of Samuel L. Clemens and William Dean Howells, 1872-1910* (2 vols., 1910), edited by H. N. Smith and W. M. Gibson. Of the many studies of Veblen published during the 'fifties, perhaps David Riesman's *Thorstein Veblen, A Critical Interpretation* (1953) is the least specialized and technical. Two biographies of Brooks Adams are worth consulting: Thornton Anderson, *Brooks Adams, Constructive Conservative* (1951) and A. F. Beringause, *Brooks Adams: a Biography* (1955). As a corrective to what I now consider my too biased estimate of Theodore Roosevelt, see John M. Blum's just and incisive study, *The Republican Roosevelt* (1954).

INDEX

. . . .

A

Absentee Ownership (Veblen), 217, 225

Adams, Brooks: (252-80) influence on Theodore Roosevelt, 252; confessions to Henry Cabot Lodge, 253; previous interpretations of, 254; early ambitions, 255-6; first book, 256-7; discovery of Middle Ages, 257-8; on Scott and Dickens, 259; on 'gold-bugs,' 259-60; campaign of 1896, 260-62; new imperialism, 262-3; the geopolitician, 263-4; political postulates, 265-7; America's economic supremacy, 267-9; friendship with Theodore Roosevelt, 269-70; dreams of empire, 270; need for new type of administrator, 270-72; advice to T.R., 272-3; opinion of World War I, 274-5; speaks at Massachusetts Constitutional Convention, 275-6; relation with Henry Adams, 276-9; miscellaneous, 74, 281, 282, 286, 292; quoted, 253ff.

Adams, Henry, 247, 253, 254, 255, 256, 257, 259, 260, 262, 264, 267, 268, 271, 274, 276, 277, 278, 279, 280; quoted, 12, 135, 276, 292

Adams, John, 16

Adams, John Q., 37, 265, 279

Addams, Jane, 149, 158, 298

Alcott, Amos Bronson, 49

Alcott, Louisa M., quoted, 22, 23

Alger, Russell A., 142

Altgeld, John P., 137, 149, 250

American, the: his faith in progress, 3-4, Tocqueville on, 4-7

America's Economic Supremacy (Brooks Adams), 262

Anarchism, 89, 181

Annie Kilburn (Howells), 190-91; 200-201

Arena, The, 149

Ashtabula Sentinel, 179

Atlantic Monthly, 149, 173, 175, 180

Austin, Henry, 106, 107

B

Bancroft, George, 26

Bare Hands and Stone Walls (C. E. Russell), 299-300

Beard, Charles, 254, 298

Bebel, F. A., 144

Beecher, Henry Ward, 88, 138

Bellamy, Edward: (92-132) Gronlund on, 93; Howells on, 94; Bellamy and George, 95; influence of Fourier on, 95-6; family background, 96-7; early life, 97; origins of *Looking Backward,* 98-100; the story of, 100; style, 101-2; reception of, 102-4; life in Chicopee, 104-6; *The Nationalist* editor, 106-7; social philosophy of, 108ff.; meaning of Nationalism, 110; interest in military, 110-11; appeal of Nationalism, 111-12; attitude toward working class, 113-14; and the Socialists, 114; on democracy, 115-16; Storiot's *History,* 116-24; criticisms of his utopia, 124-6; his religion and its social implications, 126-9; last days, 131; miscellaneous, 19, 35, 89, 174, 180, 181, 195, 198, 217, 237, 238; quoted, 92ff., 135, 187, 237

Björnson, Björnstjerne, 180, 210

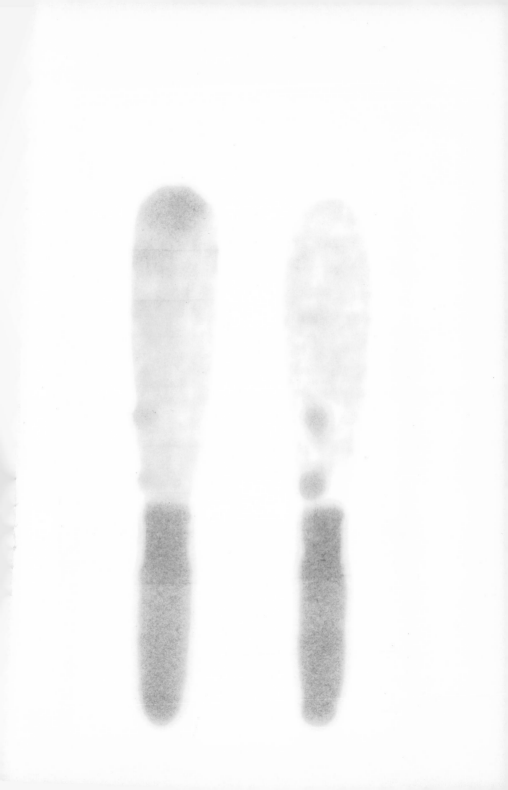